LEGAL WRITING EXERCISES

A CASE FILE AND FORMULA–BASED APPROACH TO LEGAL REASONING

■ ■ ■

By

Stephanie J. Thompson

Assistant Director, Global Lawyering Skills
University of the Pacific, McGeorge School of Law

AMERICAN CASEBOOK SERIES®

WEST®
A Thomson Reuters business

Mat #40987596

610 Opperman Drive
St. Paul, MN 55123
1–800–313–9378

Printed in the United States of America

ISBN: 978–0–314–26395–7

To my parents, friends, and colleagues who provided me with endless encouragement and support.
To my students who inspired me to write this book.

To my daughters, Kate the Great and Super Sarah, and my husband, Mike, who are the loves of my life.

ACKNOWLEDGEMENTS

This text was only made possible with the help of my past and present colleagues at Pacific McGeorge School of Law, my students, and from the inspiration I have received from the Legal Writing Institute and the Association of Legal Writing Directors.

A special thanks to my research assistants Elizabeth Kiessling and Adam Guernsey who assisted me greatly with this project.

And, a huge thank you to my good friend Adrienne Brungess, who provided me countless hours of inspiration, support, editing, and friendship through my years of teaching and in writing this book.

Table of Contents

Legal Writing Exercises

A CASE FILE AND FORMULA–BASED APPROACH TO LEGAL REASONING

Introduction

■ ■ ■

The goal of this workbook is to help you better understand the material you will learn in your legal writing course. It will provide you with a process for brainstorming and formulas for writing each component of the objective and persuasive paradigms.

Legal Writing Exercises: A Case File and Formula-Based Approach to Legal Reasoning draws upon three case files to teach the essential components of an objective memorandum and a persuasive brief. Each of the three case files begins with a fact pattern and the relevant legal authority. Each of the case files, in turn, includes a set worksheets, which are identical for each of the three case files. Each worksheet instructs on a specific part of an objective memorandum or a persuasive brief and provides a formula for completing the task. Ultimately, by using this workbook, you will develop a process for legal writing, develop good writing habits, and set goals for a lifetime of writing in the profession.

Section I

Objective Legal Writing

■ ■ ■

CASE FILE NO. 1: PEOPLE v. GIBSON

WORKSHEET NO. 1: INTRODUCTION, FACTS, AND RELEVANT AUTHORITY

Introduction

Attorneys rarely research the law and write an analysis simply to learn the law. Instead, attorneys almost always research and write in response to the specific situation faced by a client. Therefore, before you turn to the attached statutes and cases, read the Office Memorandum on the next page to give yourself an understanding of your client's situation. The Office Memorandum is an example of what you might receive when a supervising attorney asks you to work on a case.

After you read the Office Memorandum, read the statutes and cases provided in the Case File. One of your goals in reading these statutes and cases is to develop your understanding of California's law on burglary. Another goal is to find the answer to the question the supervising attorney poses in the Office Memorandum: Can Sam Gibson be convicted of first-degree burglary under California law? As you read each legal authority, consider how you can use it to determine the most likely outcome for your client. The most likely outcome, however, may not always be a favorable one. Therefore, considering the law and the facts from a neutral perspective are vital to fully advise your client.

OFFICE MEMORANDUM

TO: Legal Intern
FROM: Supervising Attorney
DATE: September 1, YEAR
RE: People v. Gibson; first or second degree burglary

Our client, Sam Gibson, recently was arrested for first-degree burglary. We would like to evaluate whether the charge of first-degree burglary against Mr. Gibson can be reduced to a charge of second-degree burglary on the legal theory that the house was not inhabited when Mr. Gibson entered it.

I recently interviewed Mr. Gibson and reviewed the police report provided by the District Attorney's Office. My notes summarizing the facts of this case are below. These are the only facts available at this time.

Notes of interview with Mr. Gibson

— *Mr. Gibson is struggling financially because of the economic downturn.*

— *He lost his job.*

— *He previously worked in construction.*

— *He has a wife and four children under the age of 10.*

— *Unemployment only provides enough money to pay rent; family does not have enough money for groceries.*

— *He has no criminal past.*

— *On August 14, YEAR, he broke into a house at 5553 Tree Lined Street in Sacramento, California. It was dark and the house appeared to be vacant. He had walked to the house from his apartment, which was only about 1/2 mile away.*

— *He used a crowbar to open the back sliding glass door. He entered the house. He admits that he went into the house to steal anything he thought he could sell for quick cash.*

— *The house was basically empty. He only found some crystal, china, and silver in a moving box in the hall closet. The box was not taped shut.*

— *He put the china, crystal, and silver in a bag he had brought with him.*

— *He left the house on foot, carrying the bag.*

— *He walked only a few yards down the sidewalk when police stopped him.*

— *Mr. Gibson said that the police said that they knew the house was empty and asked him what he was doing. Mr. Gibson admitted what he did and handed over the bag.*

— *The police opened the bag and found the china, crystal, and silver.*

— *The police arrested Mr. Gibson and he was eventually charged with first-degree burglary.*

Summary of Police Report

— *Ms. Audrey Brown owns a house at 5041 South Park Lane in Sacramento, California. She has lived in this house for six years.*

— *On July 1, YEAR, Ms. Brown's eighty-five year old mother passed away.*

— *Ms. Brown inherited her mother's house.*

— *Ms. Brown's mother's house is located at 5553 Tree Lined Street in Sacramento, California.*

— *On August 1st, Ms. Brown hired an auction house to sell the furnishings in her mother's house and a disposal company to take the unsold contents to the local Goodwill. This process was completed on August 5th.*

— *The only items that remained in the house after August 5th were some of her mother's personal items that Ms. Brown packed in a moving box before the auction and left in a hall closet. They included her mother's china, crystal, and silver.*

— *She recently listed her own house at 5041 South Park Lane for sale.*

— *Ms. Brown intended to move into her mother's house as soon as her house on 5041 South Park Lane sold.*

— *As of the date of the burglary, Ms. Brown's house on South Park Lane had not sold and Ms. Brown had not moved to her mother's house on Tree Lined Street.*

— *On August 14, YEAR, the police saw Mr. Gibson suspiciously leave the property on 5553 Tree lined Street.*

— *The officers knew that the owner recently died and were aware that the house was vacant.*

— *After Mr. Gibson walked only a few yards down the sidewalk, the police turned on their lights and siren and ordered him to stop. They also told him to drop the bag.*

— *The police asked Mr. Gibson what he was doing at the house.*

— *The police state that Mr. Gibson immediately broke down crying and admitted that he had just stole some things from the house and that they were in the bag.*

— *The police then took the bag and opened it. In it, they found the china, crystal, and silver.*

— *The police arrested Mr. Gibson; Mr. Gibson was later charged with first-degree burglary.*

PENAL CODE

Part 1. Of Crimes and Punishments
Title 13. Of Crimes Against Property
Chapter 2. Burglary

California Penal Code § 459. Burglary

Every person who enters any house, room, apartment, tenement, shop, warehouse, store, mill, barn, stable, outhouse or other building, tent, vessel, as defined in Section 21 of the Harbors and Navigation Code, floating home, as defined in subdivision (d) of Section 18075.55 of the Health and Safety Code, railroad car, locked or sealed cargo container, whether or not mounted on a vehicle, trailer coach, as defined in Section 635 of the Vehicle Code, any house car, as defined in Section 362 of the Vehicle Code, inhabited camper, as defined in Section 243 of the Vehicle Code, vehicle as defined by the Vehicle Code, when the doors are locked, aircraft as defined by Section 21012 of the Public Utilities Code, or mine or any underground portion thereof, with intent to commit grand or petit larceny or any felony is guilty of burglary. As used in this chapter, "inhabited" means currently being used for dwelling purposes, whether occupied or not. A house, trailer, vessel designed for habitation, or portion of a building is currently being used for dwelling purposes if, at the time of the burglary, it was not occupied solely because a natural or other disaster caused the occupants to leave the premises.

California Penal Code § 460. Degrees

(a) Every burglary of an inhabited dwelling house, vessel, as defined in the Harbors and Navigation Code, which is inhabited and designed for habitation, floating home, as defined in subdivision (d) of Section 18075.55 of the Health and Safety Code, or trailer coach, as defined by the Vehicle Code, or the inhabited portion of any other building, is burglary of the first degree.

(b) All other kinds of burglary are of the second degree.

(c) This section shall not be construed to supersede or affect Section 464 of the Penal Code.

THE PEOPLE, Plaintiff and Respondent

v.

ANTONIO ROMERO CARDONA, Defendant and Appellant

Court of Appeal, Fourth District, Division 1, California

142 Cal.App.3d 481

April 27, 1983

BROWN

Antonio Cardona appeals his conviction of first degree burglary (Pen. Code, § 459, 460), contending he is guilty only of second degree burglary as the house he entered was not inhabited at the time.

On September 12, 1981, Keith Fuller and his family moved out of the house they rented on Jefferson Street in Carlsbad. The Fullers spent the night of September 12 in their new home in Oceanside. They did not intend ever to spend another night at the Jefferson Street house. They, however, had paid rent on the house through September 15 and, as of September 13, had not completed moving all their belongings out of the house. On the night of September 13, Cardona broke into the Jefferson Street house with the intent to steal some of the Fullers' belongings that were still stored there. Cardona was caught red-handed by the Fullers, who had returned to the house to pick up some of their belongings. *483

Cardona was charged with first degree burglary. At trial, he argued he was guilty only of second degree burglary because the house was not inhabited at the time of the burglary. The superior court found the house was inhabited by the Fullers and found Cardona guilty of first degree burglary. The court found this is an unusual case under the criteria of California Rules of Court rule 416 and thus Penal Code section 462, prohibiting a grant of probation where defendant is convicted of first degree burglary, does not apply. Cardona was granted three years probation on the conditions he participate in an alcoholic rehabilitation program, report his employment status to his probation officer, violate no law and serve 307 days in custody with credit for 307 days served.

A burglary is of the first degree only if it is of an inhabited dwelling house during the nighttime (Pen. Code, § 460). Penal Code section 459 defines "inhabited" as it is used in section 460 as meaning "currently being used for dwelling purposes, whether occupied or not." The issue here is whether the Fullers continued to use the house on Jefferson Street for dwelling purposes after they permanently stopped sleeping there but had not yet moved all their belongings out or lost the right to possess the house.

Penal Code section 459 clearly states a house remains "inhabited" despite the fact it is empty at the time of the burglary. Furthermore, a house remains inhabited even if the burglary occurs while the residents are away for an extended period of time (*People v. Harris* (1968) 266 Cal.App.2d 426, 430 [72 Cal.Rptr. 423]; *People v. Stewart* (1952) 113 Cal.App.2d 687, 691 [248 P.2d 768]). (1) Where, however, the residents have moved out without the intent to return, the house becomes uninhabited, i.e., it is no longer being used for dwelling purposes, and a burglary of the house, even one occurring within a few days after the residents vacate, cannot be of the first degree (*People v. Valdez* (1962) 203 Cal.App.2d 559, 563 [21 Cal.Rptr. 764]). Such was the case here. Mr. Fuller testified his family had slept in their new house the night before the burglary and intended never again to occupy the Jefferson Street house. The continued use of that house for storage of belongings only was not sufficient to make the house inhabited; because a burglary is of the first degree only if it is of an inhabited house at night, the crucial element in determining whether a house is being used for dwelling purposes is whether anyone sleeps in it (*People v. Lewis* (1969) 274 Cal.App.2d 912, 921 [79 Cal.Rptr. 650]). There was no identifiable person here who used the house as sleeping quarters at the time of the burglary or intended to do so in the future.

Although no case directly on point has arisen in California, a finding the Jefferson Street house was uninhabited when the burglary occurred is supported by cases of other states. The facts of *Hayes v. State* (1937) 180 Miss. 291 [177 So.360], are identical to those involved here. The court in that case found the house was uninhabited because the prior resident no longer had any intent to *484 use the house as his residence. *State v. Ferebee* (1979) 273 S.C. 403 [257 S.E.2d 154], and *Santistevan v. People* (1972) 177 Colo. 329 [494 P.2d 75], hold a house is uninhabited as soon as the tenant vacates, despite the fact the house remains furnished; first degree burglary is a crime against habitation, not property. (See also *Tukes v. State* (Fla. 1977) 346 So.2d 1056; *Smith v. State* (1920) 80 Fla. 315 [85 So. 911].)

The superior court based its finding the Jefferson Street house was inhabited at the time of the burglary on what it found to be Cardona's intent. The court focused on the danger posed by the burglary of an occupied house and found a first degree burglary conviction is justified if there is no way for the defendant to know the house will be empty at the time of the burglary. The subjective impressions of the defendant, however, are irrelevant; a house, for example, remains inhabited although the residents are away on vacation and the burglar knows it. The dispositive element is whether the person with the possessory right to the house views the house as his dwelling. The Fullers no longer used the Jefferson Street house as their dwelling and thus it was not inhabited when the burglary occurred.

(2) Although the superior court erred in finding Cardona guilty of first degree burglary, we need not remand for resentencing. There is no doubt Cardona is guilty of second degree burglary; it is within our authority to modify the conviction to reflect the lesser offense. (See *People v. Valdez*, supra., 203 Cal.App.2d 559, 566.) The sentence imposed, probation with-

out any further custody, is as lenient as Cardona could have expected following a conviction of second degree burglary.

The judgment is modified to find Cardona guilty of second degree burglary only. As modified, the judgment is affirmed.

THE PEOPLE, Plaintiff and Respondent

v.

RAFAEL AGUIRRE HERNANDEZ, Defendant and Appellant

Court of Appeal, Fourth District, Division 2, California

9 Cal.App.4th 438

September 8, 1992

DABNEY

Defendant Rafael Aguirre Hernandez was convicted by a jury of first degree burglary (Pen. Code § 459). The court found true the special allegations that Hernandez had suffered a prior conviction for residential burglary (§ 667) and a prior conviction for possession of a controlled substance for sale (§ 667.5, subd. (b).) The court sentenced Hernandez to the middle term of four years for the burglary, a consecutive term of five years for the section 667 prior, and a consecutive term of one year for the section 667.5, subdivision (b) prior.

On appeal, Hernandez contends (1) the evidence was insufficient to support his conviction for burglary of an inhabited dwelling; (2) the court *440 gave conflicting and confusing instructions on the definition of an inhabited dwelling; (3) the court erroneously refused to give requested instructions on the definition of an inhabited dwelling; (4) the unjustified use of physical restraints violated his constitutional rights; (5) the court erred in refusing to allow him to set aside his prior conviction; (6) the court erroneously refused a requested defense instruction on the lesser related offense of unauthorized entry into a noncommercial dwelling; (7) the court erred in using prior convictions for impeachment; (8) the court erred in failing to discharge a juror for nondisclosure of her relationship to the victim; and (9) the section 667 enhancement should be stricken because it was not proved beyond a reasonable doubt.

Facts

On September 1, 1990, Stephen Kirkreit and his family moved all their furniture and personal belongings to a new apartment on Mitchell Avenue in Riverside, leaving nothing behind at their old apartment. The utilities had been turned on at the new apartment. The Kirkreits finished moving at 9 p.m. and spent the night with relatives because nothing was unpacked.

The next morning they returned to the Mitchell Avenue apartment and found the front door, which had been left locked, was wide open. Their VCR, stereo receiver, and some clothing were missing. They did not spend the night at the Mitchell Avenue apartment until September 3.

Police officers discovered fingerprints on a piece of glass from a broken rear window which was determined to have been the point of entry. An expert witness testified that the prints matched those of Hernandez. In the expert witness's opinion, the prints had been made by someone reaching through the broken window from the outside.

Defense. Hernandez knew the former tenants of the Mitchell Avenue apartment and had spent the night with them several times. During his visits, he had entered the bedroom with the broken window and had touched the window. He denied he had entered the apartment the night of the burglary and denied taking property from the apartment.

Residents of another apartment on Mitchell Avenue testified they had seen Hernandez visiting the former tenants. They testified the Kirkreits did not actually begin staying at the Mitchell Avenue apartment for more than two weeks after they moved their property there because the apartment had to be fumigated for cockroaches. *441

Discussion

I. Sufficiency of Evidence of Residential Burglary

A. Standard of Review.

(1) "When the sufficiency of the evidence is challenged on appeal, the court must review the whole record in the light most favorable to the judgment to determine whether it contains substantial evidence—i.e., evidence that is credible and of solid value—from which a rational trier of fact could have found the defendant guilty beyond a reasonable doubt." [Citations.] (*People v. Green* (1980) 27 Cal.3d 1, 55 [164 Cal.Rptr. 1, 609 P.2d 468], overruled on another ground in *People v. Hall* (1986) 41 Cal.3d 826 [226 Cal.Rptr. 112, 718 P.2d 99].)

B. Evidence That Residence Was Inhabited.

(2) Hernandez contends the evidence was insufficient to support his conviction of first degree burglary because the evidence did not show the residence was inhabited within the meaning of section 460, subdivision (a) when the burglary was committed. (Footnote omitted). The Kirkreits had never slept in the apartment before the burglary and had not unpacked their belongings. They did not begin sleeping at the apartment until after the burglary. Hernandez contends that the crucial element for whether a house is inhabited is whether anyone sleeps there. (*People v. Lewis* (1969) 274 Cal.App.2d 912, 921 [79 Cal.Rptr. 650].)

In *People v. Cardona* (1983) 142 Cal.App.3d 481 [191 Cal.Rptr. 109], the court stated, "[B]ecause a burglary is of the first degree only if it is of an inhabited house at night, the crucial element in determining whether a house is being used for dwelling purposes is whether anyone sleeps in it [citation]." (*Id.* at p. 483.) However statutory amendments have eliminated the requirement that a burglary take place at night for it to be first degree burglary. (Stats. 1982, ch. 1297, § 1, p. 4786.) Thus, the Legislature has rejected the view, expressed in prior case law, that the use of a house as sleeping quarters is critical. (Cf. *Lewis*, supra, 274 Cal.App.2d at pp. 920–921.) Rather, such use is merely one circumstance the fact finder may consider.

To support his argument that the apartment was uninhabited, Hernandez cites *People v. Valdez* (1962) 203 Cal.App.2d 559 [21 Cal.Rptr. 764]. In *Valdez*, a burglary of a house took place on March 9, 1961. The previous *442 tenant had moved out a week earlier, and the owner had rented the premises to a new tenant whose occupancy was scheduled to begin on March 13. The new tenant had not moved any belongings into the house and had not had the utilities connected. (*Id.* at pp. 562–563.) The court held that the burglary could not be of the first degree because no one resided there. (*Id.* at p. 563.)

In *Cardona*, supra, 142 Cal.App.3d 481, a burglary of a house took place on September 13, 1981. A family had moved out of the house and had spent the night of September 12 in their new residence. However, they had not completed moving their belongings from the house, and they had paid rent there until September 15. (*Id.* at p. 482.) The court held that the defendant could not have been convicted of first degree burglary, because the house was no longer inhabited. The court stated the house became uninhabited when the tenants moved out, not intending to return there to live. (*Id.* at p. 483.)

In *People v. Jackson* (1992) 6 Cal.App.4th 1185 [8 Cal.Rptr.2d 239], the court held that a dwelling continued to be inhabited because a tenant who intended to move out had never vacated the premises, but was still using the house at the time of the robbery. (*Id.* at p. 1189.)

Here, the Kirkreits had had the utilities connected and had moved all of their belongings into the Mitchell Avenue apartment, intending to occupy it as their residence. The evidence reasonably supported a jury finding that although the Kirkreits had not yet slept there, the apartment was occupied by them as a place of settled residence from which they were merely temporarily absent. We conclude the evidence was sufficient for the jury to find that the apartment was inhabited at the time of the burglary.

The judgment is affirmed.

THE PEOPLE, Respondent

v.

JOSEPH ALBERT ALLARD, Appellant

District Court of Appeal, Second District, Division 2, California

99 Cal.App. 591

June 24, 1929

CRAIG

The appellant was found guilty of first degree burglary and was sentenced accordingly. He appeals, and bases his claim for reversal upon alleged insufficiency of the evidence to sustain the verdict.

It appears that a house, the property of one R. P. Low, was burglarized by defendant who, at the time was unarmed. The crime was committed in the night-time and the house was not occupied on that particular night. Low and his family lived there, but, as testified by him, "were just away for two or three days."

[1] The argument presented by appellant is, that under these circumstances the house was not "inhabited" as required by section 460 of the Penal Code, in order that the burglary may be first degree where the person committing the crime is not armed with a deadly weapon.

An inhabitant of a house is one who resides therein, and "inhabitancy" and "residence" are synonymous terms. (*Harding v. Standard Oil Co.*, 182 Fed. 421.) It has never been held that a person loses his residence by reason of a brief absence from the house where he lives, and without evidence of an intention to depart therefrom and go to live in some other place. Under a statute similar to ours, where a family lived in the house but were away on vacation, it was held to be an inhabited dwelling-house. (*Mason v. State*, 27 Ohio C. C. 526.)

We consider the evidence in this case entirely sufficient.

The judgment is affirmed.

WORKSHEET NO. 2: CASE SYNTHESIS

Synthesis is the binding together of several rules from a collection of cases into one legal principle. It provides a collective meaning that is not apparent from the individual cases themselves.

To synthesize, you need to step back and ask yourself what the cases have in common. Many law students and lawyers use charts to help them see what the cases have in common. A chart is provided for you to use for the exercise below.

Case File Assignment:

Read and brief the cases contained in Worksheet No. 1. After you have read and briefed these cases, fill in the attached synthesis chart. After you have completed the chart, review the information you included to help you see what the cases have in common. On a separate piece of paper, start to draft a synthesized legal principle. This does not need to be a well-crafted rule at this time, as you will work on drafting rules in Worksheet No. 3.

Case names			
Facts			
Holding			
Reasoning			
What is the rule or legal principle you can take away from the case?			

WORKSHEET NO. 3: RULES

Drafting rules is the process of taking the rule or policy from a single authority or from a collection of cases you have synthesized and putting it in written form. To help you write a complete statement of the rule or policy on a particular point of law, you must first ask yourself the following brainstorming questions:

1. What is the rule, policy, or synthesized rule?
2. What are the exceptions to the rule, policy, or synthesized rule, if any?
3. Is there anything else the court will consider in applying the rule, policy, or synthesized rule?

You should always be able to answer the first question unless courts in the jurisdiction have not yet ruled on the issue or the courts in the jurisdiction have ruled inconsistently such that you cannot reconcile the rules or results. You will not always be able to answer the second and third questions, but you should always ask them.

After answering these brainstorming questions, you can begin to write your rule by cutting and pasting your answers to these questions into one or more sentences.

Once you have drafted your rule, you then need to evaluate it for completeness. To evaluate the rule you have written, answer the following questions:

1. Is the rule too specific based on the legal authorities and your client facts?
2. Is the rule too broad based on the legal authorities and your client facts?
3. Does the rule include vague terms?
4. Is the rule circular?
5. If there is more than one rule, are the rules repetitive?

Case File Assignment:

Write a synthesized rule for the issue of inhabited in the context of first-degree burglary using all of the legal authorities provided in the Case File and the information from your completed synthesis chart (Worksheet No. 2). To help you write your synthesized rule, answer the following brainstorming questions:

1. What is the rule, policy, or synthesized rule?

2. Are there any exceptions to the rule, policy, or synthesized rule?

3. Is there anything else the court would consider in applying the rule, policy, or synthesized rule?

After answering these brainstorming questions, cut and paste your answers together into one or more sentences. This is the first draft of your complete rule. Evaluate your draft rule by evaluating the following questions:

1. Is the rule too specific based on the legal authorities and your client facts?
2. Is the rule too broad based on the legal authorities and your client facts?
3. Does the rule include vague terms?
4. Is the rule circular?
5. If there is more than one rule, are the rules repetitive?

Edit your draft synthesized rule based on your answers to these questions and provide your final synthesized rule below:

WORKSHEET NO. 4: CASE ILLUSTRATIONS

Case illustrations describe a precedent case to further define the rule (the R in the objective paradigm) or provide the reader with an example of how a rule has been applied in other cases. All case illustrations include six categories of information. While all six categories should be included in each case illustration, each category of information does not require its own separate sentence. Thus, you may have a complete case illustration that only is two sentences, but you may also have a complete case illustration that is two paragraphs. The length of your case illustration depends on the information your reader needs for a complete understanding of the specific legal principle you are explaining with the case illustration.

A case illustration is substantively complete if it includes:

1. A thesis sentence stating the specific legal principle you plan to explain with the case illustration;
2. The issue before the court in the precedent case on the specific legal principle you plan to explain with the case illustration;
3. The relevant facts of the precedent case on the specific legal principle you plan to explain with the case illustration;
4. The court's holding in the precedent case on the specific legal principle you plan to explain with the case illustration;
5. The court's reasoning in the precedent case on the specific legal principle you plan to explain with the case illustration; and
6. A conclusion sentence to give closure to the case illustration; this must relate back to the thesis sentence that began the case illustration.

The above order of the six categories of information is the most common organization and tends provide the most natural flow of information. It can be modified, where appropriate, but the thesis sentence must always come first.

The most difficult part of writing a case illustration is the first sentence—the thesis sentence. Typically, this is a detailed sentence providing further explanation of how the rule (the R in your objective paradigm) operates, how the rule has been defined, or how the rule has been applied by the court in another case. Occasionally, however, this simply is the rule (the R in your objective paradigm) without a separate thesis sentence.

Example 1 begins with the rule in bold (the R in the objective paradigm) followed by the thesis sentence for the case illustration (underlined) and the rest of the case illustration categories. Example 2 begins with the rule in bold and underlined (the R in the objective paradigm), which also is the thesis sentence for the case illustration, followed by the rest of the case illustration categories. There is not a separate thesis sentence for this case illustration because the applicable rule is sufficiently narrow to serve as both the rule and the thesis sentence.

EXAMPLE 1:

Consent to use a celebrity's photograph is unnecessary if the use of a photograph is directly related to matters in the public interest. For example, consent is unnecessary if the use of a photograph is directly related to commentary on events that impact society. In Dora v. Frontline Video, Inc., the court determined whether the use of the plaintiff's photograph in a surfing documentary was proper under the public interest exception. 15 Cal. App. 4th 536 (2nd Dist. 1993). A 1950s professional surfer brought a claim against the producers of a documentary video for using his photograph, voice, and video recordings without his consent. Id. at 541. The court held that the use of the surfer's photograph, voice, and video recordings in the surfing documentary did not require consent because they were used in a manner that was directly related to a matter in the public interest. Id. at 546. It reasoned that surfing is in the public interest because "surfing is more than passing interest to some," that "it has created a lifestyle that influences speech, behavior, dress, and entertainment, among other things," and has "had a significant influence on the popular culture." Id. Because the surfer's photograph, voice, and video recordings were used in the documentary on surfing, which directly related to a matter in the public interest, the use was proper under the public interest exception and consent was unnecessary. Id.

EXAMPLE 2:

Consent to use a celebrity's photograph is required if the use of a photograph is for advertising purposes and is not directly related to a matter in the public interest. Downing v. Abercrombie & Fitch, 265 F.3d 994 (9th Cir. 2001). In Downing, the court determined whether the unauthorized use of a surfer's photograph in a surf-themed clothing catalogue was protected under the public interest exception. Id. at 999. The clothing catalog included a small number of editorials on surfing, but its primary purpose was to increase brand awareness and sell clothes. Id. at 1000. The photograph preceded two pages that advertised t-shirts designed to replicate those worn by the surfer in the photograph. The court held that the use of the surfer's photograph, although on a topic in the public interest, was not protected because the photograph was used as a "window dressing" to advance the surf-themed catalogue. Id. at 1002. It contrasted the use in the catalog from the use in the documentary in Dora, stating that although both cover the theme of surfing, the documentary's use "directly contributed to the story" while the catalog's use did not. Id. at 1003. Instead, the catalog's use was "much more commercial in nature." Therefore, the use of the surfer's photograph was not a proper use under the public interest exception and consent was required. Id.

Case File Assignment:

Write a case illustration for your client's case using the case(s) assigned to you by your professor. To help you write the case illustration, answer the following brainstorming questions. Please note, however, that before you can write a case illustration, you must know the rule or legal principle the case illustration is explaining.

For context, include the rule (the R in the objective paradigm) or legal principle you plan to explain with the case illustration here:

1. What is the specific legal principle you plan to explain with the case illustration? (NOTE: this is the thesis sentence for the case illustration that provides further explanation of how the rule (the R in your objective paradigm) operates, how the rule has been defined, or how the rule has been applied by the court in another case.)

2. What was the specific issue before the court in the precedent case as it relates to the specific legal principle you plan to explain with the case illustration? (NOTE: This must only be the issue specific to the legal principle you plan to explain with the case illustration, not all of the issues included in the precedent case. For example, focus specifically on the issue of whether a home was inhabited at the time of the burglary, not whether the defendant could be convicted of first degree burglary generally.)

3. What are the specific facts in the precedent case as they relate to the specific legal principle you plan to explain with the case illustration? (NOTE: This must only be the facts specific to the legal principle you plan to explain with the case illustration, not all of the facts included in the precedent case.)

4. What is the holding in the precedent case as it relates to the specific legal principle you plan to explain with the case illustration? (NOTE: This must only be the holding specific to the legal principle you plan to explain with the case illustration, not all of the holdings included in the precedent case.)

5. What is the reasoning in the precedent case as it relates to the specific legal principle you plan to explain with the case illustration? (NOTE: This must only be the reasoning specific to the legal principle you plan to explain with the case illustration, not all of the reasoning included in the precedent case.)

6. What additional sentence(s) might you need to provide closure to this case illustration and to connect it back to the specific legal principle identified in response to Question 1 above?

Using the answers to these brainstorming questions as your guide, write the case illustration. Start by cutting and pasting your answers into paragraph form and then mold them into a readable paragraph. Each of the six categories of information must be included for a complete case illustration. This does not mean, however, that you need to have six sentences. A complete case illustration may be as little as two sentences or as much as two full paragraphs.

WORKSHEET NO. 5: POLICY-BASED REASONING

Policy-based reasoning is analysis that applies the purpose underlying a rule to your client's case. Policy-based reasoning is most often used to strengthen an argument that already is supported by legal authorities or other types of reasoning. For example, the result is not only X because of the case law, but the result also is X because that result satisfies the purpose underlying the applicable rule. Policy-based reasoning can also be used to make an argument where there are not any applicable legal authorities or the direct application of the law provides a result that is inconsistent with the purpose underlying the rule.

To apply policy-based reasoning to your client's case, you must first determine the purpose underlying the rule: what was the goal of the legislature or the court in creating the rule? This purpose might come from the purpose section of a statute, legislative history, the court's opinion, or published legal commentary on a rule of law. It should not, however, come from your own personal view of society or your personal opinion as to why the rule was created.

Once you have determined the purpose underlying the rule, you then need to evaluate whether that purpose applies to your client's case. To determine the purpose underlying the rule and to evaluate whether it applies to your client's case, consider:

1. The conclusion you will reach by applying the policy to your client's case. (NOTE: You may need to answer this question after you have completed your analysis of the policy.)

2. The rule you are applying to your client's case.

3. The purpose underlying the rule identified in response to Question 2 above. What greater societal purpose(s) was the court or legislature trying to protect in creating the rule? (NOTE: There may be more than one purpose. If there is more than one purpose, identify if the court seems to prefer one purpose over another.) Also, the purpose behind the rule must come from legal authority, such as legislative history, case authority, or well-established public opinion, not your personal opinion.

4. The potential outcomes for your client when applying the rule.

5. The potential outcomes for the other party when applying the rule.

6. How the outcomes identified in response to Questions 4 and 5 above are or are not served by the purpose(s) of the rule you identified in response to Question 3 above.

7. The outcome that best follows the purpose of the rule.

After considering these brainstorming questions, you should have a clear understanding of whether the possible outcomes for your client do or do not serve the underlying purpose(s) of the rule. The following formula will then help you write a policy-based reasoning analysis. Each of these components must be included for a complete policy-based reasoning analysis.

A policy-based reasoning analysis is substantively complete if it:

1. Begins the paragraph(s) by stating the conclusion you will reach by applying the purpose of the rule to your client's case. (NOTE: This is the thesis sentence for this paragraph.)

2. States the rule that is the basis of the policy-based reasoning analysis.

3. Identifies and describes the purpose underlying the rule and the origin of that purpose. Remember, the purpose behind the rule must come from legal authority, such as legislative history, case authority, or well-established public opinion, not your personal opinion. Also, if there is more than one purpose, explain which purpose the courts tend to use more.

4. States whether the underlying purpose does or does not apply to the possible outcome(s) in your client's case.

5. Explains with specific detail why the possible outcome(s) in your client's case will or will not further the purpose underlying the rule.

6. Concludes with a sentence that provides closure to the policy-based reasoning analysis. This sentence must connect to the thesis sentence that began the policy-based reasoning analysis.

EXAMPLE POLICY–BASED REASONING:

The defendant's Civil Code § 3344(a) violation likely is not be actionable because the defendant's use of Ms. Anchor's photograph on its t-shirt provided commentary on a matter in the public interest and, therefore, consent was unnecessary. California Civil Code § 3344(d) provides an exception to the consent requirement contained in § 3344(a). It states that the use of a photograph in connection with "any news, public affairs, or sports broadcast or account, or any political campaign" does not require consent. § 3344(d). The courts have explained that the purpose of this exception is to protect the public's right to know about things, events, and people, such as news, celebrity activities, and sports. Eastwood, 149 Cal. App. 3d at 421; Gionfriddo v. Major League Baseball, 94 Cal. App. 4th 400 (1st Dist. 2001); Montana v. San Jose Mercury News, Inc., 34 Cal. App. 4th 790 (6th Dist. 1995). Thus, the right of a celebrity in her image is not absolute, but must be balanced against the public interest in the dissemination of news and information. Id. It is for this reason that the use of a celebrity's photograph on a matter in the public interest is exempt from the consent requirement of § 3344(a).

Ms. Anchor's claim is not furthered by the statutory purpose of protecting matters in the public interest. Rather, the defendant's use of Ms. Anchor's photograph with the Mayor's photograph as a miniature devil on her shoulder furthers the purpose because the t-shirt is part of an expressive comment on the unethical reporting on politics in Los Angeles. This is type of information the public interest exception was designed to protect. Thus, it is likely the use of Ms. Anchor's photograph on the t-shirt as a political and social commentary is not actionable due to the nature of the policy protecting the dissemination of information in the public interest.

Case File Assignment:

Write an analysis for your client's case using policy-based reasoning based on the legal authority contained in the Case File and/or the legal authority assigned by your professor. To help you write a policy-based reasoning analysis, answer the following brainstorming questions:

1. What is the conclusion you will reach by applying the policy to your client's case? (NOTE: You may need to answer this question after you have completed your analysis of the policy.)

2. What is the rule you are applying to your client's case?

3. What is the purpose underlying the rule identified in response to Question 2 above? What greater societal purpose(s) was the court or legislature trying to protect in creating the rule? (NOTE: There may be more than one purpose. If there is more than one purpose, identify if the court seems to prefer one purpose over another.) Also, the purpose behind the rule should come from legal authority, such as legislative history, case authority, or well-established public opinion, not your personal opinion.

4. What are the potential outcomes for your client when applying the rule?

5. What are the potential outcomes for the other party when applying the rule?

6. How are the outcomes identified in response to Questions 4 and 5 above served or not served by the purpose(s) of the rule you identified in response to Question 3 above?

7. Which outcome best follows the purpose(s) of the rule? Explain why.

After answering these brainstorming questions, you should have a clear understanding of whether the possible outcomes for your client do or do not serve the underlying purpose(s) of the rule. Use the following formula to write a policy-based reasoning analysis. Each of these components must be included for a complete policy-based reasoning analysis.

1. Begin the paragraph(s) by stating the conclusion you will reach by applying the purpose of the rule to your client's case. (NOTE: This is the thesis sentence for this paragraph.)
2. State the rule that is the basis of the policy-based reasoning analysis.
3. Identify and describe the purpose underlying the rule and the origin of that purpose. If there is more than one purpose, explain which one the courts tend to use more. Remember, the purpose behind the rule must come from legal authority, such as legislative history, case authority, or well-established public opinion, not your personal opinion on the purpose of the rule.
4. State whether the underlying purpose does or does not apply to the possible outcome(s) in your client's case.
5. Explain with specific detail why the possible outcome(s) in your client's case does or does not further the purpose underlying the rule.
6. Conclude with a sentence that provides closure to the policy-based reasoning analysis. This sentence must connect to the thesis sentence that began the policy-based reasoning analysis.

WORKSHEET NO. 6: ANALOGICAL REASONING

This worksheet is designed to give you a structured brainstorming process to evaluate whether analogical reasoning should be used in the analysis of your client's case. Clarity of writing comes from clarity of understanding. If you do not completely understand the structure or substance of the analogical reasoning to be included in your analysis, neither will the reader.

For an analogical reasoning analysis to be thoroughly evaluated, you must go through the following brainstorming process with as much detail as possible. This evaluation should be done for each issue and for each precedent case you plan to address with analogical reasoning.

1. Identify one issue you plan to address with analogical reasoning.

2. Identify the name of one precedent case you plan to use for the issue you selected above.

3. Identify the specific holding of the precedent case on the legal issue you plan to analyze with this analogical reasoning (NOTE: This must only be the holding specific to the legal issue you are addressing, not the overall holding of the precedent case.)

4. Describe the reasoning of the precedent case on the legal issue you plan to analyze with this analogical reasoning (NOTE: This must only be the reasoning specific to the legal issue you are addressing, not the overall reasoning of the precedent case.)

5. Make a list of the relevant facts from the precedent case on the legal issue you plan to analyze with this analogical reasoning (NOTE: This must only be the facts specific to the legal issue you are addressing, not all of the facts from the precedent case.)

6. Make a list of the relevant facts from your client's case on the legal issue you plan to analyze with this analogical reasoning (NOTE: This must only be the facts specific to the legal issue you are addressing, not all of the facts from your client's case.)

7. Group the facts of the precedent case and your client's case into facts that are similar and facts that are distinguishable.

Depending on whether the facts are similar or distinguishable or both, you may only need to consider some of the questions below. If the facts are similar, answer Questions 8–10. If the facts are distinguishable, answer Questions 11–13. If the facts are both similar and distinguishable, answer Questions 8–13.

8. Identify the fact(s) to be compared in your analysis as similar. (NOTE: this must only be the facts specific to the legal issue you are addressing, not all of the facts from the precedent case or your client's case.)

9. Explain why these facts are similar—use specific factual examples to demonstrate the similarities.

10. Explain *why* these factual similarities support your legal analysis on the issue you are addressing. This is where you must directly apply the reasoning of the precedent case to the facts of your client's case. Specifically look at why and how the precedent case ruled as it did and why that same reasoning applies to your client's case.

11. Identify the fact(s) to be compared in your analysis as distinguishable. (NOTE: This must only be the facts specific to the legal issue you are addressing, not all of the facts from the precedent case or your client's case.)

12. Explain why these facts are distinguishable—use specific factual examples to demonstrate the differences.

13. Explain *why* these factual differences support your legal analysis on the issue you are addressing. This is where you must directly apply the reasoning of the precedent case to the facts of your client's case. Specifically look at why and how the precedent case ruled as it did and why that same reasoning does not apply to your client's case.

After evaluating these brainstorming questions, you should have a clear understanding of whether this analogical reasoning should be included in the analysis of your client's case. You then must decide if the analogical reasoning will be based on a single case or multiple cases. If multiple cases are used to analyze the same legal issue, then you must provide this analysis at the same time, rather than as a separate analogical reasoning for each precedent case. Once you have decided if the analogical reasoning will be based on a single case or multiple cases, use one of the following formulas to write your analogical reasoning analysis:

<u>Analogical Reasoning Formula Using a Single Case:</u>

Component 1: The legal conclusion you want the reader to reach based on your analogical reasoning (this is the overall thesis sentence for the analogical reasoning paragraph or paragraphs—case names should not be included in this sentence).

Component 2: Sentence stating, "In client's case (use client's name) is similar to/distinguishable from _______ (insert precedent case name) based on _______ (identify the specific issue this analogical reasoning is addressing)."

Component 3: Sentence stating, "In client's case (use client's name), (insert detailed facts about your client's case that will be compared; this must only be the specific facts to be compared, not all of the facts of the case)."

Component 4: Sentence stating, "This case is similar to/distinguishable from ______ (insert precedent case name) where (insert detailed facts about the precedent case that will be compared—this must only be the specific facts to be compared, not all of the facts from the precedent case.)"

Component 5: Explain, using *specific factual detail*, why the facts you are comparing are similar or distinguishable. This is where you need to provide specific fact-to-fact comparisons, using actual facts from your client's case and the precedent case. (i.e.—"Fact X in client's case is similar to/distinguishable from Fact Y in precedent case because ______").

Component 6: Identify the likely outcome of your client's case based on the similarities or differences you discussed in Component 5. This is a re-statement of the conclusion (Component 1) but with more detail and this likely is the beginning of a new paragraph.

Component 7: Explain *why* this is the likely outcome. This is where you must directly apply the reasoning from the precedent case to your client's case.

Possible phrasing:

The court in ______ (insert precedent case name) reasoned ______ (insert the fact specific reasoning of the precedent case on the specific legal issue the analogical reasoning is addressing). This reasoning applies to your client's case (use client's name) because ______ (explain why it applies). Therefore, because the reasoning from (insert precedent case name) applies to your client's case (use client's name), the outcome in your client's case (use client's name) will likely be ______ (insert the outcome you are trying to prove with the analogical reasoning.)

Component 8: Re-state the conclusion you want the reader to reach based on your analogical reasoning. This must connect to the analysis provided by the analogical reasoning and to the conclusion stated in Component 1.

EXAMPLE SINGLE CASE ANALOGICAL REASONING:

TFF is not entitled to the public interest exception because the implication of unethical reporting created by the photographs on the t-shirt is false. Ms. Anchor's case is similar to Eastwood because both involved the dissemination of false information. 149 Cal. App. 3d 409. In Ms. Anchor's case, the t-shirt had a photograph of Ms. Anchor combined with a photograph of the Mayor as a miniature devil sitting on her shoulder. The inclusion of the Mayor on her shoulder with devil horns implied that he was influencing or controlling her reporting on his campaign, which Ms. Anchor denies. This is similar to Eastwood where the article stated that Mr. Eastwood was in a love triangle with two other celebrities, which Mr. Eastwood denied. Id. at 414. Just as Mr. Eastwood denied that he was involved in a love triangle, Ms. Anchor denies that she ever reported on the Mayor's re-election campaign and the general manager of KTV–LA stated that "there are no concerns about Ms. Anchor's ethics whatsoever." As reasoned in Eastwood, it is this type of dissemination of false information that legislature did not intend the public interest exception to protect. Id. at 425. Because the court in Eastwood reasoned that the Enquirer was not entitled to the public interest exception for its false article and TFF created a false implication by its use of Ms. Anchor's photograph on its t-shirt, TFF is not entitled to the public interest exception.

Analogical Reasoning Formula Using Multiple Cases:

Component 1: The legal conclusion you want the reader to reach based on your analogical reasoning (this is the overall thesis sentence for the analogical reasoning paragraph or paragraphs—case names should not be included in this sentence).

Component 2: Sentence stating, "Client's case (insert client's name) is similar to/distinguishable from ______ (insert first precedent case name) and/but similar to/distinguishable from ______ (insert second precedent case name) based on ______ (identify the specific issue this analogical reasoning is addressing)."

Component 3: Sentence stating, "In client's case (use client's name), (insert detailed facts about your client's case that will be compared; this must only be the specific facts to be compared, not all of the facts of the case.)"

Component 4(a): Sentence stating, "This case is similar to/distinguishable from ______ (insert first precedent case name) where (insert detailed facts about the precedent case you are relying upon—this must only be the specific facts to be compared, not all of the facts from the precedent case.)"

Component 4(b): Explain, using *specific factual detail*, why the facts you are comparing are similar/distinguishable. This is where you need to provide specific fact-to-fact comparisons, using actual facts from your client's case and the precedent case (i.e.—"Fact X in client's case is similar to/distinguishable from Fact Y in precedent case because ______ ").

Component 5(a): Sentence stating, "This case is similar to/distinguishable from ______ (insert second precedent case name) where (insert detailed facts about the precedent case you are relying upon—this also must only be the specific facts to be compared, not all of the facts from the precedent case)." [NOTE: you many need to use a transition to begin this sentence, such as "In addition," "Also," "However," or "On the other hand"]

Component 5(b): Explain, using *specific factual detail*, why the facts you are comparing are similar/distinguishable. This is where you need to provide specific fact-to-fact comparisons, using actual facts from your client's case and the precedent case. (i.e.—"Fact X in client's case is similar to/distinguishable from Fact Y in precedent case because ______ ").

Component 6: Identify the likely outcome of your client's case based on the similarities/differences you discussed previously (see Components 4(b) and 5(b)). This is a re-statement of the conclusion (Component 1) but with more detail and this likely is the beginning of a new paragraph.

Component 7: Explain *why* this is the likely outcome. This is where you must directly apply the reasoning from the precedent case to your client's case.

Possible phrasing if the reasoning of the precedent cases is the same:

The court in ______ (insert first and second precedent case names) reasoned ______ (insert the fact specific reasoning of the precedent cases on the specific legal issue the analogical reasoning is addressing). This reasoning applies to your client's case (use client's name) because ______ (explain why it applies). Therefore, because the reasoning from (insert precedent case names) applies to your client's case (use client's name), the outcome in your client's case (use client's name) will likely be ______ (insert the outcome you are trying to prove with the analogical reasoning.)

Possible phrasing if the reasoning of the precedent cases is different:

The court in _______ (insert first precedent case name) reasoned _______ (insert the fact specific reasoning of the first precedent case on the specific legal issue the analogical reasoning is addressing). This reasoning applies to your client's case (use client's name) because _______ (explain why it applies). However, the court in _______ (insert second precedent case name) reasoned _______ (insert the fact specific reasoning of the second precedent case on the specific legal issue the analogical reasoning is addressing). This reasoning does not apply to your client's case (use client's name) because _______ (explain why it does not apply). Therefore, because the reasoning from (insert first precedent case name) applies to your client's case (use client's name) and the reasoning from (insert second precedent case name) does not apply to your client's case (use client's name), the outcome in your client's case (use client's name) will likely be _______ (insert the outcome you are trying to prove with the analogical reasoning.)

Component 8: Re-state the conclusion you want the reader to reach based on your analogical reasoning. This must connect to the analysis provided by the analogical reasoning and to the conclusion stated in Component 1.

EXAMPLE MULTIPLE CASES ANALOGICAL REASONING:

The use of Ms. Anchor's photograph by TFF likely did not require consent because the use directly related to a matter in the public interest and was not commercial in nature. Ms. Anchor's case is similar to Dora but distinguishable from Downing because of the direct connection between the use of her photograph and the public interest. Ms. Anchor, a reporter for a local news station, was involved in a highly publicized relationship with the Mayor and there was a significant amount media attention alleging that she unethically reported on the Mayor's re-election campaign. TFF claims it created and sold a t-shirt with a photograph of Ms. Anchor, with a superimposed picture on her shoulder of the Mayor wearing miniature devil-horns, to provide commentary on Ms. Anchor's unethical reporting on local politics. This is similar to Dora, where Frontline Video used the image, video, and voice recordings of a well-known professional surfer in its surfing documentary to provide commentary on the early years of surfing and the cultural impact of surfing. Dora, 15 Cal. App. 4th at 541. The court in Dora reasoned that the use of the surfer's photograph in the documentary directly contributed to the story on surfing and the surfer had a significant influence on popular culture. Id. at 546. This reasoning applies here because the use of Ms. Anchor's photograph on TFF's t-shirt "directly contributed to the story" on her alleged unethical reporting on the Mayor's re-election campaign and its "significant influence" on local politics.

Furthermore, Ms. Anchor's case is distinguishable from Downing, where a well-known surfer's photograph, taken during a surfing championship, was used in a surf-themed clothing catalog. 265 F.3d 994. The surfer's photograph followed two articles that discussed the history of surfing; however, no connection was made between the articles and the surfer, and the surfer was not identified as a legend of the sport. Id. at 1002. Instead, the two pages following the surfer's photograph advertised t-shirts replicating those worn by the surfer in his photograph. Id. The court reasoned that this use was merely "window dressing to advance the [catalog's] surf theme" and promote sales based on the implied endorsement by the well-known surfer. Id. The use of the photograph was not to provide commentary on surfing like in Dora where the "point of the program" was to provide commentary on surfing. Id. at 1001. Ms. Anchor's is distinguishable from Downing in how her photograph was used because her photograph was used on a t-shirt primarily to provide commentary on her relationship with the Mayor and the alleged influence he may have had on Ms. Anchor's reporting on his re-election campaign. TFF stated that "the point of the t-shirt" was to provide commentary on Ms. Anchor's conflict of interest in reporting on the Mayor's re-election campaign; it was not a mere "window dressing" to sell the t-shirt. Consumers likely would

purchase the t-shirt because of the commentary, not because of her implied endorsement.

While the court in Dora reasoned that the use of the photograph in a surfing documentary did not require consent due to its direct contribution to public's interest in the significant influence of surfing and its cultural impact, the court in Downing reasoned that consent was required because the use of the photograph was commercial in nature, having only a tenuous relationship as a "window-dressing" with the surfing theme of the clothing catalog. Id. at 1002. Ms. Anchor's case is more analogous to Dora than Downing because of the strong connection between the use of her photograph and the public's interest in her relationship with the Mayor and possible unethical reporting on his re-election campaign. Therefore, because the reasoning from Dora more closely relates to Ms. Anchor's case than the reasoning from Downing, the use of the photograph in Ms. Anchor's case likely was directly connected to the public interest and consent was unnecessary.

Case File Assignment:

Write an analysis for your client's case using analogical reasoning based on the legal authority in the Case File and/or the legal authority assigned by your professor. To help you write your analogical reasoning, answer the following brainstorming questions:

1. Identify one specific legal issue you plan to address with analogical reasoning (or the specific issue assigned by your professor):

2. Identify the name of one precedent case you plan to use for the issue you selected above (or the case assigned by your professor).

3. Identify the specific holding of the precedent case on the legal issue you plan to analyze with this analogical reasoning. (NOTE: This must only be the holding on the specific legal issue you are addressing with this analogical reasoning, not the overall holding of the precedent case.)

4. Describe the reasoning of the precedent case you plan to analyze with this analogical reasoning. (NOTE: This must only be the reasoning on the specific legal issue you are addressing with this analogical reasoning, not the overall reasoning of the precedent case.)

5. Make a list of the relevant facts from the precedent case on the legal issue you plan to analyze with this analogical reasoning. (NOTE: This must only be the facts on the specific legal issue you are addressing with this analogical reasoning, not all of the facts from the precedent case.)

6. Make a list of the relevant facts from your client's case on the legal issue you plan to analyze with this analogical reasoning. (NOTE: This must only be the facts specific to the legal issue you are addressing with this analogical reasoning, not all of the facts from your client's case.)

7. Organize the facts of the precedent case and your client's case into the charts below:

Facts that are similar:

Your Client's Case	Precedent Case

Facts that are distinguishable:

Your Client's Case	Precedent Case

Using the information you filled into the charts above, decide whether you think your client's case and the precedent case are similar, distinguishable, or both. If they are similar, answer Questions 8–10 below. If they are distinguishable, answer Questions 11–13 below. If they are both similar and distinguishable, answer Questions 8–13 below.

8. Identify the fact(s) from your client's case and the precedent case to be compared as similar. (NOTE: This must only be facts specific to the legal issue you are addressing, not all of the facts from the precedent case or your client's case.)

9. Explain why these facts are similar—use specific factual examples to demonstrate the similarities.

10. Explain *why* these factual similarities support your legal analysis on the issue you are addressing. This is where you must directly apply the reasoning of the precedent case to the facts of your client's case. Specifically look at why and how the precedent case ruled as it did and why that same reasoning applies to your client's case.

11. Identify the fact(s) to be compared in your analysis as distinguishable. (NOTE: This must only be the facts specific to the legal issue you are addressing, not all of the facts from the precedent case or your client's case.)

12. Explain why these facts are distinguishable—use specific factual examples to demonstrate the differences.

13. Explain *why* these factual differences support your legal analysis on the issue you are addressing. This is where you must directly apply the reasoning of the precedent case to the facts of your client's case. Specifically look at why and how the precedent case ruled as it did and why that same reasoning does not apply to your client's case.

After answering these brainstorming questions, you should have a clear understanding of whether analogical reasoning should be included in the analysis of your client's case. You then must decide if the analogical reasoning will be based on a single case or multiple cases. If multiple cases are used to analyze the same legal issue, then you must provide this analysis at the same time, rather than as a separate analogical reasoning for each precedent case. Once you have decided if the analogical reasoning will be based on a single case or multiple cases, use one of the following formulas to write your analogical reasoning analysis:

<u>Analogical Reasoning Formula Using a Single Case:</u>

Component 1: The legal conclusion you want the reader to reach based on your analogical reasoning (this is the overall thesis sentence for the analogical reasoning paragraph or paragraphs—case names should not be included in this sentence).

Component 2: Sentence stating, "In client's case (use client's name) is similar to/distinguishable from ______ (insert precedent case name) based on ______ (identify the specific issue this analogical reasoning is addressing)."

Component 3: Sentence stating, In "client's case (use client's name), (insert detailed facts about your client's case that will be compared; this must only be the specific facts to be compared, not all of the facts of the case)."

Component 4: Sentence stating, "This case is similar to/distinguishable from ______ (insert precedent case name) where (insert detailed facts about the precedent case that will be compared—this must only be the specific facts to be compared, not all of the facts from the precedent case.)"

Component 5: Explain, using *specific factual detail*, why the facts you are comparing are similar or distinguishable. This is where you need to provide specific fact-to-fact comparisons, using actual facts from your client's case and the precedent case. (i.e.—"Fact X in client's case is similar to/distinguishable from Fact Y in precedent case because ______ ").

Component 6: Identify the likely outcome of your client's case based on the similarities or differences you discussed in Component 5. This is a re-statement of the conclusion (Component 1) but with more detail and this likely is the beginning of a new paragraph.

Component 7: Explain *why* this is the likely outcome. This is where you must directly apply the reasoning from the precedent case to your client's case.

Possible phrasing:

The court in ______ (insert precedent case name) reasoned ______ (insert the fact specific reasoning of the precedent case on the specific legal issue the analogical reasoning is addressing). This reasoning applies to your client's case (use client's name) because ______ (explain why it applies). Therefore, because the reasoning from (insert precedent case name) applies to your clients case (use client's name), the outcome in your client's case (use client's name) will likely be ______ (insert the outcome you are trying to prove with the analogical reasoning.)

Component 8: Re-state the conclusion you want the reader to reach based on your analogical reasoning. This must connect to the analysis provided by the analogical reasoning and the conclusion stated in Component 1.

<u>Analogical Reasoning Formula Using Multiple Cases:</u>

Component 1: The legal conclusion you want the reader to reach based on your analogical reasoning (this is the overall thesis sentence for the analogical reasoning paragraph or paragraphs—case names should not be included in this sentence).

Component 2: Sentence stating, "Client's case (insert client's name) is similar to/distinguishable from ______ (insert first precedent case name) and/but similar to/distinguishable from ______ (insert second precedent case name) based on ______ (identify the specific issue this analogical reasoning is addressing)."

Component 3: Sentence stating, "In client's case (use client's name), (insert detailed facts about your client's case that will be compared; this must only be the specific facts that will be compared, not all of the facts of the case.)"

Component 4(a): Sentence stating, "This case is similar to/distinguishable from ______ (insert first precedent case name) where (insert detailed facts about the precedent case you are relying upon—this must only be specific facts to be compared, not all of the facts from the precedent case.)"

Component 4(b): Explain, using *specific factual detail*, why the facts you are comparing are similar/distinguishable. This is

where you need to provide specific fact-to-fact comparisons, using actual facts from your client's case and the precedent case (i.e.—"Fact X in client's case is similar to/distinguishable from Fact Y in precedent case because ______ ").

Component 5(a): Sentence stating, "This case is similar to/distinguishable from ______ (insert second precedent case name) where (insert detailed facts about the precedent case you are relying upon—this also must only be the specific facts to be compared, not all of the facts from the precedent case)." [NOTE: you many need to use a transition to begin this sentence, such as "In addition," "Also," "However," or "On the other hand"]

Component 5(b): Explain, using *specific factual detail*, why the facts you are comparing are similar/distinguishable. This is where you need to provide specific fact-to-fact comparisons, using actual facts from your client's case and the precedent case. (i.e.—"Fact X in client's case is similar to/distinguishable from Fact Y in precedent case because ______ ").

Component 6: Identify the likely outcome of your client's case based on the similarities/differences you discussed previously (see Components 4(b) and 5(b)). This is a re-statement of the conclusion (Component 1) but with more detail and this likely is the beginning of a new paragraph.

Component 7: Explain *why* this is the likely outcome. This is where you must directly apply the reasoning from the precedent case to your client's case.

Possible phrasing if the reasoning of the precedent cases is the same:

The court in ______ (insert first and second precedent case names) reasoned ______ (insert the fact specific reasoning of the precedent cases on the specific legal issue the analogical reasoning is addressing). This reasoning applies to your client's case (use client's name) because ______ (explain why it applies). Therefore, because the reasoning from (insert precedent case names) applies to your client's case (use client's name), the outcome in your client's case (use client's name) will likely be ______ (insert the outcome you are trying to prove with the analogical reasoning.)

Possible phrasing if the reasoning of the precedent cases is different:

The court in ______ (insert first precedent case name) reasoned ______ (insert the fact specific reasoning of the first precedent case on the specific legal issue the analogical reasoning is addressing). This reasoning applies to your client's case (use client's name) because ______ (explain why it applies). However, the court in ______ (insert second precedent case name) reasoned ______ (insert the fact specific reasoning of the second precedent case on the specific legal issue the analogical reasoning is addressing). This reasoning does not apply to your client's case (use client's name) because ______ (explain why it does not apply). Therefore, because the reasoning from (insert first precedent case name) applies to your client's case (use client's name) and the reasoning from (insert second precedent case name) does not apply to your client's case (use client's name), the outcome in your client's case (use client's name) will likely be ______ (insert the outcome you are trying to prove with the analogical reasoning.)

Component 8: Re-state the conclusion you want the reader to reach based on your analogical reasoning. This must connect to the analysis provided by the analogical reasoning and to the conclusion in Component 1.

WORKSHEET NO. 7: QUESTION PRESENTED

The Question Presented establishes the focus of the memorandum for the reader. It identifies the applicable statute or common law rule, it sets out the legal question(s) to be addressed in your memorandum, and it summarizes the facts that will be significant in addressing the legal question(s).

The most common Question Presented formula is known as the under-does-when formula:

Under [Insert reference to applicable law],

Does/did/is/was/can/may [Insert the legal question]

When/for/if [Insert the legally significant facts]?

An "under-does-when" Question Presented is substantively correct if it:

1. Includes the applicable law. This will be the popular name of a statute (not the citation) or a general legal principle based in common law (without case names or citations);
2. Identifies the specific legal question(s) your memorandum is addressing. The legal questions(s) must not be too narrow or too broad. If it is too narrow, the question will not cover all of the issues and sub-issues the memorandum is addressing. If it is too broad, the question will not serve the function of focusing the reader's attention on the specific issue(s) the memorandum is addressing; and
3. Provides the legally significant facts. The legally significant facts are the facts used in the analysis of your memorandum.

An "under-does-when" Question Presented is technically correct if it:

1. Is only one sentence; and
2. Ends with a question mark.

EXAMPLE QUESTION PRESENTED:
Under the California statutory right of publicity, does Tasha V. Anchor, a well-known television reporter, have a right of publicity claim against T–Shirts For Fun for its use of Ms. Anchor's photograph on a t-shirt combined with a photograph of the Los Angeles Mayor in a manner that falsely implies he unethically influenced Ms. Anchor's reporting on his re-election campaign?

Case File Assignment:

Write the Question Presented for your client's case. To help you write the Question Presented for your client's case, answer the following brainstorming questions:

1. What is the applicable law? This will be the popular name of a statute (not the citation) or a general legal principle based in common law (without case names or citations).

2. What is the specific legal question(s) your memorandum is addressing? The legal question(s) must not be too narrow or too broad. If it is too narrow, the question will not cover all of the issues and sub-issues the memorandum is addressing. If it is too broad, the question will not serve the function of focusing the reader's attention on the specific issue(s) the memorandum is addressing.

3. What are the legally significant facts? The legally significant facts are the facts used in the analysis in your memorandum. If there are numerous facts, summarize them or include only the most important facts.

Using the answers to these brainstorming questions as your guide, write the Question Presented for your client's case. Start by cutting and pasting your answers into paragraph form and then mold them into a readable sentence using the following formula as your guide. Also, remember that a technically correct "under-does-when" Question Presented must only be one sentence and end with a question mark.

Under [Insert reference to applicable law], does/did/is/was/can/may [Insert the legal question] when/for/if [Insert the legally significant facts]?

WORKSHEET NO. 8: BRIEF ANSWER

The Brief Answer responds to the question posed by the Question Presented. When read together, the Question Presented and Brief Answer are the "Introduction" to an objective memorandum. After reading the Question Presented and Brief Answer, the reader should have a solid understanding of the subject, the law, and the outcome predicted in the memorandum.

The Brief Answer typically begins with a one- or two-word answer, which is followed by a period; this is called the "short answer." The words that are typically used are "yes," "probably yes," "no," and "probably no/not." If you believe the answer could go either way, it is appropriate to indicate that the outcome is a close call by using the word "probably" in your short answer. However, you must still make a prediction; thus, avoid words such as "might," "possibly," or "could."

Next, you will explain to the reader the basis for the short answer. To do this, you will first provide a statement of the applicable rule(s) that apply to your client's case. Then, you will provide a summary of the reasoning that supports the short answer based on the legally significant facts and the application of the rule(s) to those facts. Finally, the organization of the Brief Answer should parallel the organization of the Discussion section and the tone must to remain objective—do not "argue" your answer.

A Brief Answer is substantively correct if it includes:

1. A short answer:

   a. Yes.

   b. Probably yes.

   c. No.

   d. Probably no/not.

2. A statement of the applicable rule(s). This should define the applicable law(s) identified in your Question Presented. To do this, consult the rules in your analysis (the Rs in each of your objective paradigms).

3. A summary of the reasoning that supports the short answer based on the legally significant facts and the application of the rule(s) to those facts. This should summarize each of the fact-specific conclusions you reached in your analysis. To help you do this, review the analysis in your memorandum (the As in each of your objective paradigms) and try to summarize it in three to four sentences.

EXAMPLE BRIEF ANSWER (the Question Presented is included for context):

QUESTION PRESENTED

Under the California statutory right of publicity, does Tasha V. Anchor, a well-known television reporter, have a right of publicity claim against T–Shirts For Fun for its use of Ms. Anchor's photograph on a t-shirt combined with a photograph of the Los Angeles Mayor in a manner that falsely implies he unethically influenced Ms. Anchor's reporting on his re-election campaign?

BRIEF ANSWER

Probably yes. The California statutory right of publicity is violated when a person's photograph is knowingly used on a product for profit without consent. This statutory right is not absolute as consent is unnecessary if the use of the photograph contributes to the public interest. However, if the photograph or its use contains false information, the public interest exception does not apply. Here, T–Shirts For Fun knowingly used Ms. Anchor's photograph on a t-shirt it created and sold for profit without her consent. The use of the photograph, however, was likely in the public interest because the t-shirt provided commentary on the highly publicized affair between Ms. Anchor and the Mayor and the potential influence the Mayor may have had on Ms. Anchor's reporting on his re-election campaign. Because such information is in the public interest, Ms. Anchor's consent to use her photograph was not required. This exception, however, will likely not apply because, although in the public interest, the commentary was based on false information. While it is true that Ms. Anchor had an affair with the Mayor, she and the television station she works for deny that she ever reported on the Mayor's re-election campaign, showing the commentary on the t-shirt was false. Thus, Ms. Anchor likely will have a right of publicity claim against T–Shirts For Fun.

Case File Assignment:

Write the Brief Answer for your client's case. To help you write the Brief Answer for your client's case, review your Question Presented to remind yourself of the question your Brief Answer is responding to. Next, answer the following brainstorming questions to help you develop the substance of your Brief Answer:

1. What is the short answer to the question posed in your Question Presented? Remember this can only be "yes," "probably yes," "no," or "probably no/not."

2. What are the applicable rule(s)? This should define the applicable law(s) identified in your Question Presented. To do this, consult the rules in your analysis (the Rs in each of your objective paradigms).

3. Summarize the reasoning that supports the short answer based on the legally significant facts and the application of the rule(s) to those facts. This should summarize each of the fact-specific conclusions you reached in your analysis. To help you do this, review the analysis (the As in each of your objective paradigms) in your memorandum and try to summarize it in three to four sentences.

Using the answers to these brainstorming questions as your guide, write the Brief Answer for your client's case. Start by cutting and pasting your answers into paragraph form and then mold them into a readable paragraph, using the following formula:

Short answer. Statement of the applicable rule(s). Summary of the reasoning that supports the short answer based on the legally significant facts and the application of the rule(s) to those facts.

WORKSHEET NO. 9: FACTS

The four most important things to remember when writing an objective Facts section are to: (1) include the legally significant facts; (2) organize the facts in an effective manner; (3) maintain a neutral tone; and (4) provide objectively accurate facts.

The Facts section is substantively correct if it:

1. Develops the foundation or context for the reader in the first paragraph (or first couple of sentences) by:
    a. Identifying your client, the opposing party, and their relationship;
    b. Stating your client's general problem or goal;
    c. Describing the setting (e.g. the time and location of the events); and
    d. Including the procedural history or the status of the case.
2. Includes the proper substance by:
    a. Including the legally significant facts. To determine the legally significant facts, review your analysis and highlight all of the facts from your client's case that you relied upon. These are the legally significant facts. If you have not yet written your analysis, determine the legally significant facts by asking yourself what are the facts a court would consider in ruling on your client's case?
    b. Including background facts that are needed for the legally significant facts to make sense. To determine the necessary background facts, ask yourself: what else does the reader need to know to understand the story of your client's case?
    c. Describing the facts accurately;
    d. Including both favorable and unfavorable facts;
    e. Omitting factual arguments, references to the law, legal conclusions, and factual conclusions; and
    f. Maintaining an objective and neutral tone.
3. Has a strategically selected organization to best tell the story: chronological, topical, or a combination of chronological and topical. The organization you select must be a strategic choice based on the best approach to tell the reader the story of your client's case.
4. Provides closure to the Facts section by not ending abruptly (consider re-stating what the client has asked you to do or stating the procedural history of the case).

EXAMPLE FACTS:

T–Shirts for Fun (TFF) recently created and sold a t-shirt featuring a photograph of Tasha V. Anchor, a local television reporter for KTV-LA. On the t-shirt, Ms. Anchor's photograph is combined with a photograph of a miniaturized image of the Los Angeles Mayor wearing a suit and devil horns, sitting on Ms. Anchor's left shoulder. TFF, a company that designs, produces, and distributes funny t-shirts for profit, claims it created the t-shirt to provide subtle commentary on the possibility that Ms. Anchor unethically reported on the Mayor's re-election campaign. Ms. Anchor, however, did not consent to the use of her photograph on the t-shirt and is offended by its use because she denies that she ever unethically reported on the Mayor's re-election campaign.

TFF created the t-shirt soon after an affair between Ms. Anchor and the Mayor was made public. The affair was highly publicized and the ethics of both Ms Anchor and the Mayor were questioned by the media. Ms. Anchor admits that she conducted a few of interviews of the Mayor last fall, but states they were on topics unrelated to his re-election campaign. Her employer, KTV–LA, has allowed Ms. Anchor to keep her position and the general manager for the station said "There is no concern as to the ethics of Ms. Anchor whatsoever."

Ms. Anchor would like to determine if she has a claim against TFF based on its unauthorized use of her photograph in a manner that falsely implies she unethically reported on the Mayor's re-election campaign.

Case File Assignment:

Write the Facts section for you client's case. To help you write the Facts section, answer the following brainstorming questions:

1. For the first paragraph (or first couple of sentences) of the Facts section, develop the foundation or context for the reader:
   a. Who is your client? Who is the opposing party? What is their relationship (i.e.—employer/employee; buyer/seller; landlord/tenant; accused/victim)?

   b. What is your client's general problem or goal?

c. What was the setting (e.g. the time and location of the events)?

d. What is the procedural history or the status of the case?

2. For the remaining paragraphs in your Facts section, answer the following brainstorming questions to help you identify the relevant facts:

   a. What are the legally significant facts? Review your analysis section and highlight all of the facts from your client's case that you used in your analysis. These are the legally significant facts and they must be included in your Facts section. If you have not yet written your analysis, then determine the legally significant facts by asking yourself: what are the facts a court would consider in ruling on your client's case?

   b. What background facts are necessary to provide context for the legally significant facts identified in response to Question 2(a) above?

   c. What are the unfavorable facts? What are the facts the opposing party likely will rely upon?

3. Looking at your answers to these brainstorming questions and using your understanding of your client's case, identify the organization you will use to structure your Facts section? Chronological? Topical? Combination of chronological and topical? The organization you select must be a strategic choice based on the best approach to tell the story of your client's case.

Using the answers to these brainstorming questions as your guide, write the Facts section for your client's case. Start by cutting and pasting your answers into paragraph form and then mold them into readable paragraphs.

When writing the Facts section, consider the following:

1. The first paragraph must:
   - Identify all of the parties and their relationship;
   - Briefly describe your client's problem or goal;
   - Provide the setting (time and location of events); and
   - Include the status or procedural history of the case.
2. The overall substance and tone must:
   - Have a strategically selected organization (avoid stream of consciousness writing);
   - Describe the facts accurately;
   - Include both favorable and unfavorable facts;
   - Omit factual arguments, references to the law, legal conclusions, and factual conclusions; and
   - Maintain an objective and neutral tone.
3. The last paragraph must:
   - Provide closure to the Facts section by not ending abruptly (consider re-stating what the client has asked you to do or stating the procedural history of the case).

WORKSHEET NO. 10: CONCLUSION

The Conclusion summarizes the individual conclusions reached in your analysis into one or two paragraphs and provides strategic recommendations based on your analysis in the memorandum. Although the Conclusion should be self-contained, that is, the reader should be able to understand it without having to read the entire memorandum, it should not include nearly as much detail as the Discussion section.

A Conclusion is substantively correct if it includes:

1. The ultimate conclusion of your memorandum;
2. Each rule applied to your client's case (the R in each objective paradigm included in your memorandum);
3. The conclusion for each rule applied in your client's case (the C in each objective paradigm included in your memorandum);
4. A summary of the reasoning that supports those conclusions (summarize the A sections in each objective paradigm included in your memorandum); and
5. Any strategic recommendations based on the analysis provided in the memorandum.

EXAMPLE CONCLUSION:

Ms. Anchor likely has a valid right of publicity claim against TFF. Under the California statutory right of publicity, a person has a claim if another knowingly uses the person's photograph without consent. Consent is unnecessary, however, if the photograph relates to a matter in the public interest and is connected to that public interest, unless the use provides false information. In this case, TFF's knowingly used Ms. Anchor's photograph without her consent in violation of § 3344(a). However, because it was used by TFF for the purpose of providing a commentary on the affair between Ms. Anchor and the Mayor and the possible unethical reporting on the Mayor's re-election campaign, the use of the photograph relates to a matter in the public interest. Thus, it is subject to the exemption in § 3344(d) and Ms. Anchor's consent was unnecessary. Despite this, Ms. Anchor likely will still prevail because the implication created by TFF's use of Ms. Anchor's photograph on the t-shirt is false and, therefore, not entitled to protection. For these reasons, Ms. Anchor likely has a successful claim against TFF and should pursue a legal remedy in this matter.

Case File Assignment:

Write the Conclusion for you client's case. To help you write the Conclusion section, answer the following brainstorming questions:

1. What is the ultimate conclusion of your memorandum? (NOTE: This must be consistent with the information provided in your Question Presented and your Brief Answer.)

2. Identify each rule applied to your client's case (the R in each objective paradigm included in your memorandum).

3. Identify the conclusion for each rule applied in your client's case (the C in each objective paradigm included in your memorandum)?

4. Summarize the analysis that supports the conclusion on each rule (summarize the A section in each objective paradigm included in your memorandum)?

5. Identify any strategic recommendations based on the analysis provided in your memorandum.

Using the answers to these brainstorming questions as your guide, write the Conclusion for your client's case. Start by cutting and pasting your answers into paragraph form and then mold them into a readable paragraph. When writing the Conclusion, maintain an objective and neutral tone, have the organization of the Conclusion parallel the organization of the Discussion section, and avoid simply repeating the Brief Answer.

CASE FILE NO. 2: FARMER JOHN v. FARMER FORD

WORKSHEET NO. 1: INTRODUCTION, FACTS, AND RELEVANT AUTHORITY

Introduction

Attorneys rarely research the law and write an analysis simply to learn the law. Instead, attorneys almost always research and write in response to the specific situation faced by a client. Therefore, before you turn to the attached statutes and cases, read the Office Memorandum on the next page to give yourself an understanding of your client's situation. The Office Memorandum is an example of what you might receive when a supervising attorney asks you to work on a case.

After you read the Office Memorandum, read the statutes and cases provided in the Case File. One of your goals in reading these statutes and cases is to develop your understanding of Rhode Island's law on spite fences. Another goal is to find the answer to the question the supervising attorney poses in the Office Memorandum: Does Farmer John have a claim against Farmer Ford under the Rhode Island spite fence statute? As you read each legal authority, consider how you can use it to determine the most likely outcome for your client. The most likely outcome, however, may not always be a favorable one. Therefore, considering the law and the facts from a neutral perspective are vital to fully advise your client.

OFFICE MEMORANDUM

TO: Legal Intern
FROM: Supervising Attorney
DATE: September 1, YEAR
RE: Farmer John v. Farmer Ford; Spite fence

My uncle, John Campbell (who we call Farmer John), recently came to me about an issue regarding his neighbor, James Ford (who calls himself Farmer Ford). We would like to determine if the Rhode Island spite fence statute applies to my uncle's situation and allow him to bring a claim against Farmer Ford.

My notes summarizing the facts of this case are below. These are the only facts available at this time.

— *Farmer John owns a farm in southern Rhode Island.*

— *The farm has been in our family for more than a century and has always grown apples and sweet corn.*

— *There are three other farms that border Farmer John's farm.*

— *The farm on the northern side was sold three years ago to Farmer Ford. This farm has grown potatoes for more than a century, but it has not been owned by the same family. Instead, this farm has been bought and sold multiple times over the last fifty years, with Farmer Ford being its most recent owner.*

— *Farmer John does not like Farmer Ford and thinks he is destroying the farm and the farming community.*

— *Farmer Ford recently decided potatoes were not profitable for him or his farm anymore. He decided to take advantage of the federal Cash for Clunkers program and turned his farm into an auto dismantling and junk yard.*

— *The neighbors began to complain about the noise, the smells, and the traffic created by the large big rig trucks that delivered junked cars.*

— *Farmer Ford said, "it is his farm and he can do what he wants."*

— *Farmer John organized the neighbors to try to force Farmer Ford to stop his auto dismantling and junk yard business.*

— *Farmer Ford responded by offering to have a fence built between his property and the others. He said he would pay for half of the cost of the fence.*

— *Farmer John was furious at the suggestion of a fence, as farm land is supposed to be open and have a sense of community. He also was offended that Farmer Ford would only pay for half of the fence.*

— *Farmer Ford said never mind and that he would build his own fence. He then took a backhoe and dug six large holes on the edge of his property that bordered Farmer John's property. Farmer Ford then took six cars that were going to be junked and planted them nose-first into the ground so that the cars were vertically "planted" in the ground.*

— *The six cars were standard sedans, which are 16 feet in length and 6 feet wide, and were planted only one foot apart from each other.*

— *After "planting" the cars, Farmer Ford told the neighbors, "Aren't you happy now? You've got your stupid fence for free and I am growing crops again! This should be a good year to grow sedans, ha, ha!"*

— *Farmer John and the neighbors were furious at the sight of the cars and wanted them removed immediately.*

— *Farmer John told Farmer Ford that his family would turn in their grave to know that their prized farm was next to Hillbilly Stonehenge and if it was not removed, Farmer John and the other farmers would sue.*

— *Farmer Ford claims that he planted the cars out of humor and as a temporary advertising gimmick for his new business, rather than out of spite for his neighbors' complaints. But he also did say that the neighbor's frustration was an added benefit.*

R.I. Gen. Laws 34–10–1

General Laws of Rhode Island

TITLE 34. PROPERTY
CHAPTER 10. FENCES

§ 34–10–1. Lawful fences defined

The following fences shall be adjudged to be lawful fences:

(1) A hedge with a ditch shall be three feet (3') high upon the bank of the ditch, well staked, at the distance of two feet and a half (2 1/2'), bound together at the top and sufficiently filled to prevent small stock from creeping through; and the bank of the ditch shall not be less than one foot (1') above the surface of the ground.

(2) A hedge without a ditch shall be four feet (4') high, staked, bound and filled, as a hedge with a ditch.

(3) A post-and-rail fence on the bank of a ditch shall be four (4) rails high, each well set in posts, and not less than four feet and a half (4 1/2') high.

(4) A stone wall fence shall be four feet (4') high, with a flat stone hanging over the top thereof or a good rail or pole thereon, well staked or secured with crotches or posts.

(5) A stone wall without flat stones, rails or posts on the top, shall be four feet and a half (4 1/2') high.

(6) A woven wire fence of wire not less than number nine, firmly fastened to posts not more than sixteen feet (16') apart, constructed of not less than eleven (11) horizontal wires, the top wire not less than fifty-four inches (54") from the ground, the bottom wire not more than two inches (2") from the ground and with stays or uprights not more than six inches (6") apart.

(7) All other kinds of fences not herein particularly described shall be four feet and a half (4 1/2') high.

§ 34–10–20. Spite fences

A fence or other structure in the nature of a fence which unnecessarily exceeds six feet (6') in height and is maliciously erected or maintained for the purpose of annoying the owners or occupants of adjoining property, shall be deemed a private nuisance, and any owner or occupant who is injured, either in the comfort or enjoyment of his or her estate thereby, may have an action to recover damages for the injury.

MUSUMECI et ux.

v.

LEONARDO et ux.

Supreme Court of Rhode Island

75 A.2d 175

July 13, 1950

CONDON

* * *

Fundamentally, the question raised by the appeal is whether a fence erected on one's own land with the intent to deprive an adjacent landowner of light and air is a private nuisance which equity will enjoin. Such a fence is popularly called a 'spite fence.' In this state, by virtue of General Laws 1938, chapter 645, § 20, a fence substantially of that character is deemed a private nuisance and one injured thereby is expressly given a right of **176 action at law for damages.

* * *

The evidence shows that respondents' land is higher than complainants' land. On the boundary there is a cement retaining wall which is about six feet from complainants' house and varies in height from five to seven feet. At its highest point it is about on a level with the top of the lower sash of the windows on the first floor and at its lowest point is about level with the bottom of such window sash. About two feet from this wall on their own land and parallel to the whole side of complainants' house facing the wall respondents have erected a board fence varying in height from five feet four inches to five feet six inches. Some of the posts, however, are as high as six feet, but none of the boarding is of that height. The fence is considerably higher than the top of the windows on the first floor. This admittedly blocks the view from such windows, darkens the rooms on that floor, and cuts off air.

Respondent Vincenzo Leonardo erected the fence as a result of an altercation with complainants' daughter, Mrs. Anna Fascitelli, in the summer of 1948 which arose in the following manner. It seems that on several occasions during that summer respondent while watering his garden had allowed water to go beyond into complainants' premises and through the open windows of Mrs. Fascitelli's apartment on the first floor which damaged her wallpaper and curtains and caused puddles on her rugs. She testified that she complained to him about this but that he ignored such complaints. As a result, ill feeling grew up between them, and finally Mrs. Fascitelli called respondent a vile name. Whereupon, according to Mrs. Fascitelli, the respondent said: '* * * I will fix you. I will build a fence so high I won't let you see no light and no sun any more.' The respondent, however, testified that he erected the fence to protect his interests and so that no water would go over the wall when he was watering his garden, and also to keep children out of his garden and off the wall.

It is obvious from the testimony presented by both sides that the fence itself does not exceed six feet in height nor does the wall and fence together, in our opinion, constitute a 'structure in the nature of a fence.' The wall was built by complainants and is apparently a necessary structure for the mutual benefit of the adjacent proprietors, as it is intended to preserve as nearly as possible the natural contour of the land by holding in place the upper proprietor's soil, thus preventing it from eroding and being cast upon the lower proprietor's land. In itself the wall is not a fence nor does it form any part of the actual board fence which respondents have erected on their own land. This being so, chap. 645, § 20, is not applicable as is clearly evident from its language which is as follows: 'A fence, or other structure in the nature of a fence, which unnecessarily exceeds 6 feet in height, and is maliciously erected or maintained for the purpose of annoying the owners or occupants of adjoining property, shall be deemed a private nuisance, and any such owner or occupant who is injured, either in the comfort or enjoyment of his estate thereby, may have an action of trespass on the case to recover damages for such injury.'

We agree, therefore, with complainants that this statute does not make available to them a remedy at law which would preclude them from relief in equity by injunction, if they are otherwise entitled to that equitable remedy. Hence if the trial justice's decision denying and dismissing**177 the bill of complaint were dependent for its correctness solely on the ground that complainants had a remedy at law by virtue of that section, it would be erroneous. However, we are of the opinion that it can be supported on other grounds.

First, the complainants' evidence does not show that respondents erected and now maintain their fence solely out of unmixed malice toward the complainants. Even the testimony of Mrs. Fascitelli herself tends to show that there was a good reason for some such barrier as the board fence to prevent water from entering her premises when respondent watered his garden. Whether it is effective for that purpose is not important here. The close proximity of the complainants' house to the wall, a matter of a mere six feet, plus the fact that the garden was more than five feet above the level of their lot made it likely that some water might escape from time to time to the complainants' lot below and occasionally enter the open windows of the first floor of their house. That is enough to show that the fence in question can and does perform a useful purpose regardless of the motive for its erection. So that even under the law as laid down in *Burke v. Smith*, 69 Mich. 380, 37 N.W. 838, 8 L.R.A. 184, relied on by complainants, this fence could not, on the evidence here, reasonably be said to be wholly malicious and, therefore, not enjoinable as a 'spite fence' within the meaning of that case.

The authorities cited by the complainants in addition to the Burke case hold that the maintenance of such fences may be enjoined if the alleged malice of the respondents is unmixed with an otherwise useful purpose or benefit to them which the fence will reasonably subserve. 133 A.L.R. 692, Anno. The *Burke case*, 69 Mich. at page 388, 37 N.W. at page 842, states the rule to be 'that no man has a legal right to make a malicious use of his property, *not for any benefit or advantage to himself*, but for the avowed purpose of damaging his neighbor.' (Italics ours.) See also 22 Am.Jur., Fences, § 43, where it is stated that 'Some authorities take the view that a fence erected maliciously and with no purpose other than to shut out light and air from a neighbor's window is a nuisance.' A similar statement of the law is to be found in Joyce, Law of Nuisance, § 37. Tested by those statements the fence in question here is not subject to injunction as a private nuisance.

The decree denying and dismissing the bill is correct, however, for another and stronger reason than those already stated. In this state a fence erected on one's own land for the purpose of shutting off light and air to an adjacent owner is not unlawful unless it violates G.L.1938, chap. 645, § 20. Hence the maintenance of such a fence cannot be enjoined in equity as a private nuisance. It is not a nuisance. In order to be such it would have to violate some right of the adjacent landowner. Under the common law as it is generally applied in America an adjacent proprietor has no right to light and air coming to him across the land of his neighbor. *Trustees Mathewson Street M. E. Church v. Shepard*, 22 R.I. 112, 46 A. 402.

The gravamen of the instant bill of complaint is that respondents have maliciously deprived them of light and air. But if complainants have no right to such light and air, of what does the alleged nuisance consist? They answer: the malice which motivated respondents in erecting the fence. In support of their position they argue that such malicious conduct is a clear violation of that ancient maxim of the law, *sic utere tuo ut alienum non laedas*. Their contention to this effect is borne out by the authorities which they cite, but we think it an unwarranted extension of the maxim. So use your own as not to injure another's property is, indeed, a sound and salutary principle for the promotion of justice, but it may not and should not be applied so as gratuitously to confer upon an adjacent property owner incorporeal rights incidental to his ownership of land which the law does not sanction.

A landowner has no right to the light and air coming to him across his neighbor's land. True, if the light and air be shut off damage may well result to his property for residential purposes, as is alleged here, but it is *damnum absque injuria*. It is damage **178 which the law does not recognize because there is no injury. Where there is no right, a deprivation works no injury. The motive with which the deprivation is caused may well be a wrong but it is a moral wrong too subtle for the law to recognize. And where such recognition is attempted the probabilities of working an injustice to the other landowner are real.

The municipal law regulates the conduct of men in their relations with each other and affords redress where the established civil right of one has been violated by another. Violations of ethics or morals which do not harm the public weal, it wisely leaves to the sanctions of the moral law. At that bar only can the motives of men be fully appraised and fairly judged. Positive law can only approach that ideal of perfect justice when it declares that one may not do what he will with his own to the injury of his neighbor. And so where one uses his property in such a manner as to cast noxious odors, smoke, or other deleterious substances over the land of his neighbor to his injury the law deems such conduct a nuisance in violation of the obligation formulated in that maxim.

This court has applied that concept where one used his property for otherwise legitimate purposes but in such a way that it constituted an annoyance to his neighbors and a potential danger to their property on account of the vibrations caused by the nature of the industrial work being done on his property. *Blomen v. N. Barstow Co.*, 35 R.I. 198, 85 A. 924, 44 L.R.A.,N.S., 1144. Complainants cite such case in support of their position here. The difficulty is that their case in no way resembles that case on its facts. The facts in evidence in the Blomen case properly called for the application of the maxim, as well-established rights belonging to the complainants there were being violated. In the case at bar complainants have no such rights.

Respondents cite a 'spite fence' case from Ohio in which this difference is expounded in considerable detail. *Letts v. Kessler*, 54 Ohio St. 73, 42 N.E. 765, 40 L.R.A. 177. Without adopting all that was there said we nevertheless approve the reasoning therein which distinguishes a case, such as the instant one, involving a deprivation of light and air from cases involving smoke, gas, noisome smells or noises. As that court well remarked in 54 Ohio St. at page 82, 42 N.E. at page 766: 'In such cases something is produced on one's own premises, and conveyed to the premises of another; but in this case nothing is sent, but the air and light are withheld.' See also *Rideout v. Knox*, 148 Mass. 368, 19 N.E. 390, 2 L.R.A. 81, 12 Am.St.Rep. 560; *Keats v. Hugo*, 115 Mass. 204, 15 Am.Rep. 76; *Giller v. West*, 162 Ind. 17, 69 N.E. 548.

The complainants' appeal is denied and dismissed, the decree appealed from is affirmed, and the cause is remanded to the superior court for further proceedings.

BOUTHILLIER

v.

STOLARZ

Superior Court of Rhode Island

Not Reported in A.2d
1999 WL 1334924 (R.I.Super.)

December 17, 1999

THUNBERG

*1 The plaintiffs, Susan R. and James D. Bouthillier have requested that this Court preliminarily enjoin defendant, Thomas Stolarz, from entering upon their property. The intrusion includes the placement of concrete blocks and fences as well as the installation of security cameras and lights upon property the plaintiffs contend is owned by them.

The Bouthilliers purchased their land, which sits upon a very private and rural two acre lot, in August of 1991. After moving in, Mr. Bouthillier went to introduce himself to his neighbor, defendant Stolarz. His neighbor, Mr. Bouthillier testified, resided in a very attractive gambrel amid well-maintained park-like grounds.

The plaintiffs contend that they, as well as their predecessors in title have observed a boundary line established by the defendant in 1980. In May of that year, the defendant placed huge boulders, as well as a row of ornamental arbor vitae along this line. Ever since the plaintiffs moved to the area in 1991, their conduct has been consistent with an understanding that the boulders and trees in a straight line mark the boundary. The plaintiffs cleared, mowed, mulched and stored firewood in a manner which reveals their recognition of the line in question as the true boundary.

All was well until 1997 when this controversy began to erupt. The result is the present state of the area with fences, concrete blocks, cameras and lights installed by the defendant on the plaintiffs' side of the arbor vitae/ boulder boundary.

Plaintiff, James Bouthillier, has testified that the installation of these unsightly and invasive items has "wrecked his life." He and Mrs. Bouthillier are anxious and uncomfortable going to their own home at night, never knowing what to expect. The couple's residence has gone from living in "an oasis to hell." It must be noted that the 500 pound concrete blocks were not poured by the defendant until *after* this lawsuit was filed.

Plaintiff asserts that in 1976 a mistake occurred when a surveyor reversed the adjoining lots and placed a pipe at a width of 217 feet instead of 200 feet. Defendant testified that he placed the boulders 17 feet north of the boundary line because he was "trying to balance [his] lot." The evidence of what exists on defendant's property is as compelling as the evidence of what exists on the plaintiffs' property. Mr. Stolarz has done beautiful things with his property. He has designed and constructed a lovely home, thoughtfully placed in the center of his lot. He has created and maintained park-like surroundings with great care. He appears to be a meticulous man with a high appreciation for aesthetics and respect for his own property.

It is thus inconceivable to the Court that Mr. Stolarz would partake in the construction of this truly hideous concrete barrier and fence other than for sheer spite. The Court is certain that a man of his taste would be as repulsed as the plaintiffs are if he had to view this invasive eyesore in his comings and goings and while at his residence.

*2 Every property owner has the fundamental right to the fair use and enjoyment of his or her property. The defendant has interfered with the plaintiffs' property rights in a most vulgar and pernicious fashion.

The Court is satisfied by credible evidence that the plaintiffs have demonstrated a likelihood of success on the merits and that the presence of this egregious "spite fence" is causing them irreparable harm. Therefore, the Court orders that the wire fence, concrete barriers, lights and "security" cameras be removed forthwith. The boulders and arbor vitae are not to be disturbed. The Court does not deem it necessary to require the plaintiffs to post a bond and thus declines to do so.

DOWDELL

v.

BLOOMQUIST

Supreme Court of Rhode Island

847 A.2d 827

March 15, 2004

FLAHERTY

"Tree at my window, window tree, My sash is lowered when night comes on; But let there never be curtain drawn Between you and me."

—Robert Frost

In the matter before us, four western arborvitae trees are at the plaintiff's window. Sadly, however, the curtains between the neighboring parties have long since been drawn, forever dividing what was once an amicable relationship between them. The fate of the offending trees now hangs in the balance.

The plaintiff, Cheryl Dowdell, brought this action in Superior Court alleging that the defendant, Peter Bloomquist, planted four western arborvitae trees on his Charlestown property solely to exact revenge against her, to retaliate by blocking her view, and in violation of the spite fence statute, G.L.1956 § 34–10–20. [FN1] She sought legal and equitable relief. After considering the testimony and evidence presented at a nonjury trial, [FN2 Omitted] the presiding Superior Court justice found that the trees were planted to satisfy defendant's malicious intent, not his pretextual desire for privacy, and that defendant had violated § 34–10–20. The trial justice granted plaintiff injunctive relief. We affirm the judgment of the trial justice. [FN3 Omitted]

FN1. General Laws 1956 § 34–10–20 provides as follows:

"Spite fences.—A fence or other structure in the nature of a fence which unnecessarily exceeds six feet (6') in height and is maliciously erected or maintained for the purpose of annoying the owners or occupants of adjoining property, shall be deemed a private nuisance, and any owner or occupant who is injured, either in the comfort or enjoyment of his or her estate thereby, may have an action to recover damages for the injury."

The facts pertinent to this appeal are as follows. The parties' homes are on adjoining lots in a subdivision of Charlestown, each approximately one acre in size. Dowdell's *829 home sits at a higher elevation than Bloomquist's and has a distant view of the ocean over the Bloomquist property. In June 2000, defendant acquired the home from his mother, Lorraine Bloomquist. Prior to that time, the Dowdell family had an amicable relationship with defendant's mother. Change was in the wind in the fall of 2000, however, when defendant petitioned for a zoning variance from the Charlestown zoning board seeking permission to build a second-story addition to his home. The plaintiff expressed concern about the petition, anxious that the addition would compromise her view of the Atlantic Ocean. For six months the parties argued before the Charlestown Zoning Board of Review as to the merits of the addition. As a result, the relationship between the neighbors became less than friendly. In March 2001, defendant began clearing land and digging holes to plant the disputed trees in a row between their homes. In April, defendant's counsel sent a letter to plaintiff warning him against trespass onto the Bloomquist property. In May, one day after the zoning board closed its hearing on defendant's variance request, [FN4 Omitted] defendant began planting the four western arborvitae trees that now stand in a row bordering the property line. [FN5] Although the forty-foot-high trees enabled little light to pass into Dowdell's second- and third-story picture windows, testimony at trial evidenced that the vegetation was not a bar to the unkind words between the neighbors.

> FN5. The western arborvitae were planted directly behind a row of eastern arborvitae already existing on the Dowdell property near its boundary with the Bloomquist land. According to expert testimony at trial, the eastern arborvitae are smaller trees, growing to a height of eight to eleven feet. In contrast, the western arborvitae are capable of growing to a height of seventy feet. Although the Dowdell trees are in excess of six feet, there are no allegations that they were ever placed out of spite and these trees are not the subject of the instant matter. However, the trial justice noted that the Dowdell trees already offered sufficient privacy between the Dowdell and Bloomquist properties and cited this as one reason why he considered defendant's purported privacy motive to be a subterfuge for malicious intent.

After the trial justice heard four days of testimony and viewed the property, he made a finding that the row of trees were a fence, based on the language of § 34–10–1. [FN6] He further found that the objective of privacy claimed by defendant was "no more than a subterfuge for his clear intent to spite his neighbors by erecting a fence of totally out of proportion trees." Hence, the trial justice found that the trees constituted a spite fence in violation of § 34–10–20. He noted testimony that plaintiff's real estate values had depreciated by as much as $100,000. Nonetheless, he found that money damages could not adequately compensate her and that equitable relief was more appropriate. Bloomquist was ordered "to cut the four Western Arborvitae to no more than 6' in height and keep them at that level or remove them entirely with no more Western Arborvitae to be planted." [FN7]

> FN6. Section 34–10–1 includes in its definition of lawful fences "[a] hedge" of specified proportions. The trial justice concluded that the four arborvitae trees may be considered a hedge based on expert tes-

timony at trial and that, therefore, the trees constitute a fence.

FN7. In employing the language ordering that "no more Western Arborvitae [are] to be planted," we assume that the trial justice is restricting the plantings along the property lines and in the nature of a fence.

*830 The defendant timely appealed to this Court. In his appeal, defendant asserts that the offending trees do not constitute a fence. Moreover, defendant contends that even if the trees were considered a fence, the trial justice erroneously granted relief in the face of testimony that the trees serve a useful purpose of privacy for defendant. To support that contention, defendant relies on *Musumeci v. Leonardo,* 77 R.I. 255, 259–60, 75 A.2d 175, 177–78 (1950), for the proposition that when a fence is erected for a useful purpose, despite spiteful motive, no relief may be granted. Moreover, defendant alleges that the trial justice lacked the authority to award injunctive relief based on the holding of *Musumeci* as well as the specific language of the spite fence statute, which states that one "may have an action to recover damages for the injury." Section 34–10–20. Additionally, defendant urges that the trial justice erred by granting relief that amounted to an easement for light or view where no such remedy exists at common law.

Not surprisingly, plaintiff defends the lower court ruling. She asserts that the trial justice had ample authority to award injunctive relief and correctly exercised this authority based on his well-supported finding that the four trees constituted nothing more than a fence erected out of spite.

The trial justice found a violation of the spite fence statute based on his careful and deliberate findings of fact and on his credibility assessment of the testimony at trial. We are mindful that factual findings "are entitled to great weight and will not be disturbed by this Court absent proof that they are clearly wrong or that the trial justice overlooked or misconceived material evidence." *Tavares v. Beck,* 814 A.2d 346, 350 (R.I.2003) (per curiam); *Perry v. Garey,* 799 A.2d 1018, 1022 (R.I.2002). We grant the same level of deference to a trial justice's determination of credibility. *See Bogosian v. Bederman,* 823 A.2d 1117, 1120 (R.I.2003). Based on this standard, we decline to disturb the trial justice's findings that the four arborvitae trees planted in a row constitute a fence and that defendant planted them with spiteful intentions. Based on the record before us, we cannot say that the trial justice was clearly wrong or that he overlooked or misconceived material evidence with respect to his findings of fact or credibility.

This is the first occasion this Court has had to address the issue of whether a row of trees may be considered a fence within the meaning of the spite fence statute, § 34–10–20. We believe the trial justice properly referred to the definition of "lawful fences" found in § 34–10–1 to understand the simple meaning and legislative intent behind its use of the word "fence." Based upon the language of § 34–10–1, a fence clearly includes a hedge. And based upon the expert testimony relied on by the trial justice, a row of western arborvitae trees may constitute a hedge. However, even if the trees were not a hedge per se, the spite fence statute refers to "[a] fence or other structure in the nature of a fence." The trial justice considered the proximity of the four trees that touched one another, and the broad span of sixty feet across which they spread, and rationally interpreted that the trees were a fence. Although defendant argues that he presented expert testimony that the western arborvitae is not a hedge plant, we nonetheless believe that the trees, when taken as a whole, fall well within the statutory definition of a "structure in the nature of a fence." This may not be the most optimal species for the creation of a hedge owing to their enormous stature and girth. However, it is *831 specifically because of their towering presence, as well as their relative positioning on defendant's land, that we can consider the trees nothing less than a fence. We are not alone in this assessment. Recently, a California appellate court found a row of evergreen trees to be a fence within the meaning of the California spite fence statute. [FN8 Omitted] *Wilson v. Handley,* 97 Cal.App.4th 1301, 119 Cal.Rptr.2d 263 (2002). That court stated,

> "In light of this statutory purpose, a structure need not be built to prevent intrusion from without or straying from within to be a 'fence or other structure in the nature of a fence' within the meaning of the spite fence statute. Instead, the structure need only be built to separate or mark the boundary between adjoining parcels—albeit, in an unnecessarily high and annoying manner." *Id.* at 269.

We next consider defendant's contention that the trial justice erroneously discounted defendant's testimony that the trees were erected for the beneficial purpose of privacy. We recognize that some useful purpose for a fence may render the victim of one even maliciously erected without a remedy. In *Musumeci,* this Court determined that a fence served the useful purpose of preventing water from entering the premises of the first floor of the complainant's house. Hence, because the purpose of the fence was not wholly malicious, it was not enjoined as a private nuisance. *Musumeci,* 77 R.I. at 258–59, 75 A.2d at 177 (citing *Burke v. Smith,* 69 Mich. 380, 37 N.W. 838 (1888) (one of the first cases announcing the new American rule on spite fences, now considered to embody the prevailing modern view)). However, based on the turbulent history between the parties, the provocative statements made by defendant, the notice of trespass letter sent to plaintiff, and the size, timing, and placement of the trees, we cannot say that the trial justice was wrong to give defendant's testimony little weight and to find his claim that the fence was installed to enhance his privacy lacked credibility. In the circumstances of this case, we agree with the trial justice that defendant needed to provide more than just privacy as justification for the fence. This is especially true when a row of smaller arborvitae already stood between the homes. As the trial justice noted, "Accepting privacy alone would simply result in the statute being rendered meaningless and absurd." The very nature of a fence is such that privacy could always be given as the reason for erecting it. In an egregious case such as this, where evidence of malicious intent plainly outweighs the discounted benefit claimed by defendant, the court correctly found defendant's actions to violate the spite fence statute.

That said, the final issue to be determined is whether injunctive relief was an appropriate remedy for the aggrieved plaintiff. The defendant relies on *Musumeci* for the proposition that plaintiff is not entitled to injunctive relief because the loss of light and view that she alleges is not a private nuisance that equity will enjoin. Moreover, he maintains that the spite fence statute provides only for a monetary damages remedy. However, *832 upon careful review of the language of § 34–10–20, this Court's discussion in *Musumeci,* and the law of private nuisance, we believe that injunctive relief is an available remedy for a violation of the spite fence statute. Consequently, we affirm the remedy ordered by the trial justice that the offending western arborvitae trees be topped off at six feet, or otherwise removed entirely.

The defendant mischaracterizes *Musumeci* as both relevant and conclusive authority on remedy in the instant case. In *Musumeci,* it was determined that a wall standing less than six feet tall and which served a useful purpose of blocking water run off onto the plaintiff's property was not a spite fence and therefore not governed by G.L.1938 ch. 645, § 20, [FN9] the predecessor to the present spite fence statute, § 34–10–20. The Court then said that "a fence erected on one's own land for the purpose of shutting off light and air to an adjacent owner is not unlawful unless it violates G.L.1938, chap. 645, § 20." *Musumeci,* 77 R.I. at 259–60, 75 A.2d at 177. Having found no statutory violation, the *Musumeci* Court addressed the issue of whether an equitable remedy was available to the aggrieved party for the shutting off of light and air out of malice, notwithstanding the inapplicability of the spite fence statute. The Court held that absent a tangible violation to the adjacent landowner's rights, the fence could not be enjoined as a private nuisance because under the common law he has no right to light and air coming across the land. Hence, there was no nuisance. *Id.* at 260, 75 A.2d at 177–78. We distinguish *Musumeci* from the instant case based on the factual and legal distinctions at play in each case. Although *Musumeci* confirms that there is no common law right to light and air, it does not preclude equitable relief for erection of a spite fence. When the spite fence statute is violated, which was not the case in *Musumeci,* the offending action is deemed a "private nuisance." *See* § 34–10–20. Under private nuisance law, equitable relief is an appropriate remedy. *See Harris v. Town of Lincoln,* 668 A.2d 321 (R.I.1995) (private nuisance of emission of noises, odors, and vibrations by sewer-processing facility pumping station onto neighboring residential property warranted injunctive relief, in addition to monetary damages); *Weida v. Ferry,* 493 A.2d 824 (R.I.1985) (noxious smells and flies emanating from dairy farm operations more suitably classified as a private nuisance rather than negligence action; case remanded for new trial with presumption that equitable relief would be an appropriate remedy had the farm not already ceased operations by this time); *DeNucci v. Pezza,* 114 R.I. 123, 329 A.2d 807 (1974) (injunctive relief properly granted upon trial justice's finding that noise from freight trucks hitching and unhitching in parking lot during early morning hours was unreasonable private nuisance interfering with the plaintiff's use and enjoyment of his residential property).

FN9. General Laws 1938 ch. 645, § 20 closely mirrors the language of § 34–10–20 and provided the following:

"A fence, or other structure in the nature of a fence, which unnecessarily exceeds 6 feet in height, and is maliciously erected or maintained for the purpose of annoying the owners or occupants of adjoining property, shall be deemed a private nuisance, and any such owner or occupant who is injured, either in the comfort or enjoyment of his estate thereby, may have an action of trespass on the case to recover damages for such injury."

We look to the case of *Wilson* for additional support that a spite fence that blocks light, air, or view is properly considered an actionable private nuisance because the statute defines it as such. In *833 *Wilson,* the court held that a row of trees blocking the plaintiff's view of Mt. Shasta may be considered a violation of the statute even though the fence interfered with nothing more than light and air. The court acknowledged that although interference with light and air was not considered a nuisance under the general definition of "nuisance," the spite fence statute never specified that the fence need interfere with more than light and air for it to be considered a nuisance. The court concluded that "we are not at liberty to read any such additional requirement into the statute." *Wilson,* 119 Cal.Rptr.2d at 270. We agree. What makes a spite fence a nuisance under § 34–10–20 is not merely that it blocks the passage of light and view, but that it does so "unnecessarily" for the malicious purpose of "annoyance." This is a notable distinction.

Finally, defendant correctly asserts that the statute specifically allows for "an action to recover damages." Specifically, the statute states that one who is injured by a spite fence "*may* have an action to recover damages for the injury." Section 34–10–20. (Emphasis added.) However, contrary to defendant's assertion, we believe this language merely sanctions the additional remedy of damages, but does not exclude injunctive relief, which is a remedy logically rooted in the nature and purpose of the statute. To support this holding, we look to the remedial practice in other states that recognize the erection of a spite fence as actionable. Connecticut, Idaho, Indiana, Massachusetts, Montana, New Hampshire, and South Dakota all allow injunctive relief for violations of spite fence law. [FN10 Omitted] Especially illustrative is the law as it stands in Massachusetts, whose statute is strikingly similar to § 34–10–20. The Massachusetts statute provides:

> "A fence or other structure in the nature of a fence which unnecessarily exceeds six feet in height and is maliciously erected or maintained for the purpose of annoying the owners or occupants of adjoining property shall be deemed a private nuisance. Any such owner or occupant injured * * * may have an action of tort for damages * * *." Mass. Gen. Laws Ann. ch. 49, § 21 (West 1994).

In interpreting this law, the Supreme Judicial Court of Massachusetts recognized that despite the lack of explicit language, the court had the authority to order a spite fence to be "abated," in addition to damages and costs. *Rice v. Moorehouse,* 150 Mass. 482, 23 N.E. 229 (1890) (trial justice properly ordered abatement of so much of a spite fence as exceeded six feet in height). The Court relied on the law of nuisance as the basis for its decision, just as we do today.

Conclusion

For the reasons set forth above, we affirm the judgment of the Superior Court. The record shall be remanded to the Superior Court.

WORKSHEET NO. 2: CASE SYNTHESIS

Synthesis is the binding together of several rules from a collection of cases into one legal principle. It provides a collective meaning that is not apparent from the individual cases themselves.

To synthesize, you need to step back and ask yourself what the cases have in common. Many law students and lawyers use charts to help them see what the cases have in common. A chart is provided for you to use for the exercise below.

Case File Assignment:

Read and brief the cases contained in Worksheet No. 1. After you have read and briefed these cases, fill in the attached synthesis chart. After you have completed the chart, review the information you included to help you see what the cases have in common. On a separate piece of paper, start to draft a synthesized legal principle. This does not need to be a well-crafted rule at this time, as you will work on drafting rules in Worksheet No. 3.

Case names			
Facts			
Holding			
Reasoning			
What is the rule or legal principle you can take away from the case?			

WORKSHEET NO. 3: RULES

Drafting rules is the process of taking the rule or policy from a single authority or from a collection of cases you have synthesized and putting it in written form. To help you write a complete statement of the rule or policy on a particular point of law, you must first ask yourself the following brainstorming questions:

1. What is the rule, policy, or synthesized rule?
2. What are the exceptions to the rule, policy, or synthesized rule, if any?
3. Is there anything else the court will consider in applying the rule, policy, or synthesized rule?

You should always be able to answer the first question unless courts in the jurisdiction have not yet ruled on the issue or the courts in the jurisdiction have ruled inconsistently such that you cannot reconcile the rules or results. You will not always be able to answer the second and third questions, but you should always ask them.

After answering these brainstorming questions, you can begin to write your rule by cutting and pasting your answers to these questions into one or more sentences.

Once you have drafted your rule, you then need to evaluate it for completeness. To evaluate the rule you have written, answer the following questions:

1. Is the rule too specific based on the legal authorities and your client facts?
2. Is the rule too broad based on the legal authorities and your client facts?
3. Does the rule include vague terms?
4. Is the rule circular?
5. If there is more than one rule, are the rules repetitive?

Case File Assignment:

Write a synthesized rule explaining when a fence qualifies as a spite fence using all of the legal authorities provided in the Case File and the information from your completed synthesis chart (Worksheet No. 2). To help you write your synthesized rule, answer the following brainstorming questions:

1. What is the rule, policy, or synthesized rule?

2. Are there any exceptions to the rule, policy, or synthesized rule?

3. Is there anything else the court would consider in applying the rule, policy, or synthesized rule?

After answering these brainstorming questions, cut and paste your answers together into one or more sentences. This is the first draft of your complete rule. Evaluate your draft rule by evaluating the following questions:

1. Is the rule too specific based on the legal authorities and your client facts?
2. Is the rule too broad based on the legal authorities and your client facts?
3. Does the rule include vague terms?
4. Is the rule circular?
5. If there is more than one rule, are the rules repetitive?

Edit your draft synthesized rule based on your answers to these questions and provide your final synthesized rule below:

WORKSHEET NO. 4: CASE ILLUSTRATIONS

Case illustrations describe a precedent case to further define the rule (the R in the objective paradigm) or provide the reader with an example of how a rule has been applied in other cases. All case illustrations include six categories of information. While all six categories should be included in each case illustration, each category of information does not require its own separate sentence. Thus, you may have a complete case illustration that only is two sentences, but you may also have a complete case illustration that is two paragraphs. The length of your case illustration depends on the information your reader needs for a complete understanding of the specific legal principle you are explaining with the case illustration.

A case illustration is substantively complete if it includes:

1. A thesis sentence stating the specific legal principle you plan to explain with the case illustration;
2. The issue before the court in the precedent case on the specific legal principle you plan to explain with the case illustration;
3. The relevant facts of the precedent case on the specific legal principle you plan to explain with the case illustration;
4. The court's holding in the precedent case on the specific legal principle you plan to explain with the case illustration;
5. The court's reasoning in the precedent case on the specific legal principle you plan to explain with the case illustration; and
6. A conclusion sentence to give closure to the case illustration; this must relate back to the thesis sentence that began the case illustration.

The above order of the six categories of information is the most common organization and tends provide the most natural flow of information. It can be modified, where appropriate, but the thesis sentence must always come first.

The most difficult part of writing a case illustration is the first sentence—the thesis sentence. Typically, this is a detailed sentence providing further explanation of how the rule (the R in your objective paradigm) operates, how the rule has been defined, or how the rule has been applied by the court in another case. Occasionally, however, this simply is the rule (the R in your objective paradigm) without a separate thesis sentence.

Example 1 begins with the rule in bold (the R in the objective paradigm) followed by the thesis sentence for the case illustration (underlined) and the rest of the case illustration categories. Example 2 begins with the rule in bold and underlined (the R in the objective paradigm), which also is the thesis sentence for the case illustration, followed by the rest of the case illustration categories. There is not a separate thesis sentence for this case illustration because the applicable rule is sufficiently narrow to serve as both the rule and the thesis sentence.

EXAMPLE 1:

Consent to use a celebrity's photograph is unnecessary if the use of a photograph is directly related to matters in the public interest. For example, consent is unnecessary if the use of a photograph is directly related to commentary on events that impact society. In Dora v. Frontline Video, Inc., the court determined whether the use of the plaintiff's photograph in a surfing documentary was proper under the public interest exception. 15 Cal. App. 4th 536 (2nd Dist. 1993). A 1950s professional surfer brought a claim against the producers of a documentary video for using his photograph, voice, and video recordings without his consent. Id. at 541. The court held that the use of the surfer's photograph, voice, and video recordings in the surfing documentary did not require consent because they were used in a manner that was directly related to a matter in the public interest. Id. at 546. It reasoned that surfing is in the public interest because "surfing is more than passing interest to some," that "it has created a lifestyle that influences speech, behavior, dress, and entertainment, among other things," and has "had a significant influence on the popular culture." Id. Because the surfer's photograph, voice, and video recordings were used in the documentary on surfing, which directly related to a matter in the public interest, the use was proper under the public interest exception and consent was unnecessary. Id.

EXAMPLE 2:

Consent to use a celebrity's photograph is required if the use of a photograph is for advertising purposes and is not directly related to a matter in the public interest. Downing v. Abercrombie & Fitch, 265 F.3d 994 (9th Cir. 2001). In Downing, the court determined whether the unauthorized use of a surfer's photograph in a surf-themed clothing catalogue was protected under the public interest exception. Id. at 999. The clothing catalog included a small number of editorials on surfing, but its primary purpose was to increase brand awareness and sell clothes. Id. at 1000. The photograph preceded two pages that advertised t-shirts designed to replicate those worn by the surfer in the photograph. The court held that the use of the surfer's photograph, although on a topic in the public interest, was not protected because the photograph was used as a "window dressing" to advance the surf-themed catalogue. Id. at 1002. It contrasted the use in the catalog from the use in the documentary in Dora, stating that although both cover the theme of surfing, the documentary's use "directly contributed to the story" while the catalog's use did not. Id. at 1003. Instead, the catalog's use was "much more commercial in nature." Therefore, the use of the surfer's photograph was not a proper use under the public interest exception and consent was required. Id.

Case File Assignment:

Write a case illustration for your client's case using the case(s) assigned to you by your professor. To help you write the case illustration, answer the following brainstorming questions. Please note, however, that before you can write a case illustration, you must know the rule or legal principle the case illustration is explaining.

For context, include the rule (the R in the objective paradigm) or legal principle you plan to explain with the case illustration here:

1. What is the specific legal principle you plan to explain with the case illustration? (NOTE: this is the thesis sentence for the case illustration that provides further explanation of how the rule (the R in your objective paradigm) operates, how the rule has been defined, or how the rule has been applied by the court in another case.)

2. What was the specific issue before the court in the precedent case as it relates to the specific legal principle you plan to explain with the case illustration? (NOTE: This must only be the issue specific to the legal principle you plan to explain with the case illustration, not all of the issues included in the precedent case.)

3. What are the specific facts in the precedent case as they relate to the specific legal principle you plan to explain with the case illustration? (NOTE: This must only be the facts specific to the legal principle you plan to explain with the case illustration, not all of the facts included in the precedent case.)

4. What is the holding in the precedent case as it relates to the specific legal principle you plan to explain with the case illustration? (NOTE: This must only be the holding specific to the legal principle you plan to explain with the case illustration, not all of the holdings included in the precedent case.)

5. What is the reasoning in the precedent case as it relates to the specific legal principle you plan to explain with the case illustration? (NOTE: This must only be the reasoning specific to the legal principle you plan to explain with the case illustration, not all of the reasoning included in the precedent case.)

6. What additional sentence(s) might you need to provide closure to this case illustration and to connect it back to the specific legal principle identified in response to Question 1 above?

Using the answers to these brainstorming questions as your guide, write the case illustration. Start by cutting and pasting your answers into paragraph form and then mold them into a readable paragraph. Each of the six categories of information must be included for a complete case illustration. This does not mean, however, that you need to have six sentences. A complete case illustration may be as little as two sentences or as much as two full paragraphs.

WORKSHEET NO. 5: POLICY-BASED REASONING

Policy-based reasoning is analysis that applies the purpose underlying a rule to your client's case. Policy-based reasoning is most often used to strengthen an argument that already is supported by legal authorities or other types of reasoning. For example, the result is not only X because of the case law, but the result also is X because that result satisfies the purpose underlying the applicable rule. Policy-based reasoning can also be used to make an argument where there are not any applicable legal authorities or the direct application of the law provides a result that is inconsistent with the purpose underlying the rule.

To apply policy-based reasoning to your client's case, you must first determine the purpose underlying the rule: what was the goal of the legislature or the court in creating the rule? This purpose might come from the purpose section of a statute, legislative history, the court's opinion, or published legal commentary on a rule of law. It should not, however, come from your own personal view of society or your personal opinion as to why the rule was created.

Once you have determined the purpose underlying the rule, you then need to evaluate whether that purpose applies to your client's case. To determine the purpose underlying the rule and to evaluate whether it applies to your client's case, consider:

1. The conclusion you will reach by applying the policy to your client's case. (NOTE: You may need to answer this question after you have completed your analysis of the policy.)

2. The rule you are applying to your client's case.

3. The purpose underlying the rule identified in response to Question 2 above. What greater societal purpose(s) was the court or legislature trying to protect in creating the rule? (NOTE: There may be more than one purpose. If there is more than one purpose, identify if the court seems to prefer one purpose over another.) Also, the purpose behind the rule must come from legal authority, such as legislative history, case authority, or well-established public opinion, not your personal opinion on the purpose of the rule.

4. The potential outcomes for your client when applying the rule.

5. The potential outcomes for the other party when applying the rule.

6. How the outcomes identified in response to Questions 4 and 5 above are or are not served by the purpose(s) of the rule you identified in response to Question 3 above.

7. The outcome that best follows the purpose of the rule.

After considering these brainstorming questions, you should have a clear understanding of whether the possible outcomes for your client do or do not serve the underlying purpose(s) of the rule. The following formula will then help you write a policy-based reasoning analysis. Each of these components must be included for a complete policy-based reasoning analysis.

A policy-based reasoning analysis is substantively complete if it:

1. Begins the paragraph(s) by stating the conclusion you will reach by applying the purpose of the rule to your client's case. (NOTE: This is the thesis sentence for this paragraph.)

2. States the rule that is the basis of the policy-based reasoning analysis.

3. Identifies and describes the purpose underlying the rule and the origin of that purpose. Remember, the purpose behind the rule must come from legal authority, such as legislative history, case authority, or well-established public opinion, not your personal opinion. Also, if there is more than one purpose, explain which purpose the courts tend to use more.

4. States whether the underlying purpose does or does not apply to the possible outcome(s) in your client's case.

5. Explains with specific detail why the possible outcome(s) in your client's case will or will not further the purpose underlying the rule.

6. Concludes with a sentence that provides closure to the policy-based reasoning analysis. This sentence must connect to the thesis sentence that began the policy-based reasoning analysis.

EXAMPLE POLICY-BASED REASONING:

The defendant's Civil Code § 3344(a) violation likely is not be actionable because the defendant's use of Ms. Anchor's photograph on its t-shirt provided commentary on a matter in the public interest and, therefore, consent was unnecessary. California Civil Code § 3344(d) provides an exception to the consent requirement contained in § 3344(a). It states that the use of a photograph in connection with "any news, public affairs, or sports broadcast or account, or any political campaign" does not require consent. § 3344(d). The courts have explained that the purpose of this exception is to protect the public's right to know about things, events, and people, such as news, celebrity activities, and sports. Eastwood, 149 Cal. App. 3d at 421; Gionfriddo v. Major League Baseball, 94 Cal. App. 4th 400 (1st Dist. 2001); Montana v. San Jose Mercury News, Inc., 34 Cal. App. 4th 790 (6th Dist. 1995). Thus, the right of a celebrity in her image is not absolute, but must be balanced against the public interest in the dissemination of news and information. Id. It is for this reason that the use of a celebrity's photograph on a matter in the public interest is exempt from the consent requirement of § 3344(a).

Ms. Anchor's claim is not furthered by the statutory purpose of protecting matters in the public interest. Rather, the defendant's use of Ms. Anchor's photograph with the Mayor's photograph as a miniature devil on her shoulder furthers the purpose because the t-shirt is part of an expressive comment on the unethical reporting on politics in Los Angeles. This is type of information the public interest exception was designed to protect. Thus, it is likely the use of Ms. Anchor's photograph on the t-shirt as a political and social commentary is not actionable due to the nature of the policy protecting the dissemination of information in the public interest.

Case File Assignment:

Write an analysis for your client's case using policy-based reasoning based on the legal authority contained in the Case File and/or the legal authority assigned by your professor. To help you write a policy-based reasoning analysis, answer the following brainstorming questions:

1. What is the conclusion you will reach by applying the policy to your client's case? (NOTE: You may need to answer this question after you have completed your analysis of the policy.)

2. What is the rule you are applying to your client's case?

3. What is the purpose underlying the rule identified in response to Question 2 above? What greater societal purpose(s) was the court or legislature trying to protect in creating the rule? (NOTE: There may be more than one purpose. If there is more than one purpose, identify if the court seems to prefer one purpose over another.) Also, the purpose behind the rule should come from legal authority, such as legislative history, case authority, or well-established public opinion, not your personal opinion on the purpose of the rule.

4. What are the potential outcomes for your client when applying the rule?

5. What are the potential outcomes for the other party when applying the rule?

6. How are the outcomes identified in response to Questions 4 and 5 above served or not served by the purpose(s) of the rule you identified in response to Question 3 above?

7. Which outcome best follows the purpose(s) of the rule? Explain why.

After answering these brainstorming questions, you should have a clear understanding of whether the possible outcomes for your client do or do not serve the underlying purpose(s) of the rule. Use the following formula to write a policy-based reasoning analysis. Each of these components must be included for a complete policy-based reasoning analysis.

1. Begin the paragraph(s) by stating the conclusion you will reach by applying the purpose of the rule to your client's case. (NOTE: This is the thesis sentence for this paragraph)
2. State the rule that is the basis of the policy-based reasoning analysis.
3. Identify and describe the purpose underlying the rule and the origin of that purpose. If there is more than one purpose, explain which one the courts tend to use more. Remember, the purpose behind the rule must come from legal authority, such as legislative history, case authority, or well-established public opinion, not your personal opinion on the purpose of the rule.
4. State whether the underlying purpose does or does not apply to the possible outcome(s) in your client's case.
5. Explain with specific detail why the possible outcome(s) in your client's case does or does not further the purpose underlying the rule.
6. Conclude with a sentence that provides closure to the policy-based reasoning analysis. This sentence must connect to the thesis sentence that began the policy-based reasoning analysis.

WORKSHEET NO. 6: ANALOGICAL REASONING

This worksheet is designed to give you a structured brainstorming process to evaluate whether analogical reasoning should be used in the analysis of your client's case. Clarity of writing comes from clarity of understanding. If you do not completely understand the structure or substance of the analogical reasoning to be included in your analysis, neither will the reader.

For an analogical reasoning analysis to be thoroughly evaluated, you must go through the following brainstorming process with as much detail as possible. This evaluation should be done for each issue and for each precedent case you plan to address with analogical reasoning.

1. Identify one issue you plan to address with analogical reasoning.
2. Identify the name of one precedent case you plan to use for the issue you selected above.
3. Identify the specific holding of the precedent case on the legal issue you plan to analyze with this analogical reasoning (NOTE: This must only be the holding specific to the legal issue you are addressing, not the overall holding of the precedent case.)
4. Describe the reasoning of the court from the precedent case on the legal issue you plan to analyze with this analogical reasoning (NOTE: This must only be the reasoning specific to the legal issue you are addressing, not the overall reasoning of the precedent case.)
5. Make a list of the relevant facts from the precedent case on the legal issue you plan to analyze with this analogical reasoning (NOTE: This must only be the facts specific to the legal issue you are addressing, not all of the facts from the precedent case.)
6. Make a list of the relevant facts from your client's case on the legal issue you plan to analyze with this analogical reasoning (NOTE: This must only be the facts specific to the legal issue you are addressing, not all of the facts from your client's case.)
7. Group the facts of the precedent case and your client's case into facts that are similar and facts that are distinguishable.

Depending on whether the facts are similar or distinguishable or both, you may only need to consider some of the questions below. If the facts are similar, answer Questions 8–10. If the facts are distinguishable, answer Questions 11–13. If the facts are both similar and distinguishable, answer Questions 8–13.

8. Identify the fact(s) to be compared in your analysis as similar. (NOTE: this must only be the facts specific to the legal issue you are addressing, not all of the facts from the precedent case or your client's case.)

9. Explain why these facts are similar—use specific factual examples to demonstrate the similarities.

10. Explain *why* these factual similarities support your legal analysis on the issue you are addressing. This is where you must directly apply the reasoning of the precedent case to the facts of your client's case. Specifically look at why and how the precedent case ruled as it did and why that same reasoning applies to your client's case.

11. Identify the fact(s) to be compared in your analysis as distinguishable. (NOTE: This must only be the facts specific to the legal issue you are addressing, not all of the facts from the precedent case or your client's case.)

12. Explain why these facts are distinguishable—use specific factual examples to demonstrate the differences.

13. Explain *why* these factual differences support your legal analysis on the issue you are addressing. This is where you must directly apply the reasoning of the precedent case to the facts of your client's case. Specifically look at why and how the precedent case ruled as it did and why that same reasoning does not apply to your client's case.

After evaluating these brainstorming questions, you should have a clear understanding of whether this analogical reasoning should be included in the analysis of your client's case. You then must decide if the analogical reasoning will be based on a single case or multiple cases. If multiple cases are used to analyze the same legal issue, then you must provide this analysis at the same time, rather than as a separate analogical reasoning for each precedent case. Once you have decided if the analogical reasoning will be based on a single case or multiple cases, use one of the following formulas to write your analogical reasoning analysis:

Analogical Reasoning Formula Using a Single Case:

Component 1: The legal conclusion you want the reader to reach based on your analogical reasoning (this is the overall thesis sentence for the analogical reasoning paragraph or paragraphs—case names should not be included in this sentence).

Component 2: Sentence stating, "In client's case (use client's name) is similar to/distinguishable from ______ (insert precedent case name) based on ______ (identify the specific issue this analogical reasoning is addressing)."

Component 3: Sentence stating, "In client's case (use client's name), (insert detailed facts about your client's case that will be compared; this must only be the specific facts that will be compared, not all of the facts of the case)."

Component 4: Sentence stating, "This case is similar to/distinguishable from ______ (insert precedent case name) where (insert detailed facts about the precedent case that will be compared—this must only be the specific facts to be compared, not all of the facts from the precedent case.)"

Component 5: Explain, using *specific factual detail*, why the facts you are comparing are similar or distinguishable. This is where you need to provide specific fact-to-fact comparisons, using actual facts from your client's case and the precedent case. (i.e.—"Fact X in client's case is similar to/distinguishable from Fact Y in precedent case because ______ ").

Component 6: Identify the likely outcome of your client's case based on the similarities or differences you discussed in Component 5. This is a re-statement of the conclusion (Component 1) but with more detail and this likely is the beginning of a new paragraph.

Component 7: Explain *why* this is the likely outcome. This is where you must directly apply the reasoning from the precedent case to your client's case.

Possible phrasing:

The court in ______ (insert precedent case name) reasoned ______ (insert the fact specific reasoning of the precedent case on the specific legal issue the analogical reasoning is addressing). This reasoning applies to your client's case (use client's name) because ______ (explain why it applies). Therefore, because the reasoning from (insert precedent case name) applies to your client's case (use client's name), the outcome in your client's case (use client's name) will likely be ______ (insert the outcome you are trying to prove with the analogical reasoning.)

Component 8: Re-state the conclusion you want the reader to reach based on your analogical reasoning. This must connect to the analysis provided by the analogical reasoning and to the conclusion stated in Component 1.

EXAMPLE SINGLE CASE ANALOGICAL REASONING:

TFF is not entitled to the public interest exception because the implication of unethical reporting created by the photographs on the t-shirt is false. Ms. Anchor's case is similar to Eastwood because both involved the dissemination of false information. 149 Cal. App. 3d 409. In Ms. Anchor's case, the t-shirt had a photograph of Ms. Anchor combined with a photograph of the Mayor as a miniature devil sitting on her shoulder. The inclusion of the Mayor on her shoulder with devil horns implied that he was influencing or controlling her reporting on his campaign, which Ms. Anchor denies. This is similar to Eastwood where the article stated that Mr. Eastwood was in a love triangle with two other celebrities, which Mr. Eastwood denied. Id. at 414. Just as Mr. Eastwood denied that he was involved in a love triangle, Ms. Anchor denies that she ever reported on the Mayor's re-election campaign and the general manager of KTV–LA stated that "there are no concerns about Ms. Anchor's ethics whatsoever." As reasoned in Eastwood, it is this type of dissemination of false information that legislature did not intend the public interest exception to protect. Id. at 425. Because the court in Eastwood reasoned that the Enquirer was not entitled to the public interest exception for its false article and TFF created a false implication by its use of Ms. Anchor's photograph on its t-shirt, TFF is not entitled to the public interest exception.

Analogical Reasoning Formula Using Multiple Cases:

Component 1: The legal conclusion you want the reader to reach based on your analogical reasoning (this is the overall thesis sentence for the analogical reasoning paragraph or paragraphs—case names should not be included in this sentence).

Component 2: Sentence stating, "Client's case (insert client's name) is similar to/distinguishable from ______ (insert first precedent case name) and/but similar to/distinguishable from ______ (insert second precedent case name) based on ______ (identify the specific issue this analogical reasoning is addressing)."

Component 3: Sentence stating, "In client's case (use client's name), (insert detailed facts about your client's case that will be compared; this must only be the specific facts to be compared, not all of the facts of the case)."

Component 4(a): Sentence stating, "This case is similar to/distinguishable from ______ (insert first precedent case name) where (insert detailed facts about the precedent case you are relying upon—this must only be the specific facts to be compared, not all of the facts from the precedent case.)"

Component 4(b): Explain, using *specific factual detail*, why the facts you are comparing are similar/distinguishable. This is where you need to provide specific fact-to-fact comparisons, using actual facts from your client's case and the precedent case (i.e.—"Fact X in client's case is similar to/distinguishable from Fact Y in precedent case because ______ ").

Component 5(a): Sentence stating, "This case is similar to/distinguishable from ______ (insert second precedent case name) where (insert detailed facts about the precedent case you are relying upon—this also must only be the specific facts to be compared, not all of the facts from the precedent case)." [NOTE: you many need to use a transition to begin this sentence, such as "In addition," "Also," "However," or "On the other hand"]

Component 5(b): Explain, using *specific factual detail*, why the facts you are comparing are similar/distinguishable. This is where you need to provide specific fact-to-fact comparisons, using actual facts from your client's case and the precedent case. (i.e.—"Fact X in client's case is similar to/distinguishable from Fact Y in precedent case because ______ ").

Component 6: Identify the likely outcome of your client's case based on the similarities/differences you discussed previously (see Components 4(b) and 5(b))." This is a re-statement of the conclusion (Component 1) but with more detail and this likely is the beginning of a new paragraph.

Component 7: Explain *why* this is the likely outcome. This is where you must directly apply the reasoning from the precedent case to your client's case.

Possible phrasing if the reasoning of the precedent cases is the same:

The court in ______ (insert first and second precedent case names) reasoned ______ (insert the fact specific reasoning of the precedent cases on the specific legal issue the analogical reasoning is addressing). This reasoning applies to your client's case (use client's name) because ______ (explain why it applies). Therefore, because the reasoning from (insert precedent case names) applies to your client's case (use client's name), the outcome in your client's case (use client's name) will likely be ______ (insert the outcome you are trying to prove with the analogical reasoning.)

Possible phrasing if the reasoning of the precedent cases is different:

The court in _______ (insert first precedent case name) reasoned _______ (insert the fact specific reasoning of the first precedent case on the specific legal issue the analogical reasoning is addressing). This reasoning applies to your client's case (use client's name) because _______ (explain why it applies). However, the court in _______ (insert second precedent case name) reasoned _______ (insert the fact specific reasoning of the second precedent case on the specific legal issue the analogical reasoning is addressing). This reasoning does not apply to your client's case (use client's name) because _______ (explain why it does not apply). Therefore, because the reasoning from (insert first precedent case name) applies to your client's case (use client's name) and the reasoning from (insert second precedent case name) does not apply to your client's case (use client's name), the outcome in your client's case (use client's name) will likely be _______ (insert the outcome you are trying to prove with the analogical reasoning.)

Component 8: Re-state the conclusion you want the reader to reach based on your analogical reasoning. This must connect to the analysis provided by the analogical reasoning and to the conclusion in Component 1.

EXAMPLE MULTIPLE CASE ANALOGICAL REASONING:

The use of Ms. Anchor's photograph by TFF likely did not require consent because the use directly related to a matter in the public interest and was not commercial in nature. Ms. Anchor's case is similar to Dora but distinguishable from Downing because of the direct connection between the use of her photograph and the public interest. Ms. Anchor, a reporter for a local news station, was involved in a highly publicized relationship with the Mayor and there was a significant amount media attention alleging that she unethically reported on the Mayor's re-election campaign. TFF claims it created and sold a t-shirt with a photograph of Ms. Anchor, with a superimposed picture on her shoulder of the Mayor wearing miniature devil-horns, to provide commentary on Ms. Anchor's unethical reporting on local politics. This is similar to Dora, where Frontline Video used the image, video, and voice recordings of a well-known professional surfer in its surfing documentary to provide commentary on the early years of surfing and the cultural impact of surfing. Dora, 15 Cal. App. 4th at 541. The court in Dora reasoned that the use of the surfer's photograph in the documentary directly contributed to the story on surfing and the surfer had a significant influence on popular culture. Id. at 546. This reasoning applies here because the use of Ms. Anchor's photograph on TFF's t-shirt "directly contributed to the story" on her alleged unethical reporting on the Mayor's re-election campaign and its "significant influence" on local politics.

Furthermore, Ms. Anchor's case is distinguishable from Downing, where a well-known surfer's photograph, taken during a surfing championship, was used in a surf-themed clothing catalog. 265 F.3d 994. The surfer's photograph followed two articles that discussed the history of surfing, however; no connection was made between the articles and the surfer, and the surfer was not identified as a legend of the sport. Id. at 1002. Instead, the two pages following the surfer's photograph advertised t-shirts replicating those worn by the surfer in his photograph. Id. The court reasoned that this use was merely "window dressing to advance the [catalog's] surf theme" and promote sales based on the implied endorsement by the well-known surfer. Id. The use of the photograph was not to provide commentary on surfing like in Dora where the "point of the program" was to provide commentary on surfing. Id. at 1001. Ms. Anchor's is distinguishable from Downing in how her photograph was used because her photograph was used on a t-shirt primarily to provide commentary on her relationship with the Mayor and the alleged influence he may have had on Ms. Anchor's reporting on his re-election campaign. TFF stated that "the point of the t-shirt" was to provide commentary on Ms. Anchor's conflict of interest in reporting on the Mayor's re-election campaign; it was not a mere "window dressing" to sell the t-shirt. Consumers likely would

purchase the t-shirt because of the commentary, not because of her implied endorsement.

While the court in Dora reasoned that the use of the photograph in a surfing documentary did not require consent due to its direct contribution to public's interest in the significant influence of surfing and its cultural impact, the court in Downing reasoned that consent was required because the use of the photograph was commercial in nature, having only a tenuous relationship as a "window-dressing" with the surfing theme of the clothing catalog. Id. at 1002. Ms. Anchor's case is more analogous to Dora than Downing because of the strong connection between the use of her photograph and the public's interest in her relationship with the Mayor and possible unethical reporting on his re-election campaign. Therefore, because the reasoning from Dora more closely relates to Ms. Anchor's case than the reasoning from Downing, the use of the photograph in Ms. Anchor's case likely was directly connected to the public interest and consent was unnecessary.

Case File Assignment:

Write an analysis for your client's case using analogical reasoning based on the legal authority in the Case File and/or the legal authority assigned by your professor. To help you write your analogical reasoning, answer the following brainstorming questions:

1. Identify one specific legal issue you plan to address with analogical reasoning (or the specific issue assigned by your professor):

2. Identify the name of one precedent case you plan to use for the issue you selected above (or the case assigned by your professor).

3. Identify the specific holding of the precedent case on the legal issue you plan to analyze with this analogical reasoning. (NOTE: This must only be the holding on the specific legal issue you are addressing with this analogical reasoning, not the overall holding of the precedent case.)

4. Describe the reasoning of the precedent case you plan to analyze with this analogical reasoning. (NOTE: This must only be the reasoning on the specific legal issue you are addressing with this analogical reasoning, not the overall reasoning of the precedent case.)

5. Make a list of the relevant facts from the precedent case on the legal issue you plan to analyze with this analogical reasoning. (NOTE: This must only be the facts on the specific legal issue you are addressing with this analogical reasoning, not all of the facts from the precedent case.)

6. Make a list of the relevant facts from your client's case on the legal issue you plan to analyze with this analogical reasoning. (NOTE: This must only be the facts specific to the legal issue you are addressing with this analogical reasoning, not all of the facts from your client's case.)

7. Organize the facts of the precedent case and your client's case into the charts below:

Facts that are similar:

Your Client's Case	Precedent Case

Facts that are distinguishable:

Your Client's Case	Precedent Case

Using the information you filled into the charts above, decide whether you think your client's case and the precedent case are similar, distinguishable, or both. If they are similar, answer Questions 8–10 below. If they are distinguishable, answer Questions 11–13 below. If they are both similar and distinguishable, answer Questions 8–13 below.

8. Identify the fact(s) from your client's case and the precedent case to be compared as similar. (NOTE: This must only be facts specific to the legal issue you are addressing, not all of the facts from the precedent case or your client's case.)

9. Explain why these facts are similar—use specific factual examples to demonstrate the similarities.

10. Explain *why* these factual similarities support your legal analysis on the issue you are addressing. This is where you must directly apply the reasoning of the precedent case to the facts of your client's case. Specifically look at why and how the precedent case ruled as it did and why that same reasoning applies to your client's case.

11. Identify the fact(s) to be compared in your analysis as distinguishable. (NOTE: This must only be the facts specific to the legal issue you are addressing, not all of the facts from the precedent case or your client's case.)

12. Explain why these facts are distinguishable—use specific factual examples to demonstrate the differences.

13. Explain *why* these factual differences support your legal analysis on the issue you are addressing. This is where you must directly apply the reasoning of the precedent case to the facts of your client's case. Specifically look at why and how the precedent case ruled as it did and why that same reasoning does not apply to your client's case.

After answering these brainstorming questions, you should have a clear understanding of whether analogical reasoning should be included in the analysis of your client's case. You then must decide if the analogical reasoning will be based on a single case or multiple cases. If multiple cases are used to analyze the same legal issue, then you must provide this analysis at the same time, rather than as a separate analogical reasoning for each precedent case. Once you have decided if the analogical reasoning will be based on a single case or multiple cases, use one of the following formulas to write your analogical reasoning analysis:

Analogical Reasoning Formula Using a Single Case:

Component 1: The legal conclusion you want the reader to reach based on your analogical reasoning (this is the overall thesis sentence for the analogical reasoning paragraph or paragraphs—case names should not be included in this sentence).

Component 2: Sentence stating, "In client's case (use client's name) is similar to/distinguishable from ______ (insert precedent case name) based on ______ (identify the specific issue this analogical reasoning is addressing)."

Component 3: Sentence stating, "In client's case (use client's name), (insert detailed facts about your client's case that will be compared; this must only be the specific facts to be compared, not all of the facts of the case.)"

Component 4: Sentence stating, "This case is similar to/distinguishable from ______ (insert precedent case name) where (insert detailed facts about the precedent case that will be compared—this must only be the specific facts to be compared, not all of the facts from the precedent case.)"

Component 5: Explain, using *specific factual detail*, why the facts you are comparing are similar or distinguishable. This is where you need to provide specific fact-to-fact comparisons, using actual facts from your client's case and the precedent case. (i.e.—"Fact X in client's case is similar to/distinguishable from Fact Y in precedent case because ______ ").

Component 6: Identify the likely outcome of your client's case based on the similarities or differences you discussed in Component 5. This is a re-statement of the conclusion (Component 1) but with more detail and this likely is the beginning of a new paragraph.

Component 7: Explain *why* this is the likely outcome. This is where you must directly apply the reasoning from the precedent case to your client's case.

Possible phrasing:

The court in ______ (insert precedent case name) reasoned ______ (insert the fact specific reasoning of the precedent case on the specific legal issue the analogical reasoning is addressing). This reasoning applies to your client's case (use client's name) because ______ (explain why it applies). Therefore, because the reasoning from (insert precedent case name) applies to your client's case (use client's name), the outcome in your client's case (use client's name) will likely be ______ (insert the outcome you are trying to prove with the analogical reasoning.)

Component 8: Re-state the conclusion you want the reader to reach based on your analogical reasoning. This must connect to the analysis provided by the analogical reasoning and the conclusion stated in Component 1.

<u>Analogical Reasoning Formula Using Multiple Cases:</u>

Component 1: The legal conclusion you want the reader to reach based on your analogical reasoning (this is the overall thesis sentence for the analogical reasoning paragraph or paragraphs—case names should not be included in this sentence).

Component 2: Sentence stating, "Client's case (insert client's name) is similar to/distinguishable from ______ (insert first precedent case name) and/but similar to/distinguishable from ______ (insert second precedent case name) based on ______ (identify the specific issue this analogical reasoning is addressing)."

Component 3: Sentence stating, "In client's case (use client's name), (insert detailed facts about your client's case that will be compared; this must only be the specific facts that will be compared, not all of the facts of the case.)"

Component 4(a): Sentence stating, "This case is similar to/distinguishable from ______ (insert first precedent case name) where (insert detailed facts about the precedent case you are relying upon—this must only be specific facts to be compared, not all of the facts from the precedent case.)"

Component 4(b): Explain, using *specific factual detail*, why the facts you are comparing are similar/distinguishable. This is

where you need to provide specific fact-to-fact comparisons, using actual facts from your client's case and the precedent case (i.e.—"Fact X in client's case is similar to/distinguishable from Fact Y in precedent case because _______ ").

Component 5(a): Sentence stating, "This case is similar to/distinguishable from _______ (insert second precedent case name) where (insert detailed facts about the precedent case you are relying upon—this also must only be the specific facts to be compared, not all of the facts from the precedent case)." [NOTE: you many need to use a transition to begin this sentence, such as "In addition," "Also," "However," or "On the other hand"]

Component 5(b): Explain, using *specific factual detail*, why the facts you are comparing are similar/distinguishable. This is where you need to provide specific fact-to-fact comparisons, using actual facts from your client's case and the precedent case (i.e.—"Fact X in client's case is similar to/distinguishable from Fact Y in precedent case because _______ ").

Component 6: Identify the likely outcome of your client's case based on the similarities/differences you discussed previously (see Components 4(b) and 5(b)). This is a re-statement of the conclusion (the first sentence) but with more detail and this likely is the beginning of a new paragraph.

Component 7: Explain *why* this is the likely outcome. This is where you must directly apply the reasoning from the precedent case to your client's case.

Possible phrasing if the reasoning of the precedent cases is the same:

The court in _______ (insert first and second precedent case names) reasoned _______ (insert the fact specific reasoning of the precedent cases on the specific legal issue the analogical reasoning is addressing). This reasoning applies to your client's case (use client's name) because _______ (explain why it applies). Therefore, because the reasoning from (insert precedent case names) applies to your client's case (use client's name), the outcome in your client's case (use client's name) will likely be _______ (insert the outcome you are trying to prove with the analogical reasoning.)

Possible phrasing if the reasoning of the precedent cases is different:

The court in _______ (insert first precedent case name) reasoned _______ (insert the fact specific reasoning of the first precedent case on the specific legal issue the analogical reasoning is addressing). This reasoning applies to your client's case (use client's name) because _______ (explain why it applies). However, the court in _______ (insert second precedent case name) reasoned _______ (insert the fact specific reasoning of the second precedent case on the specific legal issue the analogical reasoning is addressing). This reasoning does not apply to your client's case (use client's name) because _______ (explain why it does not apply). Therefore, because the reasoning from (insert first precedent case name) applies to your client's case (use client's name) and the reasoning from (insert second precedent case name) does not apply to your client's case (use client's name), the outcome in your client's case (use client's name) will likely be _______ (insert the outcome you are trying to prove with the analogical reasoning.)

Component 8: Re-state the conclusion you want the reader to reach based on your analogical reasoning. This must connect to the analysis provided by the analogical reasoning and to the conclusion stated in Component 1.

WORKSHEET NO. 7: QUESTION PRESENTED

The Question Presented establishes the focus of the memorandum for the reader. It identifies the applicable statute or common law rule, it sets out the legal question(s) to be addressed in your memorandum, and it summarizes the facts that will be significant in addressing the legal question(s).

The most common Question Presented formula is known as the under-does-when formula:

> Under [Insert reference to applicable law],
>
> Does/did/is/was/can/may [Insert the legal question]
>
> When/for/if [Insert the legally significant facts]?

An "under-does-when" Question Presented is substantively correct if it:

1. Includes the applicable law. This will be the popular name of a statute (not the citation) or a general legal principle based in common law (without case names or citations);
2. Identifies the specific legal question(s) your memorandum is addressing. The legal questions(s) must not be too narrow or too broad. If it is too narrow, the question will not cover all of the issues and sub-issues the memorandum is addressing. If it is too broad, the question will not serve the function of focusing the reader's attention on the specific issue(s) the memorandum is addressing; and
3. Provides the legally significant facts. The legally significant facts are the facts used in the analysis of your memorandum.

An "under-does-when" Question Presented is technically correct if it:

1. Is only one sentence; and
2. Ends with a question mark.

> EXAMPLE QUESTION PRESENTED:
>
> <u>Under</u> the California statutory right of publicity, <u>does</u> Tasha V. Anchor, a well-known television reporter, have a right of publicity claim against T–Shirts For Fun <u>for</u> its use of Ms. Anchor's photograph on a t-shirt combined with a photograph of the Los Angeles Mayor in a manner that falsely implies he unethically influenced Ms. Anchor's reporting on his re-election campaign?

Case File Assignment:

Write the Question Presented for your client's case. To help you write the Question Presented for your client's case, answer the following brainstorming questions:

1. What is the applicable law? This will be the popular name of a statute (not the citation) or a general legal principle based in common law (without case names or citations).

2. What is the specific legal question(s) your memorandum is addressing? The legal question(s) must not be too narrow or too broad. If it is too narrow, the question will not cover all of the issues and sub-issues the memorandum is addressing. If it is too broad, the question will not serve the function of focusing the reader's attention on the specific issue(s) the memorandum is addressing.

3. What are the legally significant facts? The legally significant facts are the facts used in the analysis in your memorandum. If there are numerous facts, summarize them or include only the most important facts.

Using the answers to these brainstorming questions as your guide, write the Question Presented for your client's case. Start by cutting and pasting your answers into paragraph form and then mold them into a readable sentence using the following formula as your guide. Also, remember that a technically correct "under-does-when" Question Presented must only be one sentence and end with a question mark.

Under [Insert reference to applicable law], does/did/is/was/can/may [Insert the legal question] when/for/if [Insert the legally significant facts]?

WORKSHEET NO. 8: BRIEF ANSWER

The Brief Answer responds to the question posed by the Question Presented. When read together, the Question Presented and Brief Answer are the "Introduction" to an objective memorandum. After reading the Question Presented and Brief Answer, the reader should have a solid understanding of the subject, the law, and the outcome predicted in the memorandum.

The Brief Answer typically begins with a one- or two-word answer, which is followed by a period; this is called the "short answer." The words that are typically used are "yes," "probably yes," "no," and "probably no/not." If you believe the answer could go either way, it is appropriate to indicate that the outcome is a close call by using the word "probably" in your short answer. However, you must still make a prediction; thus, avoid words such as "might," "possibly," or "could."

Next, you will explain to the reader the basis for the short answer. To do this, you will first provide a statement of the applicable rule(s) that apply to your client's case. Then, you will provide a summary of the reasoning that supports the short answer based on the legally significant facts and the application of the rule(s) to those facts. Finally, the organization of the Brief Answer should parallel the organization of the Discussion section and the tone must to remain objective—do not "argue" your answer.

A Brief Answer is substantively correct if it includes:

1. A short answer:

    a. Yes.

    b. Probably yes.

    c. No.

    d. Probably no/not.

2. A statement of the applicable rule(s). This should define the applicable law(s) identified in your Question Presented. To do this, consult the rules in your analysis (the Rs in each of your objective paradigms).

3. A summary of the reasoning that supports the short answer based on the legally significant facts and the application of the rule(s) to those facts. This should summarize each of the fact-specific conclusions you reached in your analysis. To help you do this, review the analysis in your memorandum (the As in each of your objective paradigms) and try to summarize it in three to four sentences.

EXAMPLE BRIEF ANSWER (the Question Presented is included for context):

QUESTION PRESENTED

Under the California statutory right of publicity, does Tasha V. Anchor, a well-known television reporter, have a right of publicity claim against T–Shirts For Fun for its use of Ms. Anchor's photograph on a t-shirt combined with a photograph of the Los Angeles Mayor in a manner that falsely implies he unethically influenced Ms. Anchor's reporting on his re-election campaign?

BRIEF ANSWER

Probably yes. The California statutory right of publicity is violated when a person's photograph is knowingly used on a product for profit without consent. This statutory right is not absolute as consent is unnecessary if the use of the photograph contributes to the public interest. However, if the photograph or its use contains false information, the public interest exception does not apply. Here, T–Shirts For Fun knowingly used Ms. Anchor's photograph on a t-shirt it created and sold for profit without her consent. The use of the photograph, however, was likely in the public interest because the t-shirt provided commentary on the highly publicized affair between Ms. Anchor and the Mayor and the potential influence the Mayor may have had on Ms. Anchor's reporting on his re-election campaign. Because such information is in the public interest, Ms. Anchor's consent to use her photograph was not required. This exception, however, will likely not apply because, although in the public interest, the commentary was based on false information. While it is true that Ms. Anchor had an affair with the Mayor, she and the television station she works for deny that she ever reported on the Mayor's re-election campaign, showing the commentary on the t-shirt was false. Thus, Ms. Anchor likely will have a right of publicity claim against T–Shirts For Fun.

Case File Assignment:

Write the Brief Answer for your client's case. To help you write the Brief Answer for your client's case, review your Question Presented to remind yourself of the question your Brief Answer is responding to. Next, answer the following brainstorming questions to help you develop the substance of your Brief Answer:

1. What is the short answer to the question posed in your Question Presented? Remember this can only be "yes," "probably yes," "no," or "probably no/not."

2. What are the applicable rule(s)? This should define the applicable law(s) identified in your Question Presented. To do this, consult the rules in your analysis (the Rs in each of your objective paradigms).

3. Summarize the reasoning that supports the short answer based on the legally significant facts and the application of the rule(s) to those facts. This should summarize each of the fact-specific conclusions you reached in your analysis. To help you do this, review the analysis (the As in each of your objective paradigms) in your memorandum and try to summarize it in three to four sentences.

Using the answers to these brainstorming questions as your guide, write the Brief Answer for your client's case. Start by cutting and pasting your answers into paragraph form and then mold them into a readable paragraph, using the following formula:

Short answer. Statement of the applicable rule(s). Summary of the reasoning that supports the short answer based on the legally significant facts and the application of the rule(s) to those facts.

WORKSHEET NO. 9: FACTS

The four most important things to remember when writing an objective Facts section are to: (1) include the legally significant facts; (2) organize the facts in an effective manner; (3) maintain a neutral tone; and (4) provide objectively accurate facts.

The Facts section is substantively correct if it:

1. Develops the foundation or context for the reader in the first paragraph (or first couple of sentences) by:

    a. Identifying your client, the opposing party, and their relationship;

    b. Stating your client's general problem or goal;

    c. Describing the setting (e.g. the time and location of the events); and

    d. Including the procedural history or the status of the case.

2. Includes the proper substance by:

    a. Including the legally significant facts. To determine the legally significant facts, review your analysis and highlight all of the facts from your client's case that you relied upon. These are the legally significant facts. If you have not yet written your analysis, determine the legally significant facts by asking yourself what are the facts a court would consider in ruling on your client's case?

    b. Including background facts that are needed for the legally significant facts to make sense. To determine the necessary background facts, ask yourself: what else does the reader need to know to understand the story of your client's case?

    c. Describing the facts accurately;

    d. Including both favorable and unfavorable facts;

    e. Omitting factual arguments, references to the law, legal conclusions, and factual conclusions; and

    f. Maintaining an objective and neutral tone.

3. Has a strategically selected organization to best tell the story: chronological, topical, or a combination of chronological and topical. The organization you select must be a strategic choice based on the best approach to tell the reader the story of your client's case.

4. Provides closure to the Facts section by not ending abruptly (consider re-stating what the client has asked you to do or stating the procedural history of the case).

EXAMPLE FACTS:

T–Shirts for Fun (TFF) recently created and sold a t-shirt featuring a photograph of Tasha V. Anchor, a local television reporter for KTV-LA. On the t-shirt, Ms. Anchor's photograph is combined with a photograph of a miniaturized image of the Los Angeles Mayor wearing a suit and devil horns, sitting on Ms. Anchor's left shoulder. TFF, a company that designs, produces, and distributes funny t-shirts for profit, claims it created the t-shirt to provide subtle commentary on the possibility that Ms. Anchor unethically reported on the Mayor's re-election campaign. Ms. Anchor, however, did not consent to the use of her photograph on the t-shirt and is offended by its use because she denies that she ever unethically reported on the Mayor's re-election campaign.

TFF created the t-shirt soon after an affair between Ms. Anchor and the Mayor was made public. The affair was highly publicized and the ethics of both Ms Anchor and the Mayor were questioned by the media. Ms. Anchor admits that she conducted a few of interviews of the Mayor last fall, but states they were on topics unrelated to his re-election campaign. Her employer, KTV–LA, has allowed Ms. Anchor to keep her position and the general manager for the station said "There is no concern as to the ethics of Ms. Anchor whatsoever."

Ms. Anchor would like to determine if she has a claim against TFF based on its unauthorized use of her photograph in a manner that falsely implies she unethically reported on the Mayor's re-election campaign.

Case File Assignment:

Write the Facts section for you client's case. To help you write the Facts section, answer the following brainstorming questions:

1. For the first paragraph (or first couple of sentences) of the Facts section, develop the foundation or context for the reader:
    a. Who is your client? Who is the opposing party? What is their relationship (i.e.—employer/employee; buyer/seller; landlord/tenant; accused/victim)?

    b. What is your client's general problem or goal?

c. What was the setting (e.g. the time and location of the events)?

d. What is the procedural history or the status of the case?

2. For the remaining paragraphs in your Facts section, answer the following brainstorming questions to help you identify the relevant facts:

   a. What are the legally significant facts? Review your analysis section and highlight all of the facts from your client's case that you used in your analysis. These are the legally significant facts and they must be included in your Facts section. If you have not yet written your analysis, then determine the legally significant facts by asking yourself: what are the facts a court would consider in ruling on your client's case?

   b. What background facts are necessary to provide context for the legally significant facts identified in response to Question 2(a) above?

   c. What are the unfavorable facts? What are the facts the opposing party likely will rely upon?

3. Looking at your answers to these brainstorming questions and using your understanding of your client's case, identify the organization you will use to structure your Facts section? Chronological? Topical? Combination of chronological and topical? The organization you select must be a strategic choice based on the best approach to tell the story of your client's case.

Using the answers to these brainstorming questions as your guide, write the Facts section for your client's case. Start by cutting and pasting your answers into paragraph form and then mold them into readable paragraphs.

When writing the Facts section, consider the following:

1. The first paragraph must:
   - Identify all of the parties and their relationship;
   - Briefly describe your client's problem or goal;
   - Provide the setting (time and location of events); and
   - Include the status or procedural history of the case.
2. The overall substance and tone must:
   - Have a strategically selected organization (avoid stream of consciousness writing);
   - Describe the facts accurately;
   - Include both favorable and unfavorable facts;
   - Omit factual arguments, references to the law, legal conclusions, and factual conclusions; and
   - Maintain an objective and neutral tone.
3. The last paragraph must:
   - Provide closure to the Facts section by not ending abruptly (consider re-stating what the client has asked you to do or stating the procedural history of the case).

WORKSHEET NO. 10: CONCLUSION

The Conclusion summarizes the individual conclusions reached in your analysis into one or two paragraphs and provides strategic recommendations based on your analysis in the memorandum. Although the Conclusion should be self-contained, that is, the reader should be able to understand it without having to read the entire memorandum, it should not include nearly as much detail as the Discussion section.

A Conclusion is substantively correct if it includes:

1. The ultimate conclusion of your memorandum;
2. Each rule applied to your client's case (the R in each objective paradigm included in your memorandum);
3. The conclusion for each rule applied in your client's case (the C in each objective paradigm included in your memorandum);
4. A summary of the reasoning that supports those conclusions (summarize the A sections in each objective paradigm included in your memorandum); and
5. Any strategic recommendations based on the analysis provided in the memorandum.

EXAMPLE CONCLUSION:

Ms. Anchor likely has a valid right of publicity claim against TFF. Under the California statutory right of publicity, a person has a claim if another knowingly uses the person's photograph without consent. Consent is unnecessary, however, if the photograph relates to a matter in the public interest and is connected to that public interest, unless the use provides false information. In this case, TFF's knowingly used Ms. Anchor's photograph without her consent in violation of § 3344(a). However, because it was used by TFF for the purpose of providing a commentary on the affair between Ms. Anchor and the Mayor and the possible unethical reporting on the Mayor's re-election campaign, the use of the photograph relates to a matter in the public interest. Thus, it is subject to the exemption in § 3344(d) and Ms. Anchor's consent was unnecessary. Despite this, Ms. Anchor likely will still prevail because the implication created by TFF's use of Ms. Anchor's photograph on the t-shirt is false and, therefore, not entitled to protection. For these reasons, Ms. Anchor likely has a successful claim against TFF and should pursue a legal remedy in this matter.

Case File Assignment:

Write the Conclusion for you client's case. To help you write the Conclusion section, answer the following brainstorming questions:

1. What is the ultimate conclusion of your memorandum? (NOTE: This must be consistent with the information provided in your Question Presented and your Brief Answer.)

2. Identify each rule applied to your client's case (the R in each objective paradigm included in your memorandum).

3. Identify the conclusion for each rule applied in your client's case (the C in each objective paradigm included in your memorandum)?

4. Summarize the analysis that supports the conclusion on each rule (summarize the A section in each objective paradigm included in your memorandum)?

5. Identify any strategic recommendations based on the analysis provided in your memorandum.

Using the answers to these brainstorming questions as your guide, write the Conclusion for your client's case. Start by cutting and pasting your answers into paragraph form and then mold them into a readable paragraph. When writing the Conclusion, maintain an objective and neutral tone, have the organization of the Conclusion parallel the organization of the Discussion section, and avoid simply repeating the Brief Answer.

CASE FILE NO. 3: CELEBRITY v. FULLBACK STEAKHOUSES, INC.

WORKSHEET NO. 1: INTRODUCTION, FACTS, AND RELEVANT AUTHORITY

Introduction

Attorneys rarely research the law and write an analysis simply to learn the law. Instead, attorneys almost always research and write in response to the specific situation faced by a client. Therefore, before you turn to the attached statutes and cases, read the Office Memorandum on the next page to give yourself an understanding of your client's situation. The Office Memorandum is an example of what you might receive when a supervising attorney asks you to work on a case.

After you read the Office Memorandum, read the statutes and cases provided in the Case File. One of your goals in reading these statutes and cases is to develop your understanding of New York's law the right of privacy. Another goal is to find the answer to the question the supervising attorney poses in the Office Memorandum: Did the Fullback Steakhouse misappropriate Suzie Celebrity's likeness in violation of New York law? As you read each legal authority, consider how you can use it to determine the most likely outcome for your client. The most likely outcome, however, may not always be a favorable one. Therefore, considering the law and the facts from a neutral perspective are vital to fully advise your client.

OFFICE MEMORANDUM

TO: Legal Intern
FROM: Supervising Attorney
DATE: September 1, YEAR
RE: Celebrity v. Fullback Steakhouses, Inc.; Misappropriation of likeness

---

I have just met with a new client and I need you to begin to work on his case. John Ritchie is the CEO of Fullback Steakhouses, Inc. (Fullback). He is seeking advice and representation. Fullback recently received a letter from legal counsel for Suzie Celebrity that states her intent to file a lawsuit against Fullback, alleging it misappropriated her likeness under New York law.

The short version of the facts is that Suzie Celebrity is a well-known socialite in New York. Her signature look is a blonde hair, large sun glasses, over-sized purse, stiletto heals, and she always is carrying a small dog in a small pink carrier. Suzie also is known for the catch-phrase "spicy." Recently, Fullback began running an animated television commercial, featuring a cartoon robot wearing a blonde wig, carrying a small dog in a small pink carrier.

I need you to evaluate whether Fullback misappropriated Suzie's likeness under New York law.

I have attached my notes from my meeting with Mr. Ritchie below, which describes the underlying facts. These are the only facts available at this time.

Client Interview Notes

Fullback aired a TV commercial in August YEAR; Advertises new chain of sports bars.

Cartoon Robot appears in the ad; resembles Suzie Celebrity.

Viewed actual pictures and video clips of Suzie Celebrity and note the following observations:

> *Blonde, thin, sultry, winks frequently.*
>
> *Carries small dog in small pink carrier.*

Viewed a copy of TV commercial and note the following observations:

> *Robot waiter dressed as a referee brings plate of Buffalo wings to table where a blonde robot is sitting with a group of friends.*
>
> *Robot is very thin, has blonde hair, and a Chihuahua in a pink carrier.*
>
> *Waiter sets plates of Buffalo wings down on the table.*

Waiter says, "Be careful, it's spicy."

One of the friends asks, "What's spicy?"

Robot picks up a Buffalo wing, puts it in her mouth, says, "Mmm, spicy," and winks at the camera.

Suzie is apparently known for the phrase "Spicy"—might be trademarked.

The robot never expressly claims to be Suzie Celebrity, nor does the commercial use her name or photograph.

Letter from Suzie's counsel indicates she is upset and angry and feels the commercial wrongly uses her celebrity likeness without her permission.

Based on Suzie's appearance on multiple reality shows and her constant public appearances, she is one of the most Googled celebrities.

Mr. Ritchie seeks advice regarding whether Suzie can successfully sue Fullback over the use of her likeness in its commercial.

McKinney's Consolidated Laws of New York

Civil Rights Law

Chapter 6 of the Consolidated Laws

Article 5 Right of Privacy

§ 50. Right of privacy

A person, firm or corporation that uses for advertising purposes, or for the purposes of trade, the name, portrait or picture of any living person without having first obtained the written consent of such person, or if a minor of his or her parent or guardian, is guilty of a misdemeanor.

§ 51. Action for injunction and for damages

Any person whose name, portrait, picture or voice is used within this state for advertising purposes or for the purposes of trade without the written consent first obtained as above provided may maintain an equitable action in the supreme court of this state against the person, firm or corporation so using his name, portrait, picture or voice, to prevent and restrain the use thereof; and may also sue and recover damages for any injuries sustained by reason of such use and if the defendant shall have knowingly used such person's name, portrait, picture or voice in such manner as is forbidden or declared to be unlawful by section fifty of this article, the jury, in its discretion, may award exemplary damages. But nothing contained in this article shall be so construed as to prevent any person, firm or corporation from selling or otherwise transferring any material containing such name, portrait, picture or voice in whatever medium to any user of such name, portrait, picture or voice, or to any third party for sale or transfer directly or indirectly to such a user, for use in a manner lawful under this article; nothing contained in this article shall be so construed as to prevent any person, firm or corporation, practicing the profession of photography, from exhibiting in or about his or its establishment specimens of the work of such establishment, unless the same is continued by such person, firm or corporation after written notice objecting thereto has been given by the person portrayed; and nothing contained in this article shall be so construed as to prevent any person, firm or corporation from using the name, portrait, picture or voice of any manufacturer or dealer in connection with the goods, wares and merchandise manufactured, produced or dealt in by him which he has sold or disposed of with such name, portrait, picture or voice used in connection therewith; or from using the name, portrait, picture or voice of any author, composer or artist in connection with his literary, musical or artistic productions which he has sold or disposed of with such name, portrait, picture or voice used in connection therewith. Nothing contained in this section shall be construed to prohibit the copyright owner of a sound recording from disposing of, dealing in, licensing or selling that sound recording to any party, if the right to dispose of, deal in, license or sell such sound recording has been conferred by contract or other written document by such living person or the holder of such right. Nothing contained in the foregoing sentence shall be deemed to abrogate or otherwise limit any rights or remedies otherwise conferred by federal law or state law.

Jacqueline Kennedy ONASSIS, Plaintiff

v.

CHRISTIAN DIOR–NEW YORK, INC., Lansdowne Advertising, Inc., Richard Avedon, Barbara Reynolds and Ron Smith Celebrity Look–Alikes, Defendants

Supreme Court, New York County, New York,

Special Term, Part I.

472 N.Y.S.2d 254

January 11, 1984.

GREENFIELD

This case poses for judicial resolution the question of whether the use for commercial purposes of a "look-alike" of a well-known personality violates the right of privacy legislatively granted by enactment of Civil Rights Law §§ 50 and 51. Put another way, can one person enjoin the use of someone else's face? The questions appear not to have been definitively answered before.

Plaintiff, Jacqueline Kennedy Onassis, former First Lady of the United States, widow of President John F. Kennedy, one of the world's most powerful men, and of Aristotle Onassis, one of the world's wealthiest men, but a well-known personality in her own right, moves for a preliminary injunction under the Civil Rights Law to restrain defendants, all of whom were associated with an advertising campaign to promote the products and the image of Christian Dior–New York, Inc., from using or distributing a certain advertisement, and for associated relief. She alleges simply in her complaint that defendants have knowingly caused the preparation and publication of an advertisement for Dior products which includes her likeness in the form of a photograph of look-alike Barbara Reynolds; that Reynolds' picture causes her to be identified with the ad to which she has not given her consent; that this was a violation of her rights of privacy and that it caused her irreparable injury.

Defendant Christian Dior–New York, Inc. is the corporate entity which controls advertising and publicity for the 35 United States licensees who sell varied lines of merchandise under the coveted Dior label. **257

* * *

So it was that J. Walter Thompson's Lansdowne Division, in conjunction with noted photographer Richard Avedon, hit upon the idea of a running series of ads featuring a trio known as the Diors (one female and two males), who were characterized by an article in Newsweek Magazine as idle rich, suggestively decadent, and aggressively chic. Indeed, it was suggested that this *menage a trois,* putatively inspired by the characters portrayed by Noel Coward, Alfred Lunt and Lynn Fontanne in Coward's 1933 play "Design for Living", would become the most notorious personae in advertising since Brooke Shields refused to let anything come between her and her Calvins (for the uninitiated, blue jeans advertised under designer Calvin Klein's label). To emphasize the impression of the unconventional, the copy for one ad had read, "When the Diors got away from it all, they brought with them nothing except 'The Decline of the West' and one toothbrush." Evidently, to stir comment, the relationship portrayed in the ad campaign was meant to be ambiguous, "to specify nothing but suggest everything." The 16 sequential ads would depict this steadfast trio in varying situations leading to the marriage of two (but not the exclusion of the third), birth of a baby, and their ascent to Heaven (subject to resurrection on demand).

Thus, the Diors, and by association their products, would be perceived as chic, sophisticated, elite, unconventional, quirky, audacious, elegant, and unorthodox. The advertisement for the wedding, which is the one challenged here, is headed "Christian Dior: Sportswear for Women and Clothing for Men." Portrayed in the ad are the happy Dior trio attended by their ostensible intimates, all ecstatically beaming—Gene Shalit, the T.V. personality, model Shari Belafonte, actress Ruth Gordon, and Barbara Reynolds, a secretary who bears a remarkable resemblance to plaintiff Jacqueline Onassis.

* * *

Of course, what stamps it as "legendary" is the presence of this eclectic group, a frothy mix, the most legendary of which would clearly be Jacqueline Kennedy Onassis, shown discreetly behind Gordon and Shalit, obviously delighted to be in attendance at this "event."

That the person behind Gordon and Shalit bore a striking resemblance to the plaintiff was no mere happenstance. Defendants knew there was little or no likelihood that Mrs. Onassis would ever consent to be depicted in this kind of advertising campaign for Dior. She has asserted in her affidavit, and it is well-known, that she has never permitted her name or picture to be used in connection with the promotion of commercial products. Her name has been used sparingly only in connection with certain public services, civic, art and educational projects which she has supported. Accordingly, Lansdowne and Avedon, once the content of the picture and the make-up of the wedding party having been determined, contacted defendant Ron Smith Celebrity Look–Alikes to provide someone who could pass for Jacqueline Kennedy Onassis. That agency, which specializes in locating and providing persons who bear a close resemblance to well-known personalities on request (and for a fee), came up with defendant Barbara Reynolds, regularly an appointments secretary to a congressman, who, with appropriate coiffure and appointments looks remarkably like Mrs. Onassis, and has made this resemblance an adjunct to her career.

The ad was run in September and October of 1983 in several upscale publications including Esquire, Harper's Bazaar, The New Yorker, and the New York Times **258 Magazine. It received widespread circulation, and apparently was the subject of considerable comment, as was the entire series. Dior reportedly committed 2.5 million dollars to the campaign, and boasted that as a result, sales went through the roof. In opposition to the application for an injunction, defendants urge, among other things, that it is unnecessary because the ad has already appeared, and it is not scheduled for republication. However, they declined to enter into any formal stipulation to that effect, and trade papers are abuzz with speculation about the resurrection and reincarnation of the campaign, with possible television showings to reach an even wider audience. Moreover, the case presents an important question under the privacy law, and it is appropriate that it be judicially resolved. *Matter of Baumann & Son Buses Inc.,* 46 N.Y.2d 1061, 1063, 416 N.Y.S.2d 788, 390 N.E.2d 295; *Le Drugstore Etats Unis v. N.Y. State Board of Pharmacy,* 33 N.Y.2d 298, 301, 352 N.Y.S.2d 188, 307 N.E.2d 249.

Section 50 of the New York Civil Rights Law provides:

> "A person, firm or corporation that uses for advertising purposes, or for the purposes of trade, the name, portrait or picture of any living person without having first obtained the written consent of such person ... is guilty of a misdemeanor."

Having defined the offense, and declaring it to be criminal, § 51 of the Civil Rights Law goes on to provide civil remedies for violation as well, including injunction and damages.

> "Any person whose name, portrait or picture is used within this state for advertising purposes or for the purposes of trade without the written consent first obtained as above provided may maintain an equitable action in the supreme court of this state against the person, firm or corporation so using his name, portrait or picture, to prevent and restrain the use thereof; and may also sue and recover damages for any injuries sustained by reason of such use and if the defendant shall have knowingly used such person's name, portrait or picture in such manner as is forbidden or declared to be unlawful by section fifty of this article, the jury, in its discretion, may award exemplary damages.... "

* * *

Is there a violation? Defendants, urging a strict and literal compliance with the statute, say that there is not.

* * *

Plaintiff's name appears nowhere in the advertisement. Nevertheless, the picture of a well-known personality, used in an ad and instantly recognizable, will still serve as a badge of approval for that commercial product. It is designed to "catch the eye and focus it on the advertisement." *Negri v. Schering Corp.,* 333 F.Supp. 101, 105. That is why the use of a person's "portrait or picture" without consent is also proscribed.**259 Just what is comprehended by the term "portrait or picture?"

In *Negri v. Schering Corp.,* supra, plaintiff, the well-known movie actress of the 1920's, Pola Negri, objected to the publication of an advertisement in 1969 showing a scene from one of her early movies with words issuing from her mouth in the balloon caption suggesting the use of the anti-histamine drug Pola-ramine. To defendant's contention that the picture did not really show plaintiff as she was then, the Southern District court, applying New York Law, held that as long as the ad portrayed a recognizable likeness it was actionable, declaring, "If a picture so used is a clear and identifiable likeness of a living person, her or she is entitled to recover damages suffered by reason of such use * * *." (id. p. 105).

In *Ali v. Playgirl, Inc.,* 447 F.Supp. 723, the portrait or picture was not an actual photo, but a composite photo-drawing depicting a naked black man in a boxing ring, with the recognizable facial features of the former world's heavyweight champion. The Southern District court, again applying New York law, held that the phrase "portrait or picture" as used in § 51 of the Civil Rights Law is not restricted to actual photographs, but comprises any representations which are recognizable as likenesses of the complaining individual. In that case, the picture represented something short of actuality—somewhere between representational art and a cartoon.

In *Loftus v. Greenwich Lithographing Co. Inc.,* 192 App.Div. 251, 182 N.Y.S. 428 the objection again was not to an actual picture of the plaintiff, but to an advertising poster for a movie called "Shame", which showed a sketch of a female figure in a costume plaintiff had popularized in a Ziegfeld production. The court rejected defendant's contention that the poster was not an actual depiction of plaintiff. Despite changes that were made as between plaintiff's actual picture and defendant's drawing, the court found it evident that the drawing took plaintiff's appearance as its starting point, and declared that slight changes or deviations would not thwart the application of the wholesome provisions of the Civil Rights Law.

In *Young v. Greneker Studios, Inc.,* 175 Misc. 1027, 26 N.Y.S.2d 357, this court extended the literal definition of portrait or picture to include a manikin or sculpture for which plaintiff was the model. The words "portrait or picture" were construed to be broad enough to cover any likeness or representation of the plaintiff, whether two or three dimensional. On the other hand, conveying the likeness of a person, not graphically, but through sound, by means of the imitation of a distinctive voice does not come within the prohibition of the statute (possibly an oversight, since the possibility of reproducing and disseminating the sound of a voice was not contemplated in 1903 when the §§ 50 and 51 of the Civil Rights Law were first enacted). See *Lahr v. Adell Chemical Co., Inc.,* 1 Cir., 300 F.2d 256, 258. This is not because the portrayal of plaintiff's distinctive vocal delivery was by an imitator, but because a voice was not construed as the equivalent of a name or picture, and the picture used was that of a duck.

The Court of Appeals, 70 years ago, in *Binns v. Vitagraph Co. of America,* 210 N.Y. 51, 103 N.E. 1108, dealt with the question of whether the use of the picture of another person suggestive of the plaintiff is a prohibited use of a plaintiff's portrait or picture. The plaintiff was a wireless operator on a sinking ship, whose radioed distress signal, "COD", resulted in the rescue of hundreds of passengers, and made him a hero. Defendant, attempting to capitalize on the widespread public interest in the story, did a photoplay based on the event (what we would today call a "docudrama"). A professional actor was employed to portray the plaintiff, and was photographed playing the part. The court declared, "A picture within the meaning of the statute is not necessarily a photograph of the living person, but includes any representation of such person. The picture ... was intended to be, and it was, a representation of the plaintiff." **260 id, p. 57, 103 N.E. 1108. The court expressly rejected the contention of the defendant that all it used "was an actual picture of a person made up to look like and impersonate the plaintiff." While we might take a different view today as to whether a depiction of a newsworthy event (see *Murray v. New York Magazine Co.,* 27 N.Y.2d 406, 318 N.Y.S.2d 474, 267 N.E.2d 256) or a dramatized re-enactment or even a satirical portrayal is a commercial statement or protected comment (*University of Notre Dame v. Twentieth Century Fox Film Corp.,* 22 A.D.2d 452, 256 N.Y.S.2d 301, aff'd. 15 N.Y.2d 940, 259 N.Y.S.2d 832, 207 N.E.2d 508) the court was clear that the photographic portrayal by one person to simulate another without consent was forbidden by the statute.

Defendants urge as controlling *Lombardo v. Doyle, Dane & Bernbach, Inc.,* 58 A.D.2d 620, 396 N.Y.S.2d 661, in which there was a dismissal of an invasion of privacy action (by a vote of 3–2) against a television commercial which showed an actor conducting a band at a New Year's Eve party playing "Auld Lang Syne", similar to the way plaintiff bandleader had done for decades, and with which he was associated in the public mind. However, there the majority of court was refusing to equate a person's style or characteristics or musical arrangements with a "name, portrait or picture" where plaintiff's name was not mentioned and the actor did not physically resemble the plaintiff. Similarly, in *Shaw v. Time & Life Records,* 38 N.Y.2d 201, 379 N.Y.S.2d 390, 341 N.E.2d 817, plaintiff bandleader was denied the right to make claim under §§ 50 and 51 of the Civil Rights Law against defendant for simulating the "sound" and style of arrangements of his swing era band. And in *Toscani v. Hersey,* 271 App. Div. 445, 65 N.Y.S.2d 814, where the plaintiff was portrayed in the book and play "A Bell for Adano", but under a different and fictionalized name, the court held that a work inspired by the acts, events and experiences of a living person is not an unauthorized use of his "name, portrait or picture."

The principle to be distilled from a study of the statute and of the cases construing it is that all persons, of whatever station in life, from the relatively unknown to the world famous, are to be secured against rapacious commercial exploitation. While the statute may not, by its terms, cover voice or movement, characteristics or style, it is intended to protect the essence of the person, his or her identity or *persona* from being unwillingly or unknowingly misappropriated for the profit of another.

* * *

Today, the visual have superseded the verbal arts, and news photography, television, and motion pictures can accord instant world-wide recognition to a face. For some people, even without their American Express Cards, the face is total identification, more than a signature or a coat of arms. (Cf. *Orsini v. Eastern Wine Corp.,* 190 Misc. 235, 73 N.Y.S.2d 426 aff'd. 273 App.Div. 947, 78 N.Y.S.2d 224). The unauthorized use of a person's signature would not pass muster under the statute because it was claimed merely to be a facsimile. Is a picture or portrait intended to look like someone not that person's picture if it is similarly a facsimile or a simulation?

* * *

The statute is in the disjunctive. There need not be, as defendants suggest, a coupling of name *and* picture. The essence of what is prohibited, as the statute, the cases, and the dictionary definitions make clear, is the exploitation of one's identity as that is conveyed verbally or graphically. A photograph may be a depiction only of the person before the lens, but a "portrait or picture" gives wider scope, to encompass a representation which conveys the essence and likeness of an individual, not only actuality, but the close and purposeful resemblance to reality. That is how it was defined in *Binns v. Vitagraph Co. of America,* supra, as any representation, including the picture of another, which was intended to be, and did, in fact, convey the idea that it was the plaintiff.

We are dealing here with actuality and appearance, where illusion often heightens reality and all is not quite what it seems. Is the illusionist to be free to step aside, having reaped the benefits of his creation, and permitted to disclaim the very impression he sought to create? If we were to permit it, we would be sanctioning an obvious loophole to evade the statute. If a person is unwilling to give his or her endorsement to help sell a product, either at an offered price or at any price, no matter—hire a double and the same effect is achieved. The essential purpose of the statute must be carried out by giving it a common sense reading which bars easy evasion. If we truly value the right of privacy in a world of exploitation, where every mark of distinctiveness becomes grist for the mills of publicity, then we must give it more than lip service and grudging recognition. Let the word go forth—there is no free ride. The commercial hitchhiker seeking to travel on the fame of another will have to learn to pay the fare or stand on his own two feet.

There are many aspects of identity. A person may be known not only by objective indicia-name, face, and social security number, but by other characteristics as well-voice, movement, style, coiffure, typical phrases, as well as by his or her history and accomplishments. Thus far, the legislature has accorded protection only to those aspects of identity embodied in name and face. Imitators are free to simulate voice or hair-do, or characteristic clothing or accessories, and writers to comment on and actors to re-enact events. No one is free to trade on another's name or appearance and claim immunity because what he is using is similar to but not identical with the original.

* * *

The fact that even as between people who resemble one another, there are variances and points of dissimilarity is of no moment. It is the over-all impression being made that counts. The statute necessarily contemplates that a depiction may not be precise, for the words "portrait or picture" comprehend a sketch, a cartoon, or a caricature which selectively omit some features and accentuate others. There are then points of resemblance and points of difference and distortion, but if done well there is instant recognition. What difference if a sketch is used instead of a look-alike model in connection with a commercial promotion? The end result is the same-trading on the name or features of another and the unwarranted commercial exploitation of a person who has not consented to be commercially exploited.

* * *

In essence, this court finds on the undisputed facts, that plaintiff's identity was impermissibly misappropriated for the purposes of trade and advertising, and that it makes no difference if the picture used to establish that identity was genuine or counterfeit.

* * *

Plaintiff's statutory right to privacy has been trampled upon, and that is **264 all that need be shown. The motion is granted; the cross-motion is denied.

Robert BURCK d/b/a The Naked Cowboy, Plaintiff

v.

MARS, INCORPORATED and Chute Gerdeman, Inc., Defendants

United States District Court,

S.D. New York

571 F.Supp.2d 446

June 23, 2008

CHIN

This is the case of The Naked Cowboy versus The Blue M & M.

Plaintiff Robert Burck is a "street entertainer" who performs in New York City's Times Square as The Naked Cowboy, wearing only a white cowboy hat, cowboy boots, and underpants, and carrying a guitar strategically placed to give the illusion of nudity. He has registered trademarks to "The Naked Cowboy" name and likeness.

Beginning in April 2007, defendants Mars, Incorporated ("Mars") and Chute Gerdeman, Inc. ("Chute") began running an animated cartoon advertisement on two oversized video billboards in Times Square, featuring a blue M & M dressed "exactly like The Naked Cowboy," wearing only a white cowboy hat, cowboy boots, and underpants, and carrying a guitar.

In this case, Burck sues defendants for compensatory and punitive damages. He alleges that defendants have violated his "right to publicity" under New York law and infringed his trademarks under federal law by using his likeness, persona, and image for commercial purposes without his written permission and by falsely suggesting that he has endorsed M & M candy.

Three motions are before the Court: Chute moves pursuant to Fed.R.Civ.P. 12(b)(6) to dismiss the complaint; Mars moves pursuant to Fed.R.Civ.P. 12(c) for judgment on the pleadings; and Burck moves pursuant to Fed.R. Civ.P. 12(f) to strike certain of defendants' affirmative defenses.

For the reasons that follow, Burck's motion is denied and defendants' motions are denied in part and granted in part. Burck's right to privacy claim (denominated as a right of publicity claim) is dismissed, for the New York statute protects*449 the name, portrait, or picture of a "living person," not a character created or a role performed by a living person. Burck may proceed, however, with his false endorsement claim, for he plausibly alleges that consumers seeing defendants' advertisements would conclude-incorrectly-that he had endorsed M & M candy.

BACKGROUND

A. *The Facts*

As alleged in the complaint and set forth in the exhibits incorporated therein by reference, the facts are as follows:

For the past ten years, Burck "has performed as a street entertainer in New York City's Times Square under the persona known as The Naked Cowboy," wearing only "a white cowboy hat, white cowboy boots, white underpants, and an acoustic guitar." (Compl.¶ ¶ 5, 6). His street performances "have become a fixture of New York City culture, as well as one of the top tourist attractions" in Times Square. (*Id.* ¶ 7).

The Naked Cowboy has become "a prominent and well-known persona," and Burck has registered trademarks to The Naked Cowboy name and likeness. (*Id.* ¶ ¶ 20, 21). In addition to performing in Times Square, Burck has appeared as The Naked Cowboy in various television shows, movies, and video games. (*Id.* ¶ ¶ 10–19). He has also licensed his name and likeness to companies for endorsements and advertisements. (*Id.* ¶ 22). For instance, he appeared in a Chevrolet commercial that debuted during Super Bowl XLI. (*Id.* ¶ 23).

Mars sells candies and chocolate products, including the world-famous M & M's. (*Id.* ¶ 33). Mars retained Chute, an advertising and design agency, to create a video for two electronic billboards in Times Square and a mural for its M & M World store located in Times Square. (*Id.* ¶ ¶ 32, 33).

The video (an animated cartoon) featured "a blue 'M & M' dressed up exactly like The Naked Cowboy-white underwear, white cowboy hat, white cowboy boots, and white guitar." (*Id.* ¶ 26; *see* DX C).[FN1] In addition to the M & M Cowboy character, the video showed other M & Ms as famous New York figures, such as the Statue of Liberty and King Kong, as well as everyday New Yorkers and tourists engaging in typical New York activities such as hailing a cab and riding a carriage through Central Park. Beginning in April 2007 (Compl. ¶ 29), the video "played on a continuous loop every few minutes over a nine-month period" (Tr. at 22).

FN1. References to "DX" are to defendants' exhibits submitted at the oral argument on June 11, 2008. These exhibits are referred to in the complaint and are deemed incorporated therein by reference. (*See* Transcript of Proceedings of June 11, 2008 ("Tr.") at 4).

The mural inside the M & M World store was a snapshot of the heart of Times Square, transformed into an animated world populated by M & M characters. (Compl. ¶ 30; *see* DX B1). Neon lights, oversized billboards advertising Broadway shows, and familiar landmarks, such as the Cup Noodles sign, filled the scene. Many of the signs and billboards in the mural were altered to incorporate the M & M logo or candy themes, such as replacing "STOMP" (the name of a show) with the word "CHOMP" and substituting a red M & M in place of the red heart in the logo" I NY." In the middle of the mural, in the midst of a cluster of billboards, was a small billboard featuring a yellow M & M wearing The Naked Cowboy's signature costume. (DX B1).

Defendants did not request, nor did they receive, permission from Burck to use a *450 likeness of The Naked Cowboy for the M & M Cowboy characters. (Compl. ¶ 25).

* * *

DISCUSSION

I start with defendants' motions, addressing first Burck's right of privacy claim under New York law and second his trademark infringement claim under the Lanham Act. I then turn to Burck's motion to strike certain affirmative defenses.

* * *

2. *The Right of Privacy Claim*

a. *The Statute*

The right to privacy has been recognized by statute in New York for more than a century. *See Groden v. Random House, Inc.,* 61 F.3d 1045, 1048 (2d Cir.1995). The New York legislature enacted sections 50 and 51 of the Civil Rights Law to protect against "nonconsensual commercial appropriations of the name, portrait or picture of a living person." *Finger v. Omni Publ'ns. Int'l, Ltd.,* 77 N.Y.2d 138, 141, 564 N.Y.S.2d 1014, 566 N.E.2d 141 (1990); *see also Arrington v. New York Times Co.,* 55 N.Y.2d 433, 439, 449 N.Y.S.2d 941, 434 N.E.2d 1319 (1982). There is no common law right to privacy or publicity in New York, and thus sections 50 and 51 provide the only remedy for such claims. *Groden,* 61 F.3d at 1049.

*451 Section 50 of the New York Civil Rights Law makes it a misdemeanor to use "for advertising purposes, or for the purposes of trade, the name, portrait or picture of any living person without having first obtained the written consent of such person." N.Y. Civ. Rights Law § 50 (McKinney 1992). Section 51 creates a cause of action for the invasion of the "right of privacy" granted by section 50. *See Zacchini v. Scripps–Howard Broad. Co.,* 433 U.S. 562, 571 n. 6, 97 S.Ct. 2849, 53 L.Ed.2d 965 (1977). Section 51 provides:

> Any person whose name, portrait, picture or voice is used within this state for advertising purposes or for the purposes of trade without the written consent first obtained as above provided [in section 50] may maintain an equitable action ... to prevent and restrain the use thereof; and may also sue and recover damages for any injuries sustained by reason of such use.

N.Y. Civ. Rights Law § 51 (McKinney Supp.2008). To maintain a civil action under section 51, a plaintiff must show that the defendant (1) used his name, portrait, picture, or voice, (2) for advertising or trade purposes, (3) without his written consent. *Allen v. Nat'l Video, Inc.,* 610 F.Supp. 612, 621 (S.D.N.Y.1985).

Sections 50 and 51 are limited in their reach because of the First Amendment. They do not apply, for example, to "reports of newsworthy events or matters of public interest." *Messenger v. Gruner + Jahr Printing & Publ'g,* 94 N.Y.2d 436, 441, 706 N.Y.S.2d 52, 727 N.E.2d 549 (2000). Likewise, they do not apply to works of art. *Hoepker v. Kruger,* 200 F.Supp.2d 340, 349 (S.D.N.Y.2002). For example, the use of a town justice's picture without his permission was held not to violate section 50 where it was used as part of a painting that was a caricature and parody. *Altbach v. Kulon,* 302 A.D.2d 655, 657, 754 N.Y.S.2d 709 (3d Dep't 2003). Similarly, "entertainment broadcasts" that involve, for example, humor and comedy are forms of expression that may also be protected by the First Amendment, although not categorically. *See Geary v. Goldstein,* 831 F.Supp. 269, 273 (S.D.N.Y.1993) (quoting *Frank v. Nat'l Broad. Co.,* 119 A.D.2d 252, 257, 506 N.Y.S.2d 869 (2d Dep't 1986)).

Over the years there has been much litigation over what constitutes a person's "portrait" or "picture" for purposes of sections 50 and 51. It is settled that "any recognizable likeness, not just an actual photograph, may qualify as a 'portrait or picture.' "*Allen,* 610 F.Supp. at 622 (citing *Ali v. Playgirl, Inc.,* 447 F.Supp. 723, 726 (S.D.N.Y.1978)). *Ali* involved a composite photograph and drawing of a naked African–American man in a boxing ring, with facial features recognizable as those of Muhammad Ali. 447 F.Supp. at 726. The court held that this was a portrait or picture of the former world heavyweight boxing champion. *Id.* Similarly, in *Young v. Greneker Studios,* 175 Misc. 1027, 26 N.Y.S.2d 357 (N.Y.Sup.Ct.1941), the court held that a manikin that was modeled on the plaintiff was a portrait or picture of her. *Id.* at 1027–28, 26 N.Y.S.2d 357. The court explained that "[t]he words 'picture' and 'portrait' are broad enough to include any representation [of a living person], whether by photograph, painting or sculpture." *Id.* at 1028, 26 N.Y.S.2d 357.

The use in advertisements of "look-alikes"—models who look like celebrities-has generated lawsuits. The Supreme Court, New York County, held that the use in an advertisement of a model who looked like Jacqueline Kennedy Onassis violated sections 50 and 51. *452 *Onassis v. Christian Dior–New York, Inc.,* 122 Misc.2d 603, 472 N.Y.S.2d 254 (N.Y.Sup.Ct.1984). The court held that "a representation which conveys the essence and likeness of an individual, ... which was intended to be, and did, in fact, convey the idea that it was the plaintiff" was a picture or portrait for purposes of the Civil Rights Law. *Id.* at 611, 472 N.Y.S.2d 254.

In contrast, in *Allen v. National Video, Inc.,* a case involving the use in an advertisement of a Woody Allen look-alike, Judge Motley declined to apply section 51, concluding that she would have to reach a "somewhat strained construction" of the statute to hold that it governed. 610 F.Supp. at 624. The court framed the question as whether "the mixture of fantasy and reality [in the advertisement] suggested almost unavoidably the actual presence of the real-life celebrity," that is, whether "the photograph in question ... create [d], as a matter of law, the illusion of Woody Allen's actual presence in the advertisement." *Id.* at 623–24. The court concluded that the claim was more appropriately analyzed as a Lanham Act claim. *Id.* at 624.

Judge Motley recognized in *Allen* that "[t]he privacy law does not prohibit one from evoking certain aspects of another's personality." *Id.* at 623 (citing *Lombardo v. Doyle, Dane & Bernbach, Inc.,* 58 A.D.2d 620, 396 N.Y.S.2d 661 (2d Dep't 1977)). Indeed, she held that "[m]erely suggesting certain characteristics of the plaintiff, without literally using his or her name, portrait, or picture, is not actionable under the statute." 610 F.Supp. at 621.

In *Lombardo,* the court rejected a claim under section 51 by the conductor Guy Lombardo based on a commercial showing an actor conducting a band playing "Auld Lang Syne" at a New Year's Eve party much as Lombardo had done for decades. The court held that "it is clear that the Civil Rights Law is to be strictly construed and is not to be applied so as to prohibit the portrayal of an individual's personality or style of performance." 58 A.D.2d at 622, 396 N.Y.S.2d 661.

b. *Application*

There is no dispute as to the second and third elements of Burck's claim under section 51. Defendants concede that the video and mural were used, at least in part, for commercial purposes and that Burck did not give permission, written or otherwise, to defendants to use The Naked Cowboy likeness. (Tr. at 5–6). As to the first element, it is also undisputed that defendants did not invoke the name "Robert Burck" or the name of his character "The Naked Cowboy." Nor did they use Burck's voice. Rather, the sole issue is whether defendants used Burck's "portrait" or "picture."

I conclude that defendants did not.

First, defendants did not use an actual photograph or picture of Burck himself, nor did they use a recognizable likeness or representation of him. *See Allen,* 610 F.Supp. at 622. Obviously, no viewer would have thought that the M & M Cowboy characters were actually Burck or were intended to be him. *See Onassis,* 122 Misc.2d at 611, 472 N.Y.S.2d 254. The M & M Cowboy characters are not portraits or pictures of Burck, and thus defendants did not use a portrait or picture of Burck.

Second, defendants did evoke certain aspects of the character created by Burck, and they copied The Naked Cowboy's costume, but these actions were not prohibited by sections 50 and 51. Merely evoking certain aspects of another's character or role does not violate sections 50 and 51. *See Allen,* 610 F.Supp. at 623 ("The privacy law does not prohibit one from evoking certain aspects of another's personali*453ty...."); *Lombardo,* 58 A.D.2d at 622, 396 N.Y.S.2d 661.

The plain language of the Civil Rights Law makes it clear that the statutory right to privacy does not extend to fictitious characters adopted or created by celebrities. Section 51 protects "any person," and section 50 limits the statutory protection to "any living person." *See Messenger v. Gruner + Jahr Printing & Publ'g,* 208 F.3d 122, 125 (2d Cir.2000). The Naked Cowboy is not a living person, but a character Burck takes on when performing. The privacy statutes were not intended to protect a trademarked, costumed character publicly performed by a person.

The case law supports the conclusion that the M & M Cowboy characters depicted in the video and mural are merely personifications that do not fall within the literal meaning of "portrait" or "picture" of a person. In *White v. Samsung Elecs. Am., Inc.,* 971 F.2d 1395 (9th Cir.1992), Vanna White, the hostess of the popular game show "Wheel of Fortune," sued defendants for, among other things, violating her right to privacy under California's privacy statute, which is substantively similar to the New York privacy statute. FN2 (Omitted) Defendants had produced an advertisement using a robot dressed in a wig, gown, and jewelry that resembled White's hair and dress. The Ninth Circuit affirmed the lower court's dismissal of her right of privacy claim on the ground that "a robot with mechanical features [was] not, for example, a manikin molded to White's precise features." *Id.* at 1397. It thus concluded that the "caricature or impressionistic resemblance" was not a "likeness" FN3 (Omitted) within the meaning of the statute.[FN4] The M & M characters dressed to look like The Naked Cowboy here are comparable to the robot made to look like Vanna White.

FN4. The Ninth Circuit did allow White to proceed with her right to publicity claim under California common law, which the court concluded was "not so confined" as the statutory right of privacy. New York, however, does not recognize an analogous common law right to publicity. *See Allen,* 610 F.Supp. at 621.

Burck argues that his "persona" as The Naked Cowboy qualifies as a "portrait" or "picture" within the meaning of section 51. But the statutory right of privacy was not intended to protect the "property interest of the celebrity in his or her public identity." *Allen,* 610 F.Supp. at 621. Instead, sections 50 and 51 were "primarily designed to compensate for the hurt feelings of private people who find their identities usurped for another's commercial gain." *Id.* This statutory purpose is reflected in the title of Article 5 of the New York Civil Rights law, "Right of Privacy." Although public figures do not forfeit their right of privacy, *see Onassis,* 122 Misc.2d at 614, 472 N.Y.S.2d 254, aspects of their public personas not captured in their physical features or voice are not protected under the privacy statute, *see Allen,* 610 F.Supp. at 623 (under section 51, "the commercial use complained of [must] amount to a 'portrait or picture' of an individual, not merely the suggestion of some aspect of a person's public persona").

As discussed above, the "look-alike cases" are also instructive, for they emphasize*454 the point that although a representation of "any recognizable likeness, not just an actual photograph, may qualify as a 'portrait or picture,' " *id.* at 622, that likeness must be a "close and purposeful resemblance to reality" of the actual person, *Onassis,* 122 Misc.2d at 611–12, 472 N.Y.S.2d at 261. In *Onassis,* the court found that the advertisement created the overall impression that plaintiff herself was in the advertisement. The court in *Allen* distinguished *Onassis* and found that Allen's look-alike was not a portrait or picture as required by section 51. The court explained that the " 'illusion' created in *Onassis* was that plaintiff had actually appeared in the advertisement," and thus the advertisement was, "as a matter of law, a portrait of Jacqueline Onassis." *Allen,* 610 F.Supp. at 623. In contrast, there were "several physical differences" between the Allen look-alike and Allen himself, such as defendant's larger eyebrows, wider face, and more uneven complexion, and thus the court concluded that the advertisement did not use Allen's portrait or picture. *Id.* at 624. Here, of course, there was no "illusion" that Burck was actually in defendants' advertisements.

Citing *Loftus v. Greenwich Lithographing Co.,* 192 A.D. 251, 182 N.Y.S. 428 (1st Dep't 1920), Burck contends that section 51 prohibits images even where the only recognizable likeness to the plaintiff is his or her signature costume. In *Loftus,* the plaintiff was an actress who was photographed in a "red costume representing a rose." *Id.* at 252, 182 N.Y.S. 428. This costume was never worn by any person other than the plaintiff, and she was "readily recognized from the photograph, and particularly from the costume." *Id.* To promote a film, the defendant produced a poster that featured a female figure with an identical costume. Although the main identifying feature in the infringing poster was the costume, the basis of the court's decision was that the female figure in the poster was such "an accurate likeness of the plaintiff" that it was "perfectly evident that [the infringer] had and used a copy of [plaintiff's] photograph, and that he copied the features of the plaintiff." *Id.* at 254, 256, 182 N.Y.S. 428. In other words, the poster in *Loftus* violated section 51 not because it depicted a unique costume, but because it attempted to create a "portrait or picture" of the actress herself.

Here, there was no attempt to create a portrait or picture of Burck himself. Rather, the purportedly infringing images were M & M characters wearing Burck's signature outfit. The images were not portraits or pictures of Burck as The Naked Cowboy, but of M & Ms dressed as The Naked Cowboy. Thus, they do not violate sections 50 and 51, and accordingly, Burck's right of privacy claim is dismissed.

* * *

*458 *CONCLUSION*

For the reasons set forth above, Burck's motion is denied and defendants' motions are denied in part and granted in part. Chute's motion to dismiss and Mars's motion for judgment on the pleading are granted with respect to the right to privacy claim ...

SO ORDERED.

WORKSHEET NO. 2: CASE SYNTHESIS

Synthesis is the binding together of several rules from a collection of cases into one legal principle. It provides a collective meaning that is not apparent from the individual cases themselves.

To synthesize, you need to step back and ask yourself what the cases have in common. Many law students and lawyers use charts to help them see what the cases have in common. A chart is provided for you to use for the exercise below.

Case File Assignment:

Read and brief the cases contained in Worksheet No. 1. After you have read and briefed these cases, fill in the attached synthesis chart. After you have completed the chart, review the information you included to help you see what the cases have in common. On a separate piece of paper, start to draft a synthesized legal principle. This does not need to be a well-crafted rule at this time, as you will work on drafting rules in Worksheet No. 3.

Case names			
Facts			
Holding			
Reasoning			
What is the rule or legal principle you can take away from the case?			

WORKSHEET NO. 3: RULES

Drafting rules is the process of taking the rule or policy from a single authority or from a collection of cases you have synthesized and putting it in written form. To help you write a complete statement of the rule or policy on a particular point of law, you must first ask yourself the following brainstorming questions:

1. What is the rule, policy, or synthesized rule?
2. What are the exceptions to the rule, policy, or synthesized rule, if any?
3. Is there anything else the court will consider in applying the rule, policy, or synthesized rule?

You should always be able to answer the first question unless courts in the jurisdiction have not yet ruled on the issue or the courts in the jurisdiction have ruled inconsistently such that you cannot reconcile the rules or results. You will not always be able to answer the second and third questions, but you should always ask them.

After answering these brainstorming questions, you can begin to write your rule by cutting and pasting your answers to these questions into one or more sentences.

Once you have drafted your rule, you then need to evaluate it for completeness. To evaluate the rule you have written, answer the following questions:

1. Is the rule too specific based on the legal authorities and your client facts?
2. Is the rule too broad based on the legal authorities and your client facts?
3. Does the rule include vague terms?
4. Is the rule circular?
5. If there is more than one rule, are the rules repetitive?

Case File Assignment:

Write a synthesized rule for the issue of misappropriation of likeness using all of the legal authorities provided in the Case File and the information from your completed synthesis chart (Worksheet No. 2). To help you write your synthesized rule, answer the following brainstorming questions:

1. What is the rule, policy, or synthesized rule?

2. Are there any exceptions to the rule, policy, or synthesized rule?

3. Is there anything else the court would consider in applying the rule, policy, or synthesized rule?

After answering these brainstorming questions, cut and paste your answers together into one or more sentences. This is the first draft of your complete rule. Evaluate your draft rule by evaluating the following questions:

1. Is the rule too specific based on the legal authorities and your client facts?
2. Is the rule too broad based on the legal authorities and your client facts?
3. Does the rule include vague terms?
4. Is the rule circular?
5. If there is more than one rule, are the rules repetitive?

Edit your draft synthesized rule based on your answers to these questions and provide your final synthesized rule below:

WORKSHEET NO. 4: CASE ILLUSTRATIONS

Case illustrations describe a precedent case to further define the rule (the R in the objective paradigm) or provide the reader with an example of how a rule has been applied in other cases. All case illustrations include six categories of information. While all six categories should be included in each case illustration, each category of information does not require its own separate sentence. Thus, you may have a complete case illustration that only is two sentences, but you may also have a complete case illustration that is two paragraphs. The length of your case illustration depends on the information your reader needs for a complete understanding of the specific legal principle you are explaining with the case illustration.

A case illustration is substantively complete if it includes:

1. A thesis sentence stating the specific legal principle you plan to explain with the case illustration;
2. The issue before the court in the precedent case on the specific legal principle you plan to explain with the case illustration;
3. The relevant facts of the precedent case on the specific legal principle you plan to explain with the case illustration;
4. The court's holding in the precedent case on the specific legal principle you plan to explain with the case illustration;
5. The court's reasoning in the precedent case on the specific legal principle you plan to explain with the case illustration; and
6. A conclusion sentence to give closure to the case illustration; this must relate back to the thesis sentence that began the case illustration.

The above order of the six categories of information is the most common organization and tends provide the most natural flow of information. It can be modified, where appropriate, but the thesis sentence must always come first.

The most difficult part of writing a case illustration is the first sentence—the thesis sentence. Typically, this is a detailed sentence providing further explanation of how the rule (the R in your objective paradigm) operates, how the rule has been defined, or how the rule has been applied by the court in another case. Occasionally, however, this simply is the rule (the R in your objective paradigm) without a separate thesis sentence.

Example 1 begins with the rule in bold (the R in the objective paradigm) followed by the thesis sentence for the case illustration (underlined) and the rest of the case illustration categories. Example 2 begins with the rule in bold and underlined (the R in the objective paradigm), which also is the thesis sentence for the case illustration, followed by the rest of the case illustration categories. There is not a separate thesis sentence for this case illustration because the applicable rule is sufficiently narrow to serve as both the rule and the thesis sentence.

EXAMPLE 1:

Consent to use a celebrity's photograph is unnecessary if the use of a photograph is directly related to matters in the public interest. For example, consent is unnecessary if the use of a photograph is directly related to commentary on events that impact society. In Dora v. Frontline Video, Inc., the court determined whether the use of the plaintiff's photograph in a surfing documentary was proper under the public interest exception. 15 Cal. App. 4th 536 (2nd Dist. 1993). A 1950s professional surfer brought a claim against the producers of a documentary video for using his photograph, voice, and video recordings without his consent. Id. at 541. The court held that the use of the surfer's photograph, voice, and video recordings in the surfing documentary did not require consent because they were used in a manner that was directly related to a matter in the public interest. Id. at 546. It reasoned that surfing is in the public interest because "surfing is more than passing interest to some," that "it has created a lifestyle that influences speech, behavior, dress, and entertainment, among other things," and has "had a significant influence on the popular culture." Id. Because the surfer's photograph, voice, and video recordings were used in the documentary on surfing, which directly related to a matter in the public interest, the use was proper under the public interest exception and consent was unnecessary. Id.

EXAMPLE 2:

Consent to use a celebritiy's photograph is required if the use of a photograph is for advertising purposes and is not directly related to a matter in the public interest. Downing v. Abercrombie & Fitch, 265 F.3d 994 (9th Cir. 2001). In Downing, the court determined whether the unauthorized use of a surfer's photograph in a surf-themed clothing catalogue was protected under the public interest exception. Id. at 999. The clothing catalog included a small number of editorials on surfing, but its primary purpose was to increase brand awareness and sell clothes. Id. at 1000. The photograph preceded two pages that advertised t-shirts designed to replicate those worn by the surfer in the photograph. The court held that the use of the surfer's photograph, although on a topic in the public interest, was not protected because the photograph was used as a "window dressing" to advance the surf-themed catalogue. Id. at 1002. It contrasted the use in the catalog from the use in the documentary in Dora, stating that although both cover the theme of surfing, the documentary's use "directly contributed to the story" while the catalog's use did not. Id. at 1003. Instead, the catalog's use was "much more commercial in nature." Therefore, the use of the surfer's photograph was not a proper use under the public interest exception and consent was required. Id.

Case File Assignment:

Write a case illustration for your client's case using the case(s) assigned to you by your professor. To help you write the case illustration, answer the following brainstorming questions. Please note, however, that before you can write a case illustration, you must know the rule or legal principle the case illustration is explaining.

For context, include the rule (the R in the objective paradigm) or legal principle you plan to explain with the case illustration here:

1. What is the specific legal principle you plan to explain with the case illustration? (NOTE: this is the thesis sentence for the case illustration that provides further explanation of how the rule (the R in your objective paradigm) operates, how the rule has been defined, or how the rule has been applied by the court in another case.)

2. What was the specific issue before the court in the precedent case as it relates to the specific legal principle you plan to explain with the case illustration? (NOTE: This must only be the issue specific to the legal principle you plan to explain with the case illustration, not all of the issues included in the precedent case.)

3. What are the specific facts in the precedent case as they relate to the specific legal principle you plan to explain with the case illustration? (NOTE: This must only be the facts specific to the legal principle you plan to explain with the case illustration, not all of the facts included in the precedent case.)

4. What is the holding in the precedent case as it relates to the specific legal principle you plan to explain with the case illustration? (NOTE: This must only be the holding specific to the legal principle you plan to explain with the case illustration, not all of the holdings included in the precedent case.)

5. What is the reasoning in the precedent case as it relates to the specific legal principle you plan to explain with the case illustration? (NOTE: This must only be the reasoning specific to the legal principle you plan to explain with the case illustration, not all of the reasoning included in the precedent case.)

6. What additional sentence(s) might you need to provide closure to this case illustration and to connect it back to the specific legal principle identified in response to Question 1 above?

Using the answers to these brainstorming questions as your guide, write the case illustration. Start by cutting and pasting your answers into paragraph form and then mold them into a readable paragraph. Each of the six categories of information must be included for a complete case illustration. This does not mean, however, that you need to have six sentences. A complete case illustration may be as little as two sentences or as much as two full paragraphs.

WORKSHEET NO. 5: POLICY–BASED REASONING

Policy-based reasoning is analysis that applies the purpose underlying a rule to your client's case. Policy-based reasoning is most often used to strengthen an argument that already is supported by legal authorities or other types of reasoning. For example, the result is not only X because of the case law, but the result also is X because that result satisfies the purpose underlying the applicable rule. Policy-based reasoning can also be used to make an argument where there are not any applicable legal authorities or the direct application of the law provides a result that is inconsistent with the purpose underlying the rule.

To apply policy-based reasoning to your client's case, you must first determine the purpose underlying the rule: what was the goal of the legislature or the court in creating the rule? This purpose might come from the purpose section of a statute, legislative history, the court's opinion, or published legal commentary on a rule of law. It should not, however, come from your own personal view of society or your personal opinion as to why the rule was created.

Once you have determined the purpose underlying the rule, you then need to evaluate whether that purpose applies to your client's case. To determine the purpose underlying the rule and to evaluate whether it applies to your client's case, consider:

1. The conclusion you will reach by applying the policy to your client's case. (NOTE: You may need to answer this question after you have completed your analysis of the policy.)

2. The rule you are applying to your client's case.

3. The purpose underlying the rule identified in response to Question 2 above. What greater societal purpose(s) was the court or legislature trying to protect in creating the rule? (NOTE: There may be more than one purpose. If there is more than one purpose, identify if the court seems to prefer one purpose over another.) Also, the purpose behind the rule must come from legal authority, such as legislative history, case authority, or well-established public opinion, not your personal opinion.

4. The potential outcomes for your client when applying the rule.

5. The potential outcomes for the other party when applying the rule.

6. How the outcomes identified in response to Questions 4 and 5 above are or are not served by the purpose(s) of the rule you identified in response to Question 3 above.

7. The outcome that best follows the purpose of the rule.

After considering these brainstorming questions, you should have a clear understanding of whether the possible outcomes for your client do or do not serve the underlying purpose(s) of the rule. The following formula will then help you write a policy-based reasoning analysis. Each of these components must be included for a complete policy-based reasoning analysis.

A policy-based reasoning analysis is substantively complete if it:

1. Begins the paragraph(s) by stating the conclusion you will reach by applying the purpose of the rule to your client's case. (NOTE: This is the thesis sentence for this paragraph.)

2. States the rule that is the basis of the policy-based reasoning analysis.

3. Identifies and describes the purpose underlying the rule and the origin of that purpose. Remember, the purpose behind the rule must come from legal authority, such as legislative history, case authority, or well-established public opinion, not your personal opinion. Also, if there is more than one purpose, explain which purpose the courts tend to use more.

4. States whether the underlying purpose does or does not apply to the possible outcome(s) in your client's case.

5. Explains with specific detail why the possible outcome(s) in your client's case will or will not further the purpose underlying the rule.

6. Concludes with a sentence that provides closure to the policy-based reasoning analysis. This sentence must connect to the thesis sentence that began the policy-based reasoning analysis.

EXAMPLE POLICY–BASED REASONING:

The defendant's Civil Code § 3344(a) violation likely is not actionable because the defendant's use of Ms. Anchor's photograph on its t-shirt provided commentary on a matter in the public interest and, therefore, consent was unnecessary. California Civil Code § 3344(d) provides an exception to the consent requirement contained in § 3344(a). It states that the use of a photograph in connection with "any news, public affairs, or sports broadcast or account, or any political campaign" does not require consent. § 3344(d). The courts have explained that the purpose of this exception is to protect the public's right to know about things, events, and people, such as news, celebrity activities, and sports. Eastwood, 149 Cal. App. 3d at 421; Gionfriddo v. Major League Baseball, 94 Cal. App. 4th 400 (1st Dist. 2001); Montana v. San Jose Mercury News, Inc., 34 Cal. App. 4th 790 (6th Dist. 1995). Thus, the right of a celebrity in her image is not absolute, but must be balanced against the public interest in the dissemination of news and information. Id. It is for this reason that the use of a celebrity's photograph on a matter in the public interest is exempt from the consent requirement of § 3344(a).

Ms. Anchor's claim is not furthered by the statutory purpose of protecting matters in the public interest. Rather, the defendant's use of Ms. Anchor's photograph with the Mayor's photograph as a miniature devil on her shoulder furthers the purpose because the t-shirt is part of an expressive comment on the unethical reporting on politics in Los Angeles. This is type of information the public interest exception was designed to protect. Thus, it is likely the use of Ms. Anchor's photograph on the t-shirt as a political and social commentary is not actionable due to the nature of the policy protecting the dissemination of information in the public interest.

Case File Assignment:

Write an analysis for your client's case using policy-based reasoning based on the legal authority contained in the Case File and/or the legal authority assigned by your professor. To help you write a policy-based reasoning analysis, answer the following brainstorming questions:

1. What is the conclusion you will reach by applying the policy to your client's case? (NOTE: You may need to answer this question after you have completed your analysis of the policy.)

2. What is the rule you are applying to your client's case?

3. What is the purpose underlying the rule identified in response to Question 2 above? What greater societal purpose(s) was the court or legislature trying to protect in creating the rule? (NOTE: There may be more than one purpose. If there is more than one purpose, identify if the court seems to prefer one purpose over another.) Also, the purpose behind the rule should come from legal authority, such as legislative history, case authority, or well-established public opinion, not your personal opinion.

4. What are the potential outcomes for your client when applying the rule?

5. What are the potential outcomes for the other party when applying the rule?

6. How are the outcomes identified in response to Questions 4 and 5 above served or not served by the purpose(s) of the rule you identified in response to Question 3 above?

7. Which outcome best follows the purpose(s) of the rule? Explain why.

After answering these brainstorming questions, you should have a clear understanding of whether the possible outcomes for your client do or do not serve the underlying purpose(s) of the rule. Use the following formula to write a policy-based reasoning analysis. Each of these components must be included for a complete policy-based reasoning analysis.

1. Begin the paragraph(s) by stating the conclusion you will reach by applying the purpose of the rule to your client's case. (NOTE: This is the thesis sentence for this paragraph.)
2. State the rule that is the basis of the policy-based reasoning analysis.
3. Identify and describe the purpose underlying the rule and the origin of that purpose. If there is more than one purpose, explain which one the courts tend to use more. Remember, the purpose behind the rule must come from legal authority, such as legislative history, case authority, or well-established public opinion, not your personal opinion on the purpose of the rule.
4. State whether the underlying purpose does or does not apply to the possible outcome(s) in your client's case.
5. Explain with specific detail why the possible outcome(s) in your client's case does or does not further the purpose underlying the rule.
6. Conclude with a sentence that provides closure to the policy-based reasoning analysis. This sentence must connect to the thesis sentence that began the policy-based reasoning analysis.

WORKSHEET NO. 6: ANALOGICAL REASONING

This worksheet is designed to give you a structured brainstorming process to evaluate whether analogical reasoning should be used in the analysis of your client's case. Clarity of writing comes from clarity of understanding. If you do not completely understand the structure or substance of the analogical reasoning to be included in your analysis, neither will the reader.

For an analogical reasoning analysis to be thoroughly evaluated, you must go through the following brainstorming process with as much detail as possible. This evaluation should be done for each issue and for each precedent case you plan to address with analogical reasoning.

1. Identify one issue you plan to address with analogical reasoning.
2. Identify the name of one precedent case you plan to use for the issue you selected above.
3. Identify the specific holding of the precedent case on the legal issue you plan to analyze with this analogical reasoning (NOTE: This must only be the holding specific to the legal issue you are addressing, not the overall holding of the precedent case.)
4. Describe the reasoning of the precedent case on the legal issue you plan to analyze with this analogical reasoning (NOTE: This must only be the reasoning specific to the legal issue you are addressing, not the overall reasoning of the precedent case.)
5. Make a list of the relevant facts from the precedent case on the legal issue you plan to analyze with this analogical reasoning (NOTE: This must only be the facts specific to the legal issue you are addressing, not all of the facts from the precedent case.)
6. Make a list of the relevant facts from your client's case on the legal issue you plan to analyze with this analogical reasoning (NOTE: This must only be the facts specific to the legal issue you are addressing, not all of the facts from your client's case.)
7. Group the facts of the precedent case and your client's case into facts that are similar and facts that are distinguishable.

Depending on whether the facts are similar or distinguishable or both, you may only need to consider some of the questions below. If the facts are similar, answer Questions 8–10. If the facts are distinguishable, answer Questions 11–13. If the facts are both similar and distinguishable, answer Questions 8–13.

8. Identify the fact(s) to be compared in your analysis as similar. (NOTE: this must only be the facts specific to the legal issue you are addressing, not all of the facts from the precedent case or your client's case.)

9. Explain why these facts are similar—use specific factual examples to demonstrate the similarities.

10. Explain *why* these factual similarities support your legal analysis on the issue you are addressing. This is where you must directly apply the reasoning of the precedent case to the facts of your client's case. Specifically look at why and how the precedent case ruled as it did and why that same reasoning applies to your client's case.

11. Identify the fact(s) to be compared in your analysis as distinguishable. (NOTE: This must only be the facts specific to the legal issue you are addressing, not all of the facts from the precedent case or your client's case.)

12. Explain why these facts are distinguishable—use specific factual examples to demonstrate the differences.

13. Explain *why* these factual differences support your legal analysis on the issue you are addressing. This is where you must directly apply the reasoning of the precedent case to the facts of your client's case. Specifically look at why and how the precedent case ruled as it did and why that same reasoning does not apply to your client's case.

After evaluating these brainstorming questions, you should have a clear understanding of whether this analogical reasoning should be included in the analysis of your client's case. You then must decide if the analogical reasoning will be based on a single case or multiple cases. If multiple cases are used to analyze the same legal issue, then you must provide this analysis at the same time, rather than as a separate analogical reasoning for each precedent case. Once you have decided if the analogical reasoning will be based on a single case or multiple cases, use one of the following formulas to write your analogical reasoning analysis:

Analogical Reasoning Formula Using a Single Case:

Component 1: The legal conclusion you want the reader to reach based on your analogical reasoning (this is the overall thesis sentence for the analogical reasoning paragraph or paragraphs—case names should not be included in this sentence).

Component 2: Sentence stating, "In client's case (use client's name) is similar to/distinguishable from ______ (insert precedent case name) based on ______ (identify the specific issue this analogical reasoning is addressing)."

Component 3: Sentence stating, "In client's case (use client's name), (insert detailed facts about your client's case that will be compared; this must only be the specific facts to be compared, not all of the facts of the case)."

Component 4: Sentence stating, "This case is similar to/distinguishable from _______ (insert precedent case name) where (insert detailed facts about the precedent case that will be compared—this must only be the specific facts to be compared, not all of the facts from the precedent case.)"

Component 5: Explain, using *specific factual detail*, why the facts you are comparing are similar or distinguishable. This is where you need to provide specific fact-to-fact comparisons, using actual facts from your client's case and the precedent case. (i.e.—"Fact X in client's case is similar to/distinguishable from Fact Y in precedent case because _______ ").

Component 6: Identify the likely outcome of your client's case based on the similarities or differences you discussed in Component 5. This is a re-statement of the conclusion (Component 1) but with more detail and this likely is the beginning of a new paragraph.

Component 7: Explain *why* this is the likely outcome. This is where you must directly apply the reasoning from the precedent case to your client's case.

Possible phrasing:

The court in _______ (insert precedent case name) reasoned _______ (insert the fact specific reasoning of the precedent case on the specific legal issue the analogical reasoning is addressing). This reasoning applies to your client's case (use client's name) because _______ (explain why it applies). Therefore, because the reasoning from (insert precedent case name) applies to your client's case (use client's name), the outcome in your client's case (use client's name) will likely be _______ (insert the outcome you are trying to prove with the analogical reasoning.)

Component 8: Re-state the conclusion you want the reader to reach based on your analogical reasoning. This must connect to the analysis provided by the analogical reasoning and to the conclusion stated in Component 1.

EXAMPLE SINGLE CASE ANALOGICAL REASONING:

TFF is not entitled to the public interest exception because the implication of unethical reporting created by the photographs on the t-shirt is false. Ms. Anchor's case is similar to Eastwood because both involved the dissemination of false information. 149 Cal. App. 3d 409. In Ms. Anchor's case, the t-shirt had a photograph of Ms. Anchor combined with a photograph of the Mayor as a miniature devil sitting on her shoulder. The inclusion of the Mayor on her shoulder with devil horns implied that he was influencing or controlling her reporting on his campaign, which Ms. Anchor denies. This is similar to Eastwood where the article stated that Mr. Eastwood was in a love triangle with two other celebrities, which Mr. Eastwood denied. Id. at 414. Just as Mr. Eastwood denied that he was involved in a love triangle, Ms. Anchor denies that she ever reported on the Mayor's re-election campaign and the general manager of KTV–LA stated that "there are no concerns about Ms. Anchor's ethics whatsoever." As reasoned in Eastwood, it is this type of dissemination of false information that legislature did not intend the public interest exception to protect. Id. at 425. Because the court in Eastwood reasoned that the Enquirer was not entitled to the public interest exception for its false article and TFF created a false implication by its use of Ms. Anchor's photograph on its t-shirt, TFF is not entitled to the public interest exception.

Analogical Reasoning Formula Using Multiple Cases:

Component 1: The legal conclusion you want the reader to reach based on your analogical reasoning (this is the overall thesis sentence for the analogical reasoning paragraph or paragraphs—case names should not be included in this sentence).

Component 2: Sentence stating, "Client's case (insert client's name) is similar to/distinguishable from ______ (insert first precedent case name) and/but similar to/distinguishable from ______ (insert second precedent case name) based on ______ (identify the specific issue this analogical reasoning is addressing)."

Component 3: Sentence stating, "In client's case (use client's name), (insert detailed facts about your client's case that will be compared; this must only be the specific facts to be compared, not all of the facts of the case.)"

Component 4(a): Sentence stating, "This case is similar to/distinguishable from ______ (insert first precedent case name) where (insert detailed facts about the precedent case you are relying upon—this must only be the specific facts to be compared, not all of the facts from the precedent case.)"

Component 4(b): Explain, using *specific factual detail*, why the facts you are comparing are similar/distinguishable. This is where you need to provide specific fact-to-fact comparisons, using actual facts from your client's case and the precedent case (i.e.—"Fact X in client's case is similar to/distinguishable from Fact Y in precedent case because ______ ").

Component 5(a): Sentence stating, "This case is similar to/distinguishable from ______ (insert second precedent case name) where (insert detailed facts about the precedent case you are relying upon—this also must only be the specific facts to be compared, not all of the facts from the precedent case)." [NOTE: you many need to use a transition to begin this sentence, such as "In addition," "Also," "However," or "On the other hand"]

Component 5(b): Explain, using *specific factual detail*, why the facts you are comparing are similar/distinguishable. This is where you need to provide specific fact-to-fact comparisons, using actual facts from your client's case and the precedent case (i.e.—"Fact X in client's case is similar to/distinguishable from Fact Y in precedent case because ______ ").

Component 6: Identify the likely outcome of your client's case based on the similarities/differences you discussed previously (see Components 4(b) and 5(b)). This is a re-statement of the conclusion (Component 1) but with more detail and this likely is the beginning of a new paragraph.

Component 7: Explain *why* this is the likely outcome. This is where you must directly apply the reasoning from the precedent case to your client's case.

Possible phrasing if the reasoning of the precedent cases is the same:

The court in ______ (insert first and second precedent case names) reasoned ______ (insert the fact specific reasoning of the precedent cases on the specific legal issue the analogical reasoning is addressing). This reasoning applies to your client's case (use client's name) because ______ (explain why it applies). Therefore, because the reasoning from (insert precedent case names) applies to your client's case (use client's name), the outcome in your client's case (use client's name) will likely be ______ (insert the outcome you are trying to prove with the analogical reasoning.)

Possible phrasing if the reasoning of the precedent cases is different:

The court in _______ (insert first precedent case name) reasoned _______ (insert the fact specific reasoning of the first precedent case on the specific legal issue the analogical reasoning is addressing). This reasoning applies to your client's case (use client's name) because _______ (explain why it applies). However, the court in _______ (insert second precedent case name) reasoned _______ (insert the fact specific reasoning of the second precedent case on the specific legal issue the analogical reasoning is addressing). This reasoning does not apply to your client's case (use client's name) because _______ (explain why it does not apply). Therefore, because the reasoning from (insert first precedent case name) applies to your client's case (use client's name) and the reasoning from (insert second precedent case name) does not apply to your client's case (use client's name), the outcome in your client's case (use client's name) will likely be _______ (insert the outcome you are trying to prove with the analogical reasoning.)

Component 8: Re-state the conclusion you want the reader to reach based on your analogical reasoning. This must connect to the analysis provided by the analogical reasoning and to the conclusion stated in Component 1.

EXAMPLE MULTIPLE CASE ANALOGICAL REASONING:

The use of Ms. Anchor's photograph by TFF likely did not require consent because the use directly related to a matter in the public interest and was not commercial in nature. Ms. Anchor's case is similar to Dora but distinguishable from Downing because of the direct connection between the use of her photograph and the public interest. Ms. Anchor, a reporter for a local news station, was involved in a highly publicized relationship with the Mayor and there was a significant amount media attention alleging that she unethically reported on the Mayor's re-election campaign. TFF claims it created and sold a t-shirt with a photograph of Ms. Anchor, with a superimposed picture on her shoulder of the Mayor wearing miniature devil-horns, to provide commentary on Ms. Anchor's unethical reporting on local politics. This is similar to Dora, where Frontline Video used the image, video, and voice recordings of a well-known professional surfer in its surfing documentary to provide commentary on the early years of surfing and the cultural impact of surfing. Dora, 15 Cal. App. 4th at 541. The court in Dora reasoned that the use of the surfer's photograph in the documentary directly contributed to the story on surfing and the surfer had a significant influence on popular culture. Id. at 546. This reasoning applies here because the use of Ms. Anchor's photograph on TFF's t-shirt "directly contributed to the story" on her alleged unethical reporting on the Mayor's re-election campaign and its "significant influence" on local politics.

Furthermore, Ms. Anchor's case is distinguishable from Downing, where a well-known surfer's photograph, taken during a surfing championship, was used in a surf-themed clothing catalog. 265 F.3d 994. The surfer's photograph followed two articles that discussed the history of surfing; however, no connection was made between the articles and the surfer, and the surfer was not identified as a legend of the sport. Id. at 1002. Instead, the two pages following the surfer's photograph advertised t-shirts replicating those worn by the surfer in his photograph. Id. The court reasoned that this use was merely "window dressing to advance the [catalog's] surf theme" and promote sales based on the implied endorsement by the well-known surfer. Id. The use of the photograph was not to provide commentary on surfing like in Dora where the "point of the program" was to provide commentary on surfing. Id. at 1001. Ms. Anchor's is distinguishable from Downing in how her photograph was used because her photograph was used on a t-shirt primarily to provide commentary on her relationship with the Mayor and the alleged influence he may have had on Ms. Anchor's reporting on his re-election campaign. TFF stated that "the point of the t-shirt" was to provide commentary on Ms. Anchor's conflict of interest in reporting on the Mayor's re-election campaign; it was not a mere "window dressing" to sell the t-shirt. Consumers likely would

purchase the t-shirt because of the commentary, not because of her implied endorsement.

While the court in Dora reasoned that the use of the photograph in a surfing documentary did not require consent due to its direct contribution to public's interest in the significant influence of surfing and its cultural impact, the court in Downing reasoned that consent was required because the use of the photograph was commercial in nature, having only a tenuous relationship as a "window-dressing" with the surfing theme of the clothing catalog. Id. at 1002. Ms. Anchor's case is more analogous to Dora than Downing because of the strong connection between the use of her photograph and the public's interest in her relationship with the Mayor and possible unethical reporting on his re-election campaign. Therefore, because the reasoning from Dora more closely relates to Ms. Anchor's case than the reasoning from Downing, the use of the photograph in Ms. Anchor's case likely was directly connected to the public interest and consent was unnecessary.

Case File Assignment:

Write an analysis for your client's case using analogical reasoning based on the legal authority in the Case File and/or the legal authority assigned by your professor. To help you write your analogical reasoning, answer the following brainstorming questions:

1. Identify one specific legal issue you plan to address with analogical reasoning (or the specific issue assigned by your professor):

2. Identify the name of one precedent case you plan to use for the issue you selected above (or the case assigned by your professor).

3. Identify the specific holding of the precedent case on the legal issue you plan to analyze with this analogical reasoning. (NOTE: This must only be the holding on the specific legal issue you are addressing with this analogical reasoning, not the overall holding of the precedent case.)

4. Describe the reasoning of the precedent case you plan to analyze with this analogical reasoning. (NOTE: This must only be the reasoning on the specific legal issue you are addressing with this analogical reasoning, not the overall reasoning of the precedent case.)

5. Make a list of the relevant facts from the precedent case on the legal issue you plan to analyze with this analogical reasoning. (NOTE: This must only be the facts on the specific legal issue you are addressing with this analogical reasoning, not all of the facts from the precedent case.)

6. Make a list of the relevant facts from your client's case on the legal issue you plan to analyze with this analogical reasoning. (NOTE: This must only be the facts specific to the legal issue you are addressing with this analogical reasoning, not all of the facts from your client's case.)

7. Organize the facts of the precedent case and your client's case into the charts below:

Facts that are similar:

Your Client's Case	Precedent Case

Facts that are distinguishable:

Your Client's Case	Precedent Case

Using the information you filled into the charts above, decide whether you think your client's case and the precedent case are similar, distinguishable, or both. If they are similar, answer Questions 8–10 below. If they are distinguishable, answer Questions 11–13 below. If they are both similar and distinguishable, answer Questions 8–13 below.

8. Identify the fact(s) from your client's case and the precedent case to be compared as similar. (NOTE: This must only be facts specific to the legal issue you are addressing, not all of the facts from the precedent case or your client's case.)

9. Explain why these facts are similar—use specific factual examples to demonstrate the similarities.

10. Explain *why* these factual similarities support your legal analysis on the issue you are addressing. This is where you must directly apply the reasoning of the precedent case to the facts of your client's case. Specifically look at why and how the precedent case ruled as it did and why that same reasoning applies to your client's case.

11. Identify the fact(s) to be compared in your analysis as distinguishable. (NOTE: This must only be the facts specific to the legal issue you are addressing, not all of the facts from the precedent case or your client's case.)

12. Explain why these facts are distinguishable—use specific factual examples to demonstrate the differences.

13. Explain *why* these factual differences support your legal analysis on the issue you are addressing. This is where you must directly apply the reasoning of the precedent case to the facts of your client's case. Specifically look at why and how the precedent case ruled as it did and why that same reasoning does not apply to your client's case.

After answering these brainstorming questions, you should have a clear understanding of whether analogical reasoning should be included the analysis of your client's case. You then must decide if the analogical reasoning will be based on a single case or multiple cases. If multiple cases are used to analyze the same legal issue, then you must provide this analysis at the same time, rather than as a separate analogical reasoning for each precedent case. Once you have decided if the analogical reasoning will be based on a single case or multiple cases, use one of the following formulas to write your analogical reasoning analysis:

<u>Analogical Reasoning Formula Using a Single Case:</u>

Component 1: The legal conclusion you want the reader to reach based on your analogical reasoning (this is the overall thesis sentence for the analogical reasoning paragraph or paragraphs—case names should not be included in this sentence).

Component 2: Sentence stating, "In client's case (use client's name) is similar to/distinguishable from _______ (insert precedent case name) based on _______ (identify the specific issue this analogical reasoning is addressing)."

Component 3: Sentence stating, "In client's case (use client's name), (insert detailed facts about your client's case that will be compared; this must only be the specific facts to be compared, not all of the facts of the case.)"

Component 4: Sentence stating, "This case is similar to/distinguishable from _______ (insert precedent case name) where (insert detailed facts about the precedent case that will be compared—this must only be the specific facts to be compared, not all of the facts from the precedent case.)"

Component 5: Explain, using *specific factual detail*, why the facts you are comparing are similar or distinguishable. This is where you need to provide specific fact-to-fact comparisons, using actual facts from your client's case and the precedent case. (i.e.—"Fact X in client's case is similar to/distinguishable from Fact Y in precedent case because _______ ").

Component 6: Identify the likely outcome of your client's case based on the similarities or differences you discussed in Component 5. This is a re-statement of the conclusion (Component 1) but with more detail and this likely is the beginning of a new paragraph.

Component 7: Explain *why* this is the likely outcome. This is where you must directly apply the reasoning from the precedent case to your client's case.

Possible phrasing:

The court in _______ (insert precedent case name) reasoned _______ (insert the fact specific reasoning of the precedent case on the specific legal issue the analogical reasoning is addressing). This reasoning applies to your client's case (use client's name) because _______ (explain why it applies). Therefore, because the reasoning from (insert precedent case name) applies to your client's case (use client's name), the outcome in your client's case (use client's name) will likely be _______ (insert the outcome you are trying to prove with the analogical reasoning.)

Component 8: Re-state the conclusion you want the reader to reach based on your analogical reasoning. This must connect to the analysis provided by the analogical reasoning and to the conclusion stated in Component 1.

Analogical Reasoning Formula Using Multiple Cases:

Component 1: The legal conclusion you want the reader to reach based on your analogical reasoning (this is the overall thesis sentence for the analogical reasoning paragraph or paragraphs—case names should not be included in this sentence).

Component 2: Sentence stating, "Client's case (insert client's name) is similar to/distinguishable from _______ (insert first precedent case name) and/but similar to/distinguishable from _______ (insert second precedent case name) based on _______ (identify the specific issue this analogical reasoning is addressing)."

Component 3: Sentence stating, "In client's case (use client's name), (insert detailed facts about your client's case that will be compared; this must only be the specific facts that will be compared, not all of the facts of the case.)"

Component 4(a): Sentence stating, "This case is similar to/distinguishable from _______ (insert first precedent case name) where (insert detailed facts about the precedent case you are relying upon—this must only be specific facts to be compared, not all of the facts from the precedent case.)"

Component 4(b): Explain, using *specific factual detail*, why the facts you are comparing are similar/distinguishable. This is where you need to provide specific fact-to-fact comparisons, using actual facts from your client's case and the precedent case (i.e.—"Fact X in client's case is similar to/distinguishable from Fact Y in precedent case because _______ ").

Component 5(a): Sentence stating, "This case is similar to/distinguishable from _______ (insert second precedent case name) where (insert detailed facts about the precedent case you are relying upon—this also must only be the specific facts to be compared, not all of the facts from the precedent case)." [NOTE: you many need to use a transition to begin this sentence, such as "In addition," "Also," "However," or "On the other hand"]

Component 5(b): Explain, using *specific factual detail*, why the facts you are comparing are similar/distinguishable. This is where you need to provide specific fact-to-fact comparisons, using actual facts from your client's case and the precedent case (i.e.—"Fact X in client's case is similar to/distinguishable from Fact Y in precedent case because _______ ").

Component 6: Identify the likely outcome of your client's case based on the similarities/differences you discussed previously (see Components 4(b) and 5(b)). This is a re-statement of the conclusion (Component 1) but with more detail and this likely is the beginning of a new paragraph.

Component 7: Explain *why* this is the likely outcome. This is where you must directly apply the reasoning from the precedent case to your client's case.

Possible phrasing if the reasoning of the precedent cases is the same:

The court in _______ (insert first and second precedent case names) reasoned _______ (insert the fact specific reasoning of the precedent cases on the specific legal issue the analogical reasoning is addressing). This reasoning applies to your client's case (use client's name) because _______ (explain why it applies). Therefore, because the reasoning from (insert precedent case names) applies to your client's case (use client's name), the outcome in your client's case (use client's name) will likely be _______ (insert the outcome you are trying to prove with the analogical reasoning.)

Possible phrasing if the reasoning of the precedent cases is different:

The court in _______ (insert first precedent case name) reasoned _______ (insert the fact specific reasoning of the first precedent case on the specific legal issue the analogical reasoning is addressing). This reasoning applies to your client's case (use client's name) because _______ (explain why it applies). However, the court in _______ (insert second precedent case name) reasoned _______ (insert the fact specific reasoning of the second precedent case on the specific legal issue the analogical reasoning is addressing). This reasoning does not apply to your client's case (use client's name) because _______ (explain why it does not apply). Therefore, because the reasoning from (insert first precedent case name) applies to your client's case (use client's name) and the reasoning from (insert second precedent case name) does not apply to your client's case (use client's name), the outcome in your client's case (use client's name) will likely be _______ (insert the outcome you are trying to prove with the analogical reasoning.)

Component 8: Re-state the conclusion you want the reader to reach based on your analogical reasoning. This must connect to the analysis provided by the analogical reasoning and to the conclusion in Component 1.

WORKSHEET NO. 7: QUESTION PRESENTED

The Question Presented establishes the focus of the memorandum for the reader. It identifies the applicable statute or common law rule, it sets out the legal question(s) to be addressed in your memorandum, and it summarizes the facts that will be significant in addressing the legal question(s).

The most common Question Presented formula is known as the under-does-when formula:

> Under [Insert reference to applicable law],
>
> Does/did/is/was/can/may [Insert the legal question]
>
> When/for/if [Insert the legally significant facts]?

An "under-does-when" Question Presented is substantively correct if it:

1. Includes the applicable law. This will be the popular name of a statute (not the citation) or a general legal principle based in common law (without case names or citations);
2. Identifies the specific legal question(s) your memorandum is addressing. The legal questions(s) must not be too narrow or too broad. If it is too narrow, the question will not cover all of the issues and sub-issues the memorandum is addressing. If it is too broad, the question will not serve the function of focusing the reader's attention on the specific issue(s) the memorandum is addressing; and
3. Provides the legally significant facts. The legally significant facts are the facts used in the analysis of your memorandum.

An "under-does-when" Question Presented is technically correct if it:

1. Is only one sentence; and
2. Ends with a question mark.

> EXAMPLE QUESTION PRESENTED:
>
> <u>Under</u> the California statutory right of publicity, <u>does</u> Tasha V. Anchor, a well-known television reporter, have a right of publicity claim against T–Shirts For Fun <u>for</u> its use of Ms. Anchor's photograph on a t-shirt combined with a photograph of the Los Angeles Mayor in a manner that falsely implies he unethically influenced Ms. Anchor's reporting on his re-election campaign?

Case File Assignment:

Write the Question Presented for your client's case. To help you write the Question Presented for your client's case, answer the following brainstorming questions:

1. What is the applicable law? This will be the popular name of a statute (not the citation) or a general legal principle based in common law (without case names or citations).

2. What is the specific legal question(s) your memorandum is addressing? The legal question(s) must not be too narrow or too broad. If it is too narrow, the question will not cover all of the issues and sub-issues the memorandum is addressing. If it is too broad, the question will not serve the function of focusing the reader's attention on the specific issue(s) the memorandum is addressing.

3. What are the legally significant facts? The legally significant facts are the facts used in the analysis in your memorandum. If there are numerous facts, summarize them or include only the most important facts.

Using the answers to these brainstorming questions as your guide, write the Question Presented for your client's case. Start by cutting and pasting your answers into paragraph form and then mold them into a readable sentence using the following formula as your guide. Also, remember that a technically correct "under-does-when" Question Presented must only be one sentence and end with a question mark.

Under [Insert reference to applicable law], does/did/is/was/can/may [Insert the legal question] when/for/if [Insert the legally significant facts]?

WORKSHEET NO. 8: BRIEF ANSWER

The Brief Answer responds to the question posed by the Question Presented. When read together, the Question Presented and Brief Answer are the "Introduction" to an objective memorandum. After reading the Question Presented and Brief Answer, the reader should have a solid understanding of the subject, the law, and the outcome predicted in the memorandum.

The Brief Answer typically begins with a one- or two-word answer, which is followed by a period; this is called the "short answer." The words that are typically used are "yes," "probably yes," "no," and "probably no/not." If you believe the answer could go either way, it is appropriate to indicate that the outcome is a close call by using the word "probably" in your short answer. However, you must still make a prediction; thus, avoid words such as "might," "possibly," or "could."

Next, you will explain to the reader the basis for the short answer. To do this, you will first provide a statement of the applicable rule(s) that apply to your client's case. Then, you will provide a summary of the reasoning that supports the short answer based on the legally significant facts and the application of the rule(s) to those facts. Finally, the organization of the Brief Answer should parallel the organization of the Discussion section and the tone must to remain objective—do not "argue" your answer.

A Brief Answer is substantively correct if it includes:

1. A short answer:

    a. Yes.

    b. Probably yes.

    c. No.

    d. Probably no/not.

2. A statement of the applicable rule(s). This should define the applicable law(s) identified in your Question Presented. To do this, consult the rules in your analysis (the Rs in each of your objective paradigms).

3. A summary of the reasoning that supports the short answer based on the legally significant facts and the application of the rule(s) to those facts. This should summarize each of the fact-specific conclusions you reached in your analysis. To help you do this, review the analysis in your memorandum (the As in each of your objective paradigms) and try to summarize it in three to four sentences.

EXAMPLE BRIEF ANSWER (the Question Presented is included for context):

QUESTION PRESENTED

Under the California statutory right of publicity, does Tasha V. Anchor, a well-known television reporter, have a right of publicity claim against T–Shirts For Fun for its use of Ms. Anchor's photograph on a t-shirt combined with a photograph of the Los Angeles Mayor in a manner that falsely implies he unethically influenced Ms. Anchor's reporting on his re-election campaign?

BRIEF ANSWER

Probably yes. The California statutory right of publicity is violated when a person's photograph is knowingly used on a product for profit without consent. This statutory right is not absolute as consent is unnecessary if the use of the photograph contributes to the public interest. However, if the photograph or its use contains false information, the public interest exception does not apply. Here, T–Shirts For Fun knowingly used Ms. Anchor's photograph on a t-shirt it created and sold for profit without her consent. The use of the photograph, however, was likely in the public interest because the t-shirt provided commentary on the highly publicized affair between Ms. Anchor and the Mayor and the potential influence the Mayor may have had on Ms. Anchor's reporting on his re-election campaign. Because such information is in the public interest, Ms. Anchor's consent to use her photograph was not required. This exception, however, will likely not apply because, although in the public interest, the commentary was based on false information. While it is true that Ms. Anchor had an affair with the Mayor, she and the television station she works for deny that she ever reported on the Mayor's re-election campaign, showing the commentary on the t-shirt was false. Thus, Ms. Anchor likely will have a right of publicity claim against T–Shirts For Fun.

Case File Assignment:

Write the Brief Answer for your client's case. To help you write the Brief Answer for your client's case, review your Question Presented to remind yourself of the question your Brief Answer is responding to. Next, answer the following brainstorming questions to help you develop the substance of your Brief Answer:

1. What is the short answer to the question posed in your Question Presented? Remember this can only be "yes," "probably yes," "no," or "probably no/not."

2. What are the applicable rule(s)? This should define the applicable law(s) identified in your Question Presented. To do this, consult the rules in your analysis (the Rs in each of your objective paradigms).

3. Summarize the reasoning that supports the short answer based on the legally significant facts and the application of the rule(s) to those facts. This should summarize each of the fact-specific conclusions you reached in your analysis. To help you do this, review the analysis (the As in each of your objective paradigms) in your memorandum and try to summarize it in three to four sentences.

Using the answers to these brainstorming questions as your guide, write the Brief Answer for your client's case. Start by cutting and pasting your answers into paragraph form and then mold them into a readable paragraph, using the following formula:

Short answer. Statement of the applicable rule(s). Summary of the reasoning that supports the short answer based on the legally significant facts and the application of the rule(s) to those facts.

WORKSHEET NO. 9: FACTS

The four most important things to remember when writing an objective Facts section are to: (1) include the legally significant facts; (2) organize the facts in an effective manner; (3) maintain a neutral tone; and (4) provide objectively accurate facts.

The Facts section is substantively correct if it:

1. Develops the foundation or context for the reader in the first paragraph (or first couple of sentences) by:

   a. Identifying your client, the opposing party, and their relationship;

   b. Stating your client's general problem or goal;

   c. Describing the setting (e.g. the time and location of the events); and

   d. Including the procedural history or the status of the case.

2. Includes the proper substance by:

   a. Including the legally significant facts. To determine the legally significant facts, review your analysis and highlight all of the facts from your client's case that you relied upon. These are the legally significant facts. If you have not yet written your analysis, determine the legally significant facts by asking yourself what are the facts a court would consider in ruling on your client's case?

   b. Including background facts that are needed for the legally significant facts to make sense. To determine the necessary background facts, ask yourself: what else does the reader need to know to understand the story of your client's case?

   c. Describing the facts accurately;

   d. Including both favorable and unfavorable facts;

   e. Omitting factual arguments, references to the law, legal conclusions, and factual conclusions; and

   f. Maintaining an objective and neutral tone.

3. Has a strategically selected organization to best tell the story: chronological, topical, or a combination of chronological and topical. The organization you select must be a strategic choice based on the best approach to tell the reader the story of your client's case.

4. Provides closure to the Facts section by not ending abruptly (consider re-stating what the client has asked you to do or stating the procedural history of the case).

EXAMPLE FACTS:

T–Shirts for Fun (TFF) recently created and sold a t-shirt featuring a photograph of Tasha V. Anchor, a local television reporter for KTV-LA. On the t-shirt, Ms. Anchor's photograph is combined with a photograph of a miniaturized image of the Los Angeles Mayor wearing a suit and devil horns, sitting on Ms. Anchor's left shoulder. TFF, a company that designs, produces, and distributes funny t-shirts for profit, claims it created the t-shirt to provide subtle commentary on the possibility that Ms. Anchor unethically reported on the Mayor's re-election campaign. Ms. Anchor, however, did not consent to the use of her photograph on the t-shirt and is offended by its use because she denies that she ever unethically reported on the Mayor's re-election campaign.

TFF created the t-shirt soon after an affair between Ms. Anchor and the Mayor was made public. The affair was highly publicized and the ethics of both Ms Anchor and the Mayor were questioned by the media. Ms. Anchor admits that she conducted a few of interviews of the Mayor last fall, but states they were on topics unrelated to his re-election campaign. Her employer, KTV-LA, has allowed Ms. Anchor to keep her position and the general manager for the station said "There is no concern as to the ethics of Ms. Anchor whatsoever."

Ms. Anchor would like to determine if she has a claim against TFF based on its unauthorized use of her photograph in a manner that falsely implies she unethically reported on the Mayor's re-election campaign.

Case File Assignment:

Write the Facts section for you client's case. To help you write the Facts section, answer the following brainstorming questions:

1. For the first paragraph (or first couple of sentences) of the Facts section, develop the foundation or context for the reader:

   a. Who is your client? Who is the opposing party? What is their relationship (i.e.—employer/employee; buyer/seller; landlord/tenant; accused/victim)?

   b. What is your client's general problem or goal?

c. What was the setting (e.g. the time and location of the events)?

d. What is the procedural history or the status of the case?

2. For the remaining paragraphs in your Facts section, answer the following brainstorming questions to help you identify the relevant facts:

    a. What are the legally significant facts? Review your analysis section and highlight all of the facts from your client's case that you used in your analysis. These are the legally significant facts and they must be included in your Facts section. If you have not yet written your analysis, then determine the legally significant facts by asking yourself: what are the facts a court would consider in ruling on your client's case?

    b. What background facts are necessary to provide context for the legally significant facts identified in response to Question 2(a) above?

    c. What are the unfavorable facts? What are the facts the opposing party likely will rely upon?

3. Looking at your answers to these brainstorming questions and using your understanding of your client's case, identify the organization you will use to structure your Facts section? Chronological? Topical? Combination of chronological and topical? The organization you select must be a strategic choice based on the best approach to tell the story of your client's case.

Using the answers to these brainstorming questions as your guide, write the Facts section for your client's case. Start by cutting and pasting your answers into paragraph form and then mold them into readable paragraphs.

When writing the Facts section, consider the following:

1. The first paragraph must:
   - Identify all of the parties and their relationship;
   - Briefly describe your client's problem or goal;
   - Provide the setting (time and location of events); and
   - Include the status or procedural history of the case.
2. The overall substance and tone must:
   - Have a strategically selected organization (avoid stream of consciousness writing);
   - Describe the facts accurately;
   - Include both favorable and unfavorable facts;
   - Omit factual arguments, references to the law, legal conclusions, and factual conclusions; and
   - Maintain an objective and neutral tone.
3. The last paragraph must:
   - Provide closure to the Facts section by not ending abruptly (consider re-stating what the client has asked you to do or stating the procedural history of the case).

WORKSHEET NO. 10: CONCLUSION

The Conclusion summarizes the individual conclusions reached in your analysis into one or two paragraphs and provides strategic recommendations based on your analysis in the memorandum. Although the Conclusion should be self-contained, that is, the reader should be able to understand it without having to read the entire memorandum, it should not include nearly as much detail as the Discussion section.

A Conclusion is substantively correct if it includes:

1. The ultimate conclusion of your memorandum;
2. Each rule applied to your client's case (the R in each objective paradigm included in your memorandum);
3. The conclusion for each rule applied in your client's case (the C in each objective paradigm included in your memorandum);
4. A summary of the reasoning that supports those conclusions (summarize the A sections in each objective paradigm included in your memorandum); and
5. Any strategic recommendations based on the analysis provided in the memorandum.

EXAMPLE CONCLUSION:

Ms. Anchor likely has a valid right of publicity claim against TFF. Under the California statutory right of publicity, a person has a claim if another knowingly uses the person's photograph without consent. Consent is unnecessary, however, if the photograph relates to a matter in the public interest and is connected to that public interest, unless the use provides false information. In this case, TFF's knowingly used Ms. Anchor's photograph without her consent in violation of § 3344(a). However, because it was used by TFF for the purpose of providing a commentary on the affair between Ms. Anchor and the Mayor and the possible unethical reporting on the Mayor's re-election campaign, the use of the photograph relates to a matter in the public interest. Thus, it is subject to the exemption in § 3344(d) and Ms. Anchor's consent was unnecessary. Despite this, Ms. Anchor likely will still prevail because the implication created by TFF's use of Ms. Anchor's photograph on the t-shirt is false and, therefore, not entitled to protection. For these reasons, Ms. Anchor likely has a successful claim against TFF and should pursue a legal remedy in this matter.

Case File Assignment:

Write the Conclusion for you client's case. To help you write the Conclusion section, answer the following brainstorming questions:

1. What is the ultimate conclusion of your memorandum? (NOTE: This must be consistent with the information provided in your Question Presented and your Brief Answer.)

2. Identify each rule applied to your client's case (the R in each objective paradigm included in your memorandum).

3. Identify the conclusion for each rule applied in your client's case (the C in each objective paradigm included in your memorandum)?

4. Summarize the analysis that supports the conclusion on each rule (summarize the A section in each objective paradigm included in your memorandum)?

5. Identify any strategic recommendations based on the analysis provided in your memorandum.

Using the answers to these brainstorming questions as your guide, write the Conclusion for your client's case. Start by cutting and pasting your answers into paragraph form and then mold them into a readable paragraph. When writing the Conclusion, maintain an objective and neutral tone, have the organization of the Conclusion parallel the organization of the Discussion section, and avoid simply repeating the Brief Answer.

SAMPLE OBJECTIVE MEMORANDUM

OFFICE MEMORANDUM

TO: Supervising Attorney

FROM: Legal Intern

DATE: August 1, YEAR

RE: Anchor v. T–Shirts for Fun; Right of Publicity

QUESTION PRESENTED

Under the California statutory right of publicity, does Tasha V. Anchor, a well-known television reporter, have a right of publicity claim against T–Shirts For Fun for its use of Ms. Anchor's photograph on a t-shirt combined with a photograph of the Los Angeles Mayor in a manner that falsely implies he unethically influenced Ms. Anchor's reporting on his re-election campaign?

BRIEF ANSWER

Probably yes. The California statutory right of publicity is violated when a person's photograph is knowingly used on a product for profit without consent. This statutory right is not absolute as consent is unnecessary if the use of the photograph contributes to the public interest. However, if the photograph or its use contains false information, the public interest exception does not apply. Here, T–Shirts For Fun knowingly used Ms. Anchor's photograph on a t-shirt it created and sold for profit without her consent. The use of the photograph, however, was likely in the public interest because the t-shirt provided commentary on the highly publicized affair between Ms. Anchor and the Mayor and the potential influence the Mayor may have had on Ms. Anchor's reporting on his re-election campaign. Because such information is in the public interest, Ms. Anchor's consent to use her photograph was not required. This exception, however, will likely not apply because, although in the public interest, the commentary was based on false information. While it is true that Ms. Anchor had an affair with the Mayor, she and the television station she works for deny that she ever reported on the Mayor's re-election campaign, showing the commentary on the t-shirt was false. Thus, Ms. Anchor likely will have a right of publicity claim against T–Shirts For Fun.

FACTS

T–Shirts for Fun (TFF) recently created and sold a t-shirt featuring a photograph of Tasha V. Anchor, a local television reporter for KTV-LA. On the t-shirt, Ms. Anchor's photograph is combined with a photograph of a miniaturized image of the Los Angeles Mayor wearing a suit and devil horns, sitting on Ms. Anchor's left shoulder. TFF, a company that designs, produces, and distributes funny t-shirts for profit, claims it created the t-shirt to provide subtle commentary on the possibility that Ms. Anchor unethically reported on the Mayor's re-election campaign. Ms. Anchor, however, did not consent to the use of her photograph on the t-shirt and is offended by its use because she denies that she ever unethically reported on the Mayor's re-election campaign.

TFF created the t-shirt soon after an affair between Ms. Anchor and the Mayor was made public. The affair was highly publicized and the ethics of both Ms Anchor and the Mayor were questioned by the media. Ms. Anchor admits that she conducted a few of interviews of the Mayor last fall, but states they were on topics unrelated to his re-election campaign. Her employer, KTV-LA, has allowed Ms. Anchor to keep her position and the general manager for the station said "There is no concern as to the ethics of Ms. Anchor whatsoever."

Ms. Anchor would like to determine if she has a claim against TFF based on its unauthorized use of her photograph in a manner that falsely implies she unethically reported on the Mayor's re-election campaign.

DISCUSSION

Ms. Anchor likely has a statutory right of publicity claim against TFF for using her photograph without her consent. California Civil Code § 3344(a) requires a celebrity's consent for the knowing use of her photograph on a product for profit. Cal. Civ. Code Ann. § 3344(a) (West 2009). The consent requirement may be unnecessary if the use of the photograph is in the public interest—"any news, public affairs, or sports broadcast or account, or any political campaign." Id. at § 3344(d); Downing v. Abercrombie & Fitch, 265 F.3d 994 (9th Cir. 2001). However, false information is never protected, even if the matter is in the public interest. Eastwood v. Super. Ct. of L.A. Co., 149 Cal. App. 3d 409 (2nd Dist. 1983). This memorandum will evaluate: (1) whether Ms. Anchor has a right of publicity claim against TFF under § 3344(a); (2) if TFF required Ms. Anchor's consent to use her photograph under § 3344(d); (3) whether TFF's use of Ms. Anchor's photograph was in connection with the public interest; and (4) whether TFF's use of Ms. Anchor's photograph was truthful.

Right of Publicity Claim Under § 3344(a)

Ms. Anchor has a right of publicity claim against TFF under California Civil Code § 3344(a). Section 3344(a) provides that the knowing use of another's photograph for commercial purposes without the person's prior consent is a violation of that person's right of publicity. See Downing, 265 F.3d at 1002 (right of publicity violated when a clothing retailer's surf-themed catalog knowingly used a photograph of professional surfers in a surfing competition without their consent); Eastwood, 149 Cal. App. 3d at 421 (right of publicity violated when a newspaper knowingly published a love triangle story about Clint Eastwood without his consent). TFF knowingly used Ms. Anchor's photograph on t-shirts it produced and sold without her consent. Thus, TFF violated Ms. Anchor's right of publicity under California Civil Code § 3344(a).

Whether Consent is Needed For Use of Photograph Under § 3344(d)

TFF's Civil Code § 3344(a) violation likely is not actionable because its use of Ms. Anchor's photograph on the t-shirt provided commentary on a matter in the public interest and, therefore, consent was unnecessary. California Civil Code § 3344(d) provides an exception to the consent requirement contained in § 3344(a). It states that the use of a photograph in connection with "any news, public affairs, or sports broadcast or account, or any political campaign" does not require consent. § 3344(d). The courts have explained that the purpose of this exception is to protect the public's right to know about things, events, and people, such as news, celebrity activities, and sports. Eastwood, 149 Cal. App. 3d at 421; Gionfriddo v. Major League Baseball, 94 Cal. App. 4th 400 (1st Dist. 2001); Montana v. San Jose Mercury News, Inc., 34 Cal. App. 4th 790 (6th Dist. 1995). Thus, the right of a celebrity in her image is not absolute, but must be balanced against the public interest in the dissemination of news and information. Id. It is for this reason that the use of a celebrity's photograph on a matter in the public interest is exempt from the consent requirement of § 3344(a).

Ms. Anchor's claim is not furthered by the statutory purpose of protecting matters in the public interest. Rather, TFF's use of Ms. Anchor's photograph with the Mayor's photograph as a miniature devil on her shoulder furthers the purpose because the t-shirt is part of an expressive comment on the unethical reporting on politics in Los Angeles. This is type of information the public interest exception was designed to protect. Thus, it is likely the use of Ms. Anchor's photograph on the t-shirt as a political and social commentary is not actionable due to the nature of the policy protecting the dissemination of information in the public interest.

Use of the Photograph In Connection With a Matter in the Public Interest

Consent may be unnecessary because TFF's use of Ms. Anchor's photograph was likely connected to the public's interest. Consent is unnecessary if the use of a celebrity's photograph is directly related to matters in the public interest. For example, consent is unnecessary if the use of a celebrity's photograph is directly related to commentary on events that impact society. In Dora v. Frontline Video, Inc., the court determined whether the use of the plaintiff's photograph in a surfing documentary was proper under the public interest exception. 15 Cal. App. 4th 536 (2nd Dist. 1993). A 1950s professional surfer brought a claim against the producers of a documentary video for using his photograph, voice, and video recordings without his consent. Id. at 541. The court held that the use of the surfer's photograph, voice, and video recordings in the surfing documentary did not require consent because they were used in a manner that was directly related to a matter in the public interest. Id. at 546. It reasoned that surfing is in the public interest because "surfing is more than passing interest to some," that "it has created a lifestyle that influences speech, behavior, dress, and entertainment, among other things," and has "had a significant influence on the popular culture." Id. Because the surfer's photograph, voice, and video recordings was used in the documentary on surfing, which directly related to a matter in the public interest, the use was proper under the public interest exception and consent was unnecessary. Id.

However, consent is required if the use of a photograph is for advertising purposes and is not directly related to a matter in the public interest. Downing, 265 F.3d 994. In Downing, the court determined whether the unauthorized use of a surfer's photograph in a surf-themed clothing catalogue was protected under the public interest exception. Id. at 999. The clothing catalog included a small number of editorials on surfing, but its primary purpose was to increase brand awareness and sell clothes. Id. at 1000. The photograph preceded two pages that advertised t-shirts designed to replicate those worn by the surfer in the photograph. The court held that the use of the surfer's photograph, although on a topic in the public interest, was not protected because the photograph was used as a "window dressing" to advance the surf-themed catalogue. Id. at 1002. It contrasted the use in the catalog from the use in the documentary in Dora, stating that although both cover the theme of surfing, the documentary's use "directly contributed to the story" while the catalog's use did not. Id. at 1003. Instead, the catalog's use was "much more commercial in nature." Therefore, the use of the surfer's photograph was not a proper use under the public interest exception and consent was required. Id.

The use of Ms. Anchor's photograph by TFF likely did not require consent because the use directly related to a matter in the public interest and was not commercial in nature. Ms. Anchor's case is similar to Dora but distinguishable from Downing because of the direct connection between the use of her photograph and the public interest. Ms. Anchor, a reporter for a local news station, was involved in a highly publicized relationship with the Mayor and there was a significant amount media attention alleging that she unethically reported on the Mayor's re-election campaign. TFF claims it created and sold a t-shirt with a photograph of Ms. Anchor with a superimposed picture on her shoulder of the Mayor wearing miniature devil-horns to provide commentary on Ms. Anchor's unethical reporting on local politics. This is similar to Dora, where Frontline Video used the image, video, and voice recordings of a well-known professional surfer in its surfing documentary to provide commentary on the early years of surfing and the cultural impact of surfing. Dora, 15 Cal. App. 4th at 541. The court in Dora reasoned that the use of the surfer's photograph in the documentary directly contributed to the story on surfing and the surfer had a significant influence on popular culture. Id. at 546. This reasoning applies here because the use of Ms. Anchor's photograph on TFF's t-shirt directly contributed to the story on her alleged unethical reporting on the Mayor's re-election campaign and its significant influence on local politics.

Furthermore, Ms. Anchor's case is distinguishable from Downing, where a well-known surfer's photograph, taken during a surfing championship, was used in a surf-themed clothing catalog. 265 F.3d 994. The surfer's photograph followed two articles that discussed the history of surfing, however, no connection was made between the articles and the surfer, and the surfer was not identified as a legend of the sport. Id. at 1002. Instead, the two pages following the surfer's photograph advertised t-shirts replicating those worn by the surfer in his photograph. Id. The court reasoned that this use was merely "window dressing to advance the [catalog's] surf theme" and promote sales based on the implied endorsement by the well-known surfer. Id. The use of the photograph was not to provide commentary on surfing like in Dora where the "point of the program" was to provide commentary on surfing. Id. at 1001. Ms. Anchor's is distinguishable from Downing in how her photograph was used because her photograph was used on a t-shirt primarily to provide commentary on her relationship with the Mayor and the alleged influence he may have had on Ms. Anchor's reporting on his re-election campaign. TFF stated that "the point of the t-shirt" was to provide commentary on Ms. Anchor's conflict of interest in reporting on the Mayor's re-election campaign; it was not a mere "window dressing" to sell the t-shirt. Consumers likely would purchase the t-shirt because of the commentary, not because of her implied endorsement.

While the court in Dora reasoned that the use of the photograph in a surfing documentary did not require consent due to its direct contribution to public's interest in the significant influence of surfing and its cultural impact, the court in Downing reasoned that consent was required because the use of the photograph was commercial in nature, having only a tenuous relationship as a "window-dressing" with the surfing theme of the clothing catalog. Id. at 1002. Ms. Anchor's case is more analogous to Dora than Downing because of the strong connection between the use of her photograph and the public's interest in her relationship with the Mayor and possible unethical reporting on his re-election campaign. Therefore, because the reasoning from Dora more closely relates to Ms. Anchor's case than the reasoning from Downing, the use of the photograph in Ms. Anchor's case likely was directly connected to the public interest and consent was unnecessary.

Implication of False Information is Not Protected

Even though the implication that Ms. Anchor unethically reported on the Mayor's campaign is likely in the public interest, it is false and therefore not protected. Use of a celebrity's photograph can constitute infringement of a celebrity's right of publicity, even if involves matters in the public interest, if the information is false. In Eastwood, the court determined whether Clint Eastwood's right of publicity was infringed when the National Enquirer published an article about Mr. Eastwood's alleged romantic involvement with two other celebrities. 149 Cal. App. 3d at 414. Mr. Eastwood disputed the truthfulness of the article. Id. The court held that the Enquirer was not entitled to the public interest exception because the article it printed was false. Id. at 425. The court reasoned that even if there is a public interest a celebrity's conduct, the dissemination of false information is not protected because the legislature did not intend the public interest exception to preclude liability when a falsehood is presented as news. Id. Thus, the Enquirer was not entitled to the public interest exception. Id.

TFF also is not entitled to the public interest exception because the implication of unethical reporting created by the photographs on the t-shirt is false. Ms. Anchor's case is similar to Eastwood because both involved the dissemination of false information. 149 Cal. App. 3d 409. In Ms. Anchor's case, the t-shirt had a photograph of Ms. Anchor combined with a photograph of the Mayor as a miniature devil sitting on her shoulder. The inclusion of the Mayor on her shoulder with devil horns implied that he was influencing or controlling her reporting on his campaign, which Ms. Anchor denies. This is similar to Eastwood where the article stated that Mr. Eastwood was in a love triangle with two other celebrities, which Mr. Eastwood denied. Id. at 414. Just as Mr. Eastwood denied that he was involved in a love triangle, Ms. Anchor denies that she ever reported on the Mayor's re-election campaign and the general manager of KTV-LA stated that "there are no concerns about Ms. Anchor's ethics whatsoever." As explained in Eastwood, it is this type of dissemination of false information that legislature did not intend the public interest exception to protect. Id. at 425. Because the court in Eastwood reasoned that the Enquirer was not entitled to the public interest exception for its false article and TFF created a false implication by its use of Ms. Anchor's photograph on its t-shirt, TFF is not entitled to the public interest exception.

CONCLUSION

Ms. Anchor likely has a valid right of publicity claim against TFF. Under the California statutory right of publicity, a person has a claim if another knowingly uses the person's photograph without consent. Consent is unnecessary, however, if the photograph relates to a matter in the public interest and is connected to that public interest, unless the use provides false information. In this case, TFF's knowingly used Ms. Anchor's photograph without her consent in violation of § 3344(a). However, because it was used by TFF for the purpose of providing a commentary on the affair between Ms. Anchor and the Mayor and the possible unethical reporting on the Mayor's re-election campaign, the use of the photograph relates to a matter in the public interest. Thus, it is subject to the exemption in § 3344(d) and Ms. Anchor's consent was unnecessary. Despite this, Ms. Anchor likely will still prevail because the implication created by TFF's use of Ms. Anchor's photograph on the t-shirt is false and, therefore, not entitled to protection. For these reasons, Ms. Anchor likely has a successful claim against TFF and should pursue a legal remedy in this matter.

Section II

Persuasive Legal Writing

■ ■ ■

CASE FILE NO. 1: PEOPLE v. GIBSON

WORKSHEET NO. 1: INTRODUCTION, FACTS, AND RELEVANT AUTHORITY

Introduction

Attorneys rarely research the law and write an analysis simply to learn the law. Instead, attorneys almost always research and write in response to the specific situation faced by a client. Therefore, before you turn to the attached statutes and cases, read the Office Memorandum on the next page to give yourself an understanding of your client's situation. The Office Memorandum is an example of what you might receive when a supervising attorney asks you to work on a case.

After you have read the Office Memorandum, re-read the statutes and cases in the Case File. When re-reading the statutes and cases, begin to strategize on how to persuasively argue the relief requested by your client in the form of a motion to reduce the charge from first to second degree burglary.

OFFICE MEMORANDUM

TO: Legal Intern

FROM: Supervising Attorney

DATE: September 1, YEAR

RE: People v. Gibson; motion to reduce the change from first to second degree burglary

---

Thank you for your hard work on the objective memorandum for our client, Sam Gibson. Based on your analysis, I am confident that we can prevail on a motion to reduce the charge from first to second degree burglary, which I need you to write. Please review the factual record below; these are the only facts available at this time.

Declaration of Sam Gibson

I, Sam Gibson, declare as follows:

1. I have personal knowledge of the facts stated herein and, if called upon, I could testify to those facts competently.

2. I recently lost my job in construction. My family and I have gone through just about all of our savings. We currently are living on my wife's minimum wage job and welfare. It is not enough money to pay all of our bills.

3. I am married and have been for the last ten years. My wife and I have four children, aged 1, 3, 5, and 8.

4. I have never been arrested or convicted of a crime.

5. On August 14, YEAR, I did not have enough money to pay for the basic groceries I needed for my family.

6. I went for a walk to clear my head from all of my life stress. I walked by the house at 5553 Tree Lined Street in Sacramento, California. The house was dark and appeared to be vacant. But, I thought maybe there might be some belongings someone had left behind that I might be able to sell. I figured if they did not want them, I could sell them—I really needed the money.

7. I went back to my apartment and got a bag and a crowbar. I then returned to the house at 5553 Tree Lined Street. It is only about a 1/2 mile away from my apartment.

8. I used a crowbar to open the back sliding glass door and I went inside.

9. The house was basically empty. I opened every door, drawer, and cupboard. In the hall closet, I found a moving box with stuff inside of them. They were not taped shut and the stuff seemed to have been thrown in the box.

10. In the box, I found some crystal, china, and silver. I put all of it in my bag and I left the house through the same sliding door I came in.

11. I walked down the driveway and then a few yards down the sidewalk when I saw a police car with its lights on and siren running.

12. The police drove up next to me and I stopped.

13. The police told me that they knew the house was empty and asked me what I was doing.

14. I told them that I broke into the house and took some things left in the hall closet. I gave them my bag. The police opened the bad and found the china, crystal, and silver.

15. I started crying and told them that I was just trying to find a way to get food for my family. I know what I did was wrong, but I was desperate.

16. The police arrested me and I was later charged with first-degree burglary.

I declare under penalty of perjury under the laws of the State of California that the above is true and correct to the best of my recollection and understanding.

Sam Gibson

Sam Gibson

Sacramento County Police Report

Suspect	*Sam Gibson* *42 years old/Caucasian*
Date	*August 14, YEAR*
Location	*5553 Tree Lined Street in Sacramento, California 95813*
Crime	*Burglary in the First Degree*
Officers	*Lance Sullivan* *Joe Stadler*

Incident Report: *Officer Sullivan*
— *On August 14, YEAR, approached middle-aged Caucasian man leaving property on 5553 Tree lined Street.* — *Suspect carrying bag; the bag appeared to be heavy.*

— *We knew that the owner recently died and that the home was vacant.*

— *After the suspect walked only a few yards down the sidewalk, we turned on our lights and siren and ordered the suspect to stop.*

— *We told him to drop the bag; he complied.*

— *We asked the suspect what he was doing and that we knew the property was vacant.*

— *The suspect immediately began crying and admitted that just stole some things from the house and that they were in the bag.*

— *We opened the bag and in it we found china, crystal, and silver the suspect said he took from the house.*

— *We arrested the suspect and he was later charged with first-degree burglary.*

Witness Interview: *Audrey Brown*

— *Ms. Audrey Brown owns a house at 5041 South Park Lane in Sacramento, California. She has lived in this house for six years.*

— *On July 1, YEAR, Ms. Brown's eighty-five year old mother passed away.*

— *Ms. Brown inherited her mother's house.*

— *Ms. Brown's mother's house is located at 5553 Tree Lined Street in Sacramento, California.*

— *On August 1st, Ms. Brown hired an auction house to sell the furnishings in her mother's house and a disposal company to take the unsold contents to the local Goodwill. This process was completed on August 5th.*

— *The only items that remained in the house after August 5th were some of her mother's personal items that Ms. Brown packed in a moving box before the auction and left them in a hall closet. They included her mother's china, crystal, and silver*

— *She recently listed her own house at 5041 South Park Lane for sale.*

— *Ms. Brown intended to move into her mother's house as soon as her house on 5041 South Park Lane sold.*

— *As of the date of the burglary, Ms. Brown's house on South Park Lane had not sold and Ms. Brown had not moved to her mother's house on Tree Lined Street.*

— *Ms. Brown identified the contents of the suspect's bag and confirmed they belonged to her deceased mother and that they had been in the house at 5553 Tree lined Street.*

PENAL CODE

Part 1. Of Crimes and Punishments
Title 13. Of Crimes Against Property
Chapter 2. Burglary

California Penal Code § 459. Burglary

Every person who enters any house, room, apartment, tenement, shop, warehouse, store, mill, barn, stable, outhouse or other building, tent, vessel, as defined in Section 21 of the Harbors and Navigation Code, floating home, as defined in subdivision (d) of Section 18075.55 of the Health and Safety Code, railroad car, locked or sealed cargo container, whether or not mounted on a vehicle, trailer coach, as defined in Section 635 of the Vehicle Code, any house car, as defined in Section 362 of the Vehicle Code, inhabited camper, as defined in Section 243 of the Vehicle Code, vehicle as defined by the Vehicle Code, when the doors are locked, aircraft as defined by Section 21012 of the Public Utilities Code, or mine or any underground portion thereof, with intent to commit grand or petit larceny or any felony is guilty of burglary. As used in this chapter, "inhabited" means currently being used for dwelling purposes, whether occupied or not. A house, trailer, vessel designed for habitation, or portion of a building is currently being used for dwelling purposes if, at the time of the burglary, it was not occupied solely because a natural or other disaster caused the occupants to leave the premises.

California Penal Code § 460. Degrees

(a) Every burglary of an inhabited dwelling house, vessel, as defined in the Harbors and Navigation Code, which is inhabited and designed for habitation, floating home, as defined in subdivision (d) of Section 18075.55 of the Health and Safety Code, or trailer coach, as defined by the Vehicle Code, or the inhabited portion of any other building, is burglary of the first degree.

(b) All other kinds of burglary are of the second degree.

(c) This section shall not be construed to supersede or affect Section 464 of the Penal Code.

THE PEOPLE, Plaintiff and Respondent

v.

ANTONIO ROMERO CARDONA, Defendant and Appellant

Court of Appeal, Fourth District, Division 1, California

142 Cal.App.3d 481

April 27, 1983

BROWN

Antonio Cardona appeals his conviction of first degree burglary (Pen. Code, § 459, 460), contending he is guilty only of second degree burglary as the house he entered was not inhabited at the time.

On September 12, 1981, Keith Fuller and his family moved out of the house they rented on Jefferson Street in Carlsbad. The Fullers spent the night of September 12 in their new home in Oceanside. They did not intend ever to spend another night at the Jefferson Street house. They, however, had paid rent on the house through September 15 and, as of September 13, had not completed moving all their belongings out of the house. On the night of September 13, Cardona broke into the Jefferson Street house with the intent to steal some of the Fullers' belongings that were still stored there. Cardona was caught red-handed by the Fullers, who had returned to the house to pick up some of their belongings. *483

Cardona was charged with first degree burglary. At trial, he argued he was guilty only of second degree burglary because the house was not inhabited at the time of the burglary. The superior court found the house was inhabited by the Fullers and found Cardona guilty of first degree burglary. The court found this is an unusual case under the criteria of California Rules of Court rule 416 and thus Penal Code section 462, prohibiting a grant of probation where defendant is convicted of first degree burglary, does not apply. Cardona was granted three years probation on the conditions he participate in an alcoholic rehabilitation program, report his employment status to his probation officer, violate no law and serve 307 days in custody with credit for 307 days served.

A burglary is of the first degree only if it is of an inhabited dwelling house during the nighttime (Pen. Code, § 460). Penal Code section 459 defines "inhabited" as it is used in section 460 as meaning "currently being used for dwelling purposes, whether occupied or not." The issue here is whether the Fullers continued to use the house on Jefferson Street for dwelling purposes after they permanently stopped sleeping there but had not yet moved all their belongings out or lost the right to possess the house.

Penal Code section 459 clearly states a house remains "inhabited" despite the fact it is empty at the time of the burglary. Furthermore, a house remains inhabited even if the burglary occurs while the residents are away for an extended period of time (*People v. Harris* (1968) 266 Cal.App.2d 426, 430 [72 Cal.Rptr. 423]; *People v. Stewart* (1952) 113 Cal.App.2d 687, 691 [248 P.2d 768]). (1)Where, however, the residents have moved out without the intent to return, the house becomes uninhabited, i.e., it is no longer being used for dwelling purposes, and a burglary of the house, even one occurring within a few days after the residents vacate, cannot be of the first degree (*People v. Valdez* (1962) 203 Cal.App.2d 559, 563 [21 Cal.Rptr. 764]). Such was the case here. Mr. Fuller testified his family had slept in their new house the night before the burglary and intended never again to occupy the Jefferson Street house. The continued use of that house for storage of belongings only was not sufficient to make the house inhabited; because a burglary is of the first degree only if it is of an inhabited house at night, the crucial element in determining whether a house is being used for dwelling purposes is whether anyone sleeps in it (*People v. Lewis* (1969) 274 Cal.App.2d 912, 921 [79 Cal.Rptr. 650]). There was no identifiable person here who used the house as sleeping quarters at the time of the burglary or intended to do so in the future.

Although no case directly on point has arisen in California, a finding the Jefferson Street house was uninhabited when the burglary occurred is supported by cases of other states. The facts of Hayes v. State (1937) 180 Miss. 291 [177 So.360], are identical to those involved here. The court in that case found the house was uninhabited because the prior resident no longer had any intent to *484 use the house as his residence. *State v. Ferebee* (1979) 273 S.C. 403 [257 S.E.2d 154], and *Santistevan v. People* (1972) 177 Colo. 329 [494 P.2d 75], hold a house is uninhabited as soon as the tenant vacates, despite the fact the house remains furnished; first degree burglary is a crime against habitation, not property. (See also *Tukes v. State* (Fla. 1977) 346 So.2d 1056; *Smith v. State* (1920) 80 Fla. 315 [85 So. 911].)

The superior court based its finding the Jefferson Street house was inhabited at the time of the burglary on what it found to be Cardona's intent. The court focused on the danger posed by the burglary of an occupied house and found a first degree burglary conviction is justified if there is no way for the defendant to know the house will be empty at the time of the burglary. The subjective impressions of the defendant, however, are irrelevant; a house, for example, remains inhabited although the residents are away on vacation and the burglar knows it. The dispositive element is whether the person with the possessory right to the house views the house as his dwelling. The Fullers no longer used the Jefferson Street house as their dwelling and thus it was not inhabited when the burglary occurred.

(2) Although the superior court erred in finding Cardona guilty of first degree burglary, we need not remand for resentencing. There is no doubt Cardona is guilty of second degree burglary; it is within our authority to modify the conviction to reflect the lesser offense. (See *People v. Valdez*, supra., 203 Cal.App.2d 559, 566.) The sentence imposed, probation with-

out any further custody, is as lenient as Cardona could have expected following a conviction of second degree burglary.

The judgment is modified to find Cardona guilty of second degree burglary only. As modified, the judgment is affirmed.

THE PEOPLE, Plaintiff and Respondent

v.

RAFAEL AGUIRRE HERNANDEZ, Defendant and Appellant

Court of Appeal, Fourth District, Division 2, California

9 Cal.App.4th 438

September 8, 1992

DABNEY

Defendant Rafael Aguirre Hernandez was convicted by a jury of first degree burglary (Pen. Code § 459). The court found true the special allegations that Hernandez had suffered a prior conviction for residential burglary (§ 667) and a prior conviction for possession of a controlled substance for sale (§ 667.5, subd. (b).) The court sentenced Hernandez to the middle term of four years for the burglary, a consecutive term of five years for the section 667 prior, and a consecutive term of one year for the section 667.5, subdivision (b) prior.

On appeal, Hernandez contends (1) the evidence was insufficient to support his conviction for burglary of an inhabited dwelling; (2) the court *440 gave conflicting and confusing instructions on the definition of an inhabited dwelling; (3) the court erroneously refused to give requested instructions on the definition of an inhabited dwelling; (4) the unjustified use of physical restraints violated his constitutional rights; (5) the court erred in refusing to allow him to set aside his prior conviction; (6) the court erroneously refused a requested defense instruction on the lesser related offense of unauthorized entry into a noncommercial dwelling; (7) the court erred in using prior convictions for impeachment; (8) the court erred in failing to discharge a juror for nondisclosure of her relationship to the victim; and (9) the section 667 enhancement should be stricken because it was not proved beyond a reasonable doubt.

Facts

On September 1, 1990, Stephen Kirkreit and his family moved all their furniture and personal belongings to a new apartment on Mitchell Avenue in Riverside, leaving nothing behind at their old apartment. The utilities had been turned on at the new apartment. The Kirkreits finished moving at 9 p.m. and spent the night with relatives because nothing was unpacked.

The next morning they returned to the Mitchell Avenue apartment and found the front door, which had been left locked, was wide open. Their VCR, stereo receiver, and some clothing were missing. They did not spend the night at the Mitchell Avenue apartment until September 3.

Police officers discovered fingerprints on a piece of glass from a broken rear window which was determined to have been the point of entry. An expert witness testified that the prints matched those of Hernandez. In the expert witness's opinion, the prints had been made by someone reaching through the broken window from the outside.

Defense. Hernandez knew the former tenants of the Mitchell Avenue apartment and had spent the night with them several times. During his visits, he had entered the bedroom with the broken window and had touched the window. He denied he had entered the apartment the night of the burglary and denied taking property from the apartment.

Residents of another apartment on Mitchell Avenue testified they had seen Hernandez visiting the former tenants. They testified the Kirkreits did not actually begin staying at the Mitchell Avenue apartment for more than two weeks after they moved their property there because the apartment had to be fumigated for cockroaches. *441

Discussion

I. Sufficiency of Evidence of Residential Burglary

A. Standard of Review.

(1) "When the sufficiency of the evidence is challenged on appeal, the court must review the whole record in the light most favorable to the judgment to determine whether it contains substantial evidence—i.e., evidence that is credible and of solid value—from which a rational trier of fact could have found the defendant guilty beyond a reasonable doubt." [Citations.] (*People v. Green* (1980) 27 Cal.3d 1, 55 [164 Cal.Rptr. 1, 609 P.2d 468], overruled on another ground in *People v. Hall* (1986) 41 Cal.3d 826 [226 Cal.Rptr. 112, 718 P.2d 99].)

B. Evidence That Residence Was Inhabited.

(2) Hernandez contends the evidence was insufficient to support his conviction of first degree burglary because the evidence did not show the residence was inhabited within the meaning of section 460, subdivision (a) when the burglary was committed. (Footnote omitted). The Kirkreits had never slept in the apartment before the burglary and had not unpacked their belongings. They did not begin sleeping at the apartment until after the burglary. Hernandez contends that the crucial element for whether a house is inhabited is whether anyone sleeps there. (*People v. Lewis* (1969) 274 Cal.App.2d 912, 921 [79 Cal.Rptr. 650].)

In *People v. Cardona* (1983) 142 Cal.App.3d 481 [191 Cal.Rptr. 109], the court stated, "[B]ecause a burglary is of the first degree only if it is of an inhabited house at night, the crucial element in determining whether a house is being used for dwelling purposes is whether anyone sleeps in it [citation]." (*Id.* at p. 483.) However statutory amendments have eliminated the requirement that a burglary take place at night for it to be first degree burglary. (Stats. 1982, ch. 1297, § 1, p. 4786.) Thus, the Legislature has rejected the view, expressed in prior case law, that the use of a house as sleeping quarters is critical. (Cf. *Lewis*, supra, 274 Cal.App.2d at pp. 920–921.) Rather, such use is merely one circumstance the fact finder may consider.

To support his argument that the apartment was uninhabited, Hernandez cites *People v. Valdez* (1962) 203 Cal.App.2d 559 [21 Cal.Rptr. 764]. In Valdez, a burglary of a house took place on March 9, 1961. The previous *442 tenant had moved out a week earlier, and the owner had rented the premises to a new tenant whose occupancy was scheduled to begin on March 13. The new tenant had not moved any belongings into the house and had not had the utilities connected. (*Id.* at pp. 562–563.) The court held that the burglary could not be of the first degree because no one resided there. (*Id.* at p. 563.)

In *Cardona*, supra, 142 Cal.App.3d 481, a burglary of a house took place on September 13, 1981. A family had moved out of the house and had spent the night of September 12 in their new residence. However, they had not completed moving their belongings from the house, and they had paid rent there until September 15. (*Id.* at p. 482.) The court held that the defendant could not have been convicted of first degree burglary, because the house was no longer inhabited. The court stated the house became uninhabited when the tenants moved out, not intending to return there to live. (*Id.* at p. 483.)

In *People v. Jackson* (1992) 6 Cal.App.4th 1185 [8 Cal.Rptr.2d 239], the court held that a dwelling continued to be inhabited because a tenant who intended to move out had never vacated the premises, but was still using the house at the time of the robbery. (*Id.* at p. 1189.)

Here, the Kirkreits had had the utilities connected and had moved all of their belongings into the Mitchell Avenue apartment, intending to occupy it as their residence. The evidence reasonably supported a jury finding that although the Kirkreits had not yet slept there, the apartment was occupied by them as a place of settled residence from which they were merely temporarily absent. We conclude the evidence was sufficient for the jury to find that the apartment was inhabited at the time of the burglary.

The judgment is affirmed.

THE PEOPLE, Respondent

v.

JOSEPH ALBERT ALLARD, Appellant

District Court of Appeal, Second District, Division 2, California

99 Cal.App. 591

June 24, 1929

CRAIG

The appellant was found guilty of first degree burglary and was sentenced accordingly. He appeals, and bases his claim for reversal upon alleged insufficiency of the evidence to sustain the verdict.

It appears that a house, the property of one R. P. Low, was burglarized by defendant who, at the time was unarmed. The crime was committed in the night-time and the house was not occupied on that particular night. Low and his family lived there, but, as testified by him, "were just away for two or three days."

[1] The argument presented by appellant is, that under these circumstances the house was not "inhabited" as required by section 460 of the Penal Code, in order that the burglary may be first degree where the person committing the crime is not armed with a deadly weapon.

An inhabitant of a house is one who resides therein, and "inhabitancy" and "residence" are synonymous terms. (*Harding v. Standard Oil Co.*, 182 Fed. 421.) It has never been held that a person loses his residence by reason of a brief absence from the house where he lives, and without evidence of an intention to depart therefrom and go to live in some other place. Under a statute similar to ours, where a family lived in the house but were away on vacation, it was held to be an inhabited dwelling-house. (*Mason v. State*, 27 Ohio C. C. 526.)

We consider the evidence in this case entirely sufficient.

The judgment is affirmed.

WORKSHEET NO. 2: THE PERSUASIVE RULE

Rule drafting in persuasive writing is different from rule drafting in objective writing. The main differences are in the organization, the breadth and depth of the rule, and the persuasive tone.

Before writing a persuasive rule, however, you should write the rule objectively first to ensure accuracy. Crafting an objective rule first will also offer perspective on the neutral rule the judge will consider when evaluating your persuasive rule. To write the rule objectively, use the approach explained in Worksheet No. 2 for Objective Writing, which is summarized below:

To determine rules of law from a single source or multiple sources of law, including the elements, definitions, and/or exceptions, answer the following brainstorming questions:

1. What is the rule?

2. What are the exceptions to the rule, if any?

3. What else will the court consider, if anything?

After answering these three questions, put your answers together in one or more sentences to write the rule. Once you have written a rule, evaluate it to ensure it is complete and appropriate in scope. To evaluate the rule(s), answer the following questions:

1. Is the rule too specific based on the legal authority and your client facts?

2. Is the rule too broad based on the legal authority and your client facts?

3. Does the rule include vague terms?

4. Is the rule circular?

5. If there is more than one rule, are the rules repetitive?

After answering the above questions, you should have a complete objective rule. Now you need to start thinking about how to write your objective rule persuasively. To help you do this, consider the following brainstorming questions:

1. Who is your client?

2. What outcome do you want for your client based on this rule?

3. What part of the rule do you want to emphasize for your client?

4. What part of the rule do you want to de-emphasize for your client?

Using the answers to these brainstorming questions as your guide, convert your objective rule into a persuasive rule. To write your persuasive rule, look at your objective rule, your answers to the above brainstorming questions, and the following considerations:

1. Begin the rule with the outcome you want for your client; that is, if you want an injunction to be granted begin by stating "An injunction will be granted when ..."
2. Begin the rule with your client's role in the litigation; that is, Plaintiff or Defendant. For example, "A plaintiff is entitled to an injunction when ..."
3. Include the favorable part of the rule at the beginning to provide emphasis.
4. Include unfavorable parts of the rule in the middle to bury them.
5. Emphasize the opposing party's requirements of proof (burdens, elements, evidence, etc.). For example, "For a defendant to prevail on his motion, he must prove five elements with substantial evidence." Or, "Defendant has the burden of proof."

Once you have written your rule persuasively, evaluate it for persuasive tone and presentation. To evaluate whether your rule is persuasively written for your client's case, answer the following questions:

1. Did you use active or passive voice? (Consider the benefits of each.)
2. Did you put your client's position in a point of emphasis in the rule?
3. If the rule is favorable, did you state it broadly?
4. If the rule is unfavorable, did you state it narrowly?
5. If there is an exception to the rule, did you include it in a way that is favorable to your client?

EXAMPLE OBJECTIVE RULE:

California Civil Code Section 3344(a) provides that the knowing use of another's photograph for commercial purposes without the person's prior consent is a violation of that person's right of publicity. Section 3344(d) provides an exception to the consent requirement contained in § 3344(a), which states that the use of a photograph in connection with "any news, public affairs, or sports broadcast or account, or any political campaign" does not require consent.

EXAMPLE PERSUASIVE RULE:

The knowing use of another's photograph for commercial purposes without the person's consent violates California Civil Code Section 3344(a). The only exception to the statutory consent requirement is if the defendant can prove that the use of a photograph was in connection with a matter in the public interest. Cal. Civ. Code § 3344(d).

Case File Assignment:

Write a persuasive rule for your client's case on the issue of inhabited in the context of first-degree burglary using the legal authorities in the Case File. To help you write a persuasive rule, begin by writing an objective rule, or use the objective rule you wrote for Worksheet No. 2 for Objective Writing.

State your objective rule here:

Convert the objective rule into a persuasive rule. To help do this, answer the following brainstorming questions:

1. Who is your client?

2. What outcome do you want for your client based on this rule?

3. What part of the rule do you want to emphasize for your client?

4. What part of the rule do you want to de-emphasize for your client?

Using the answers to these brainstorming questions as your guide, convert your objective rule into a persuasive rule. To write your persuasive rule, look at your objective rule, your answers to the above brainstorming questions, and the following considerations:

1. Begin the rule with the outcome you want for your client; that is, if you want an injunction to be granted begin by stating "An injunction will be granted when ..."
2. Begin the rule with your client's role in the litigation; that is, Plaintiff or Defendant. For example, "A plaintiff is entitled to an injunction when ..."
3. Include the favorable part of the rule at the beginning to provide emphasis.
4. Include unfavorable parts of the rule in the middle to bury them.
5. Emphasize the opposing party's requirements of proof (burdens, elements, evidence, etc.). For example, "For a defendant to prevail on his motion, he must prove five elements with substantial evidence." Or, "Defendant has the burden of proof."

Once you have written the rule persuasively, evaluate it for persuasive tone and presentation. To evaluate whether your rule is persuasively written for your client, answer the following questions:

1. Did you use active or passive voice? (Consider the benefits of each.)
2. Did you put your client's position in a point of emphasis in the rule?
3. If the rule is favorable, did you state it broadly?
4. If the rule is unfavorable, did you state it narrowly?
5. If there is an exception to the rule, did you include it in a way that is favorable to your client?

WORKSHEET NO. 3: PARENTHETICALS

Parentheticals are a quick way to provide the reader with illustrations of a legal principle without having to include an objective case illustration. Writing parentheticals, however, can be tricky because you must include enough information for the reader to understand the significance of the precedent case and its connection to the legal principle the parenthetical is explaining, but not include so much information that you effectively have written an objective case illustration.

A parenthetical is substantively correct if it includes:

1. The legal principle or rule you plan to explain with the parenthetical;
2. The relevant facts from the precedent case that support the legal principle you plan to explain with the parenthetical; and
3. The key words and phrases from the precedent case that support the legal principle you plan to explain with the parenthetical.

A parenthetical is technically correct if it:

1. Asserts a legal principle prior to the parentheticals;
2. Follows the legal principle with a proper citation;
3. Has proper capitalization within the parenthetical—do not capitalize the first word of a parenthetical if it is only a word, phase, or clause; but do capitalize the first word of a parenthetical if it is a complete sentence;
4. Uses parallel construction for string parentheticals—if you use one form for one parenthetical, use that same form for all of the parentheticals in the string; and
5. Is kept short—if the information you want to provide cannot be provided in a phase, clause, or a single sentence, do not use a parenthetical.

Here are some examples that demonstrate parentheticals with "not enough" information and parentheticals with "enough" information. Please note the legal principle that precedes the parentheticals.

EXAMPLE PARENTHETICALS:

NOT ENOUGH INFORMATION IN THE PARENTHETICALS:

Although celebrities have the right to First Amendment protection from the unauthorized exploitation of their photographs under the right of publicity, the statutory cause of action specifically exempts from liability the use of a photograph in connection with a matter in the public interest. California Civil Code 3344(d) states that no prior consent is required for use of a photograph in the public interest, such as news, public affairs, or sports broadcast or account, or any political campaign. Public interest has been defined as "recent events or publications about people who, by their accomplishments, mode of living, professional standing or calling, create a legitimate and widespread attention to their activities." Dora v. Frontline Video, Inc., 15 Cal. App. 4th 536 (2nd Dist. 1993) (a 1987 surfing documentary); Gionfriddo v. Major League Baseball, 94 Cal. App. 4th 400 (1st Dist. 2001) (web cast of baseball statistics).

ENOUGH INFORMATION IN THE PARENTHETICALS:

Although celebrities have the right to First Amendment protection from the unauthorized exploitation of their photographs under the right of publicity, the statutory cause of action specifically exempts from liability the use of a photograph in connection with a matter in the public interest. California Civil Code 3344(d) states that no prior consent is required for use of a photograph in the public interest, such as news, public affairs, or sports broadcast or account, or any political campaign. Public interest has been defined as "recent events or publications about people who, by their accomplishments, mode of living, professional standing or calling, create a legitimate and widespread attention to their activities." Dora v. Frontline Video, Inc., 15 Cal. App. 4th 536 (2nd Dist. 1993) (a 1987 surfing documentary that included footage of a famous surfer was in the public interest and no prior consent was needed); Gionfriddo v. Major League Baseball, 94 Cal. App. 4th 400 (1st Dist. 2001) (web cast of baseball statistics that included a photograph of a famous baseball player was in the public interest and no prior consent was needed).

Case File Assignment:

Write a parenthetical(s) for your client's case using the legal authority in the Case File and/or the legal authority assigned by your professor. To help you write a parenthetical(s), answer the following brainstorming questions for each precedent case you plan to explain with a parenthetical:

1. What is the legal principle you plan to explain with a parenthetical(s)? Please note that this legal principle may precede more than one parenthetical (see examples above).

2. For each precedent case you plan to explain with a parenthetical, answer the following brainstorming questions:

   a. What is the proper citation for the precedent case you plan to explain with the parenthetical?

   b. What are the relevant facts from the precedent case that support the legal principle you plan to explain with the parenthetical?

   c. What is the legal conclusion from the precedent case that supports the legal principle you plan to explain with the parenthetical?

d. What are the key words and phrases from the precedent case that support the legal principle you plan to explain with the parenthetical?

Using your answers to these brainstorming questions as your guide, you now are ready to write a parenthetical(s). Use one of the formulas below to organize your parenthetical(s). The order of the information contained inside the parentheticals can be reversed.

One Parenthetical:

Legal Principle. Cite (relevant facts + legal conclusion to support the legal principle, using the key words and phrases from the precedent case).

Multiple Parentheticals:

Legal Principle. Cite (relevant facts + legal conclusion to support the legal principle, using the key words and phrases from the precedent case); Cite (relevant facts + legal conclusion to support the legal principle, using the key words and phrases from the precedent case); Cite (relevant facts + legal conclusion to support the legal principle, using the key words and phrases from the precedent case).

When writing parenthetical(s), consider the following technical requirements:

1. Use proper capitalization within the parenthetical—do not capitalize the first word of a parenthetical if it is only a word, phase, or clause; but do capitalize the first word of a parenthetical if it is a complete sentence;

2. Use parallel construction for string parentheticals—if you use one form for one parenthetical use that same form for all of the parentheticals in the string; and

3. Keep it short—if the information you want to provide cannot be provided in a phase, clause, or a single sentence, do not use a parenthetical.

WORKSHEET NO. 4: DEDUCTIVE REASONING

Deductive reasoning justifies a result by directly applying a legal principle to the facts of your client's case. The result is the result simply because the law mandates it. There is no in-depth analysis, but rather a straightforward application of the legal principle to the facts of the client's case.

Deductive reasoning is substantively correct if it includes:

1. The legal principle or rule you are applying;
2. The legal conclusion you seek to establish by the application of the legal principle or rule; and
3. The relevant facts from your client's case needed to justify that legal conclusion.

* Please note that 2 and 3 can be reversed and that deductive reasoning is frequently paired with parentheticals.

EXAMPLE DEDUCTIVE REASONING:

It is illegal for anyone under the age of sixteen to operate a motor vehicle. (Citation omitted). The defendant illegally operated a motor vehicle because she was only thirteen years old at the time she drove her father's car.

EXAMPLE DEDUCTIVE REASONING WITH PARENTHETICALS:

Although celebrities have the right to First Amendment protection from the unauthorized exploitation of their photographs under the right of publicity, the statutory cause of action specifically exempts from liability the use of a photograph in connection with a matter in the public interest. California Civil Code 3344(d) states that no prior consent is required for use of a photograph in the public interest, such as news, public affairs, or sports broadcast or account, or any political campaign. Public interest has been defined as "recent events or publications about people who, by their accomplishments, mode of living, professional standing or calling, create a legitimate and widespread attention to their activities." Dora v. Frontline Video, Inc., 15 Cal. App. 4th 536 (2nd Dist. 1993) (a 1987 surfing documentary that included footage of a famous surfer was in the public interest and no prior consent was needed); Gionfriddo v. Major League Baseball, 94 Cal. App. 4th 400 (1st Dist. 2001) (web cast of baseball statistics that included a photograph of a famous baseball player in the public interest and no prior consent was needed). Because the use of Mr. Quarterback's photograph was used in connection with his fourth Superbowl victory in ten years, it is in the public interest and his consent was not required.

Case File Assignment:

Write an argument for your client's case using deductive reasoning based on the legal authority in the Case File and/or the legal authority assigned by your professor. To help you write a deductive reasoning argument, answer the following brainstorming questions:

1. What is the legal principle or rule that you want to apply to your client's case?

2. What is the legal conclusion you seek to establish by the application of the legal principle or rule?

3. What are the relevant facts from your client's case needed to justify that legal conclusion?

Using the answers to these brainstorming questions as your guide, write an argument using deductive reasoning. Start by cutting and pasting your answers into paragraph form and then mold them into a readable sentence or paragraph. Consider whether the deductive reasoning will follow a simple legal principle or a legal principle with parentheticals.

WORKSHEET NO. 5: POLICY-BASED REASONING

Policy-based reasoning in persuasive writing is not that different from policy-based reasoning in objective writing. The organization of the substance is the same; however, the presentation of the substance is different.

To write a persuasive policy-based argument, start by evaluating the policy-based argument objectively (as explained in Worksheet No. 5 for Objective Writing). To do this, consider:

1. The conclusion you will reach by applying the policy to your client's case. (You may need to answer this question after you have completed your analysis of the policy.)
2. The rule you are applying to your client's case.
3. The purpose underlying the rule identified in response to Question 2 above and the origin of that purpose. What greater societal purpose(s) was the court or legislature trying to protect in creating the rule? (NOTE: There may be more than one purpose. If there is more than one purpose, identify if the court seems to prefer one purpose over another.) Also, the purpose behind the rule should come from legal authority, such as legislative history, case authority, or well-established public opinion, not your personal opinion.
4. The potential outcomes for your client when applying the rule.
5. The potential outcomes for the other party when applying the rule.
6. How the outcomes identified in response to Questions 4 and 5 above are or are not served by the purpose(s) of the rule you identified in response to Question 3 above.
7. The outcome that best follows the purpose of the rule.

After evaluating these questions, you should have an objective understanding of whether the purpose(s) of the rule supports the arguments for your client's case. If it does, use the following formula to write a policy-based reasoning argument for your client's case. If it does not support the arguments for your client's case, do not include a policy-based argument.

A persuasive policy-based reasoning argument is substantively complete if it:

1. Begins the argument by stating the conclusion you want to argue by applying the purpose of the rule to your client's case. (This is the thesis sentence for argument).
2. States the rule that is the basis of the policy-based reasoning argument.
3. Identifies and describes the purpose underlying the rule and the origin of that purpose. Remember, the purpose behind the rule must come from legal authority, such as legislative history, case authority,

or well-established public opinion, not your personal opinion. Also, if there is more than one purpose, explain which one the courts tend to use more.

4. States persuasively that the purpose underlying the rule applies to your client's case.
5. Explains with specific detail why the possible outcome(s) for your client furthers the purpose underlying the rule.
6. Concludes with a sentence that provides closure to the policy-based reasoning argument. This sentence must connect to the thesis sentence that began the policy-based reasoning argument.

EXAMPLE POLICY–BASED REASONING ARGUMENT:

Ms. Anchor's claim is supported by the purpose underlying the statute. While § 3344(d) protects information that is directly related to matters in the public interest, the legislature did not intend to protect false information that is presented as news. Eastwood, 149 Cal. App. 3d at 425. The Legislature stated that the public interest exception cannot be exercised so as to abuse the rights of individuals. Id. This policy applies to Ms. Anchor's case. Ms. Anchor denies that she ever reported on the Mayor's campaign and the general manager of her news station stated that "there are no concerns about Ms. Anchor's ethics whatsoever." Yet, TFF created a t-shirt that directly challenged Ms. Anchor's ethics. It is exactly this type of dissemination of false information the Legislature did not intend the public interest exception to protect. Id. Therefore, Ms. Anchor's right of publicity supported by the policy behind the statute and TFF's unauthorized use of her photograph is not protected.

Case File Assignment:

Write an argument for your client's case using policy-based reasoning based on the legal authority in the Case File and/or the legal authority assigned by your professor. To help you write a policy-based reasoning argument, answer the following brainstorming questions:

1. What is the conclusion you want to argue by applying the policy to your client's case? (You may need to answer this question last.)

2. What is the rule you are applying to your client's case?

3. What is the purpose underlying the rule identified in response to Question 2 above and the origin of that purpose? What greater societal purpose(s) was the court or legislature trying to protect in creating the rule? (NOTE: There may be more than one purpose. If there is more than one purpose, identify if the court seems to prefer one purpose over another.) Also, the purpose behind the rule should come from legal authority, such as legislative history, case authority, or well-established public opinion, not your personal opinion.

4. What are the potential outcomes for your client when applying the rule?

5. What are the potential outcomes for the other party when applying the rule?

6. How are the outcomes identified in response to Questions 4 and 5 above served or not served by the purpose(s) of the rule identified in response to Question 3 above?

7. Which outcome best follows the purpose(s) of the rule? Explain why.

After answering these brainstorming questions, you should have a clear understanding of whether the possible outcomes for your client do or do not serve the underlying purpose of the rule. If the purpose of the rule is served by your client's case, then use the following formula to write a policy-based reasoning argument. Each of these six parts must be included for a complete policy-based reasoning argument. This does not mean, however, that you need to have six sentences; a complete policy-based reasoning argument may be less than three sentences or as much as two full paragraphs.

1. Begin the paragraph(s) by stating the conclusion you want to argue by applying the purpose of the rule to your client's case. (This is the thesis sentence for this paragraph).
2. State the rule that is the basis of the policy-based reasoning argument.
3. Identify and describe the purpose underlying the rule and the origin of that purpose. Remember, the purpose behind the rule must come from legal authority, such as legislative history, case authority, or well-established public opinion. It is not your personal opinion on the purpose of the rule. Also, if there is more than one purpose, explain which one the courts tend to use more.
4. State persuasively that the purpose underlying the rule applies to your client's case.
5. Explain with specific detail why the possible outcome(s) for your client furthers the purpose underlying the rule.
6. Conclude with a sentence that provides closure to the policy-based reasoning argument. This sentence must connect to the thesis sentence that began the policy-based reasoning argument.

WORKSHEET NO. 6: ANALOGICAL REASONING

Analogical reasoning in persuasive writing is not that different from analogical reasoning in objective writing. The organization of the substance is essentially the same; however, to effectively persuade the reader, the content and presentation of the substance is different.

The two main differences between analogical reasoning in persuasive writing and objective writing are: (1) the depth of the substance provided and (2) the tone.

First, the depth of the substance provided is different in persuasive writing because there are no case illustrations or a traditional E section in persuasive writing as there is in objective writing. Instead, in persuasive writing the law is explained in the context of the analysis. Thus, the description of the precedent case in the persuasive analogical reasoning formula is more detailed than the description of the precedent case in the objective analogical reasoning formula.

Second, the tone must be more argumentative. Unlike objective writing, where the goal is to demonstrate to the reader all possible arguments and counter-arguments from a neutral perspective, in persuasive writing the goal is to persuade the reader to agree with your argument. Thus, in persuasive writing, you must state the arguments affirmatively and conclusively, begin with your strongest argument (or strongest analogy or distinction), and really prove the connection between the client's case and the precedent case(s).

To write analogical reasoning in persuasive writing, start by first evaluating the analogical reasoning argument objectively using the same brainstorming process used for analogical reasoning in objective writing (see Worksheet No. 6 for Objective Writing), which is provided below:

1. Identify one issue you plan to address with analogical reasoning.
2. Identify the name of one precedent case you plan to use for the issue you selected above.
3. Identify the specific holding of the precedent case on the legal issue you plan to argue with this analogical reasoning (NOTE: This must only be the holding specific to the legal issue you are addressing, not the overall holding of the precedent case).
4. Describe the reasoning of the precedent case on the legal issue you plan to argue with this analogical reasoning (NOTE: This must only be the reasoning specific to the legal issue you are addressing, not the overall reasoning of the precedent case).
5. Make a list of the relevant facts from the precedent case on the legal issue you plan to argue with this analogical reasoning (NOTE: This must only be the facts specific to the legal issue you are addressing, not all of the facts from the precedent case).

6. Make a list of the relevant facts from your client's case on the legal issue you plan to argue with this analogical reasoning (NOTE: This must only be the facts specific to the legal issue you are addressing, not all of the facts from your client's case).

7. Group the facts of the precedent case and your client's case into facts that are similar and facts that are distinguishable.

Depending on whether the facts are the similar or distinguishable or both, you may only need to consider some of the questions below. If the facts are similar, answer Questions 8–10. If the facts are distinguishable, answer Questions 11–13. If the facts are both similar and distinguishable, answer Questions 8–13.

8. Identify the fact(s) to be compared in your analysis as similar. (NOTE: This must only be the facts specific to the legal issue you are addressing, not all of the facts from the precedent case or your client's case.)

9. Explain why you think these facts are similar—use specific factual examples to demonstrate the similarities.

10. Explain *why* these factual similarities support your legal analysis on the issue you are addressing. This is where you must directly apply the reasoning of the precedent case to the facts of your client's case. Specifically look at why and how the precedent case ruled as it did and why that same reasoning applies to your client's case.

11. Identify the fact(s) to be compared in your analysis as distinguishable. (NOTE: This must only be the facts specific to the legal issue you are addressing and not all of the facts from the precedent case or your client's case.)

12. Explain why you think these facts are distinguishable—use specific factual examples to demonstrate the differences.

13. Explain *why* these factual differences support your legal analysis on the issue you are addressing. This is where you must directly apply the reasoning of the precedent case to the facts of your client's case. Specifically look at why and how the precedent case ruled as it did and why that same reasoning does not apply to your client's case.

After evaluating these brainstorming questions, you should have a clear understanding of whether an analogical reasoning argument should be made in your client's case. You then must decide if the analogical reasoning will be based on a single case or multiple cases. If multiple cases are used to argue the same legal issue, then you must make these arguments at the same time, rather than as a separate analogical reasoning for each precedent case. Once you have decided if the analogical reasoning will be based on a single case or multiple cases, use one of the following formulas to write your analogical reasoning argument:

Analogical Reasoning Formula Using a Single Case:

Component 1: Persuasively state the legal conclusion you want the reader to reach based on your analogical reasoning (this is the overall thesis sentence for the analogical reasoning paragraph or paragraphs—case names should not be included in this sentence).

Component 2: Sentence stating, "In client's case (use client's name) is similar to/distinguishable from ______ (insert precedent case name) based on ______ (identify the specific issue this analogical reasoning is addressing)."

Component 3: Sentence stating, "In client's case (use client's name), (insert the specific facts about your client's case that will be compared; these are not all of the facts of the case but only the specific facts that will be compared)."

Component 4: Sentence stating, "This case is similar to/distinguishable from ______ (insert precedent case name). In ______ (insert precedent case name) where (insert detailed information about the facts, the holding, and the reasoning from the precedent case you are relying upon that are related to the specific issue to be compared)." Remember to describe the precedent case in a way that is favorable to your client's position.

Component 5: Explain, using *specific factual detail*, why the facts you are comparing are similar or distinguishable. This is where you need to provide specific fact-to-fact comparisons, using actual facts from your client's case and the precedent case. (i.e.—"Fact X in client's case is similar to/distinguishable from Fact Y in precedent case because ______"). Remember to make these factual comparisons in a way that is favorable to your client's position.

Component 6: Persuasively re-state the likely outcome of your client's case based on the similarities or differences you discussed in Component 5. This is a re-statement of the conclusion (Component 1) but with more detail and this likely is the beginning of a new paragraph.

Component 7: Explain *why* this is the likely outcome. This is where you must directly apply the reasoning from the precedent case to your client's case.

Possible phrasing:

The court in ______ (insert precedent case name) reasoned ______ (insert the fact specific reasoning of the precedent case on the specific legal issue the analogical

reasoning is addressing). This reasoning applies to your client's case (use client's name) because ______ (explain why it applies). Therefore, because the reasoning from (insert precedent case name) applies to your client's case (use client's name), the outcome in your client's case (use client's name) is ______ (insert the outcome you are trying to prove with the analogical reasoning.)

Component 8: Persuasively re-state the conclusion you want the reader to reach based on your analogical reasoning. This must connect to the argument provided by the analogical reasoning and to the conclusion stated in Component 1.

EXAMPLE SINGLE CASE ANALOGICAL REASONING:

The implication that Ms. Anchor unethically reported on the Mayor's campaign is false and therefore unprotected. If the defendant uses a celebrity photograph in a manner that disseminates false information, the defendant violates the celebrity's right of publicity and the use is unprotected. Eastwood v. Super. Ct. of L.A. Co., 149 Cal. App. 3d 409 (2nd Dist. 1983). In Eastwood, for example, the court held Clint Eastwood's right of publicity was infringed when the National Enquirer published an article about Mr. Eastwood's alleged romantic involvement with two other celebrities; an article that was completely false. Id. at 414. Similarly, the implication that Ms. Anchor engaged in unethical reporting is also false. Ms. Anchor did not engage in any unethical reporting. Instead, and as alleged in her Complaint, Ms. Anchor never reported on the Mayor's re-election campaign and the general manager of her news station stated that "there are no concerns about Ms. Anchor's ethics whatsoever." The court in Eastwood reasoned that the veil of the public interest exception does not protect dissemination false information. Id. at 425. This reasoning applies to TFF's dissemination of false information regarding Ms. Anchor's reporting. Therefore, TFF's dissemination of false information is not protected.

Analogical Reasoning Formula Using Multiple Cases:

Component 1: Persuasively state legal conclusion you want the reader to reach based on your analogical reasoning (this is the overall thesis sentence for the analogical reasoning paragraph or paragraphs—case names should not be included in this sentence).

Component 2: Sentence stating, "Client's case (insert client's name) is similar to/distinguishable from _______ (insert first precedent case name) and/but similar to/distinguishable from _______ (insert second precedent case name) based on _______ (identify the specific issue this analogical reasoning is addressing)."

Component 3: Sentence stating, "In client's case (use client's name), (insert the specific facts about your client's case that will be compared; these are not all of the facts of the case but only the specific facts that will be compared)."

Component 4(a): Sentence stating, "This case is similar to/distinguishable from _______ (insert first precedent case name). In _______ (insert precedent case name) where (insert detailed information about the facts, the holding, and the reasoning from the precedent case you are relying upon that are related to the specific issue to be compared)." Remember to describe the precedent case in a way that is favorable to your client's position.

Component 4(b): Explain, using *specific factual detail*, why the facts you are comparing are similar/distinguishable. This is where you need to provide specific fact-to-fact comparisons, using actual facts from your client's case and the precedent case. (i.e.—"Fact X in client's case is similar to/distinguishable from Fact Y in precedent case because _______ "). Remember to make these factual comparisons in a way that is favorable to your client's position.

Component 5(a): Sentence stating, "This case is similar/distinguishable than _______ (insert second precedent case name). In (insert precedent case name) where (insert detailed information about the facts, the holding, and the reasoning from the precedent case you are relying upon that are related to the specific issue to be compared)." Remember to describe the precedent case in a way that is favorable to your client's position.

Component 5(b): Explain, using *specific factual detail*, why the facts you are comparing are similar/distinguishable. This is where you need to provide specific fact-to-fact comparisons, using actual facts from your client's case and the precedent case. (i.e.—"Fact X in client's case is similar to/distinguishable from Fact Y in precedent case because _______ "). Remember to make these factual comparisons in a way that is favorable to your client's position. [NOTE: you many need to use a transition to begin this sentence, such as "In addition," "Also," "However," or "On the other hand".]

Component 6: Persuasively re-state the likely outcome of your client's case based on the similarities/differences you discussed previously (see Components 4(b) and 5(b)). This is a re-statement of the conclusion (Component 1) but with more detail and likely is the beginning of a new paragraph.

Component 7: Explain *why* this is the likely outcome. This is where you must directly apply the reasoning from the precedent case to your client's case.

Possible phrasing if the reasoning of the precedent cases is the same:

The court in _______ (insert first and second precedent case names) reasoned _______ (insert the fact specific reasoning of the precedent cases on the specific legal issue the analogical reasoning is addressing). This reasoning applies to your client's case (use client's name) because _______ (explain why it applies). Therefore, because the reasoning from (insert precedent case names) applies to your client's case (use client's name), the outcome in your client's case (use client's name) will likely will be _______ (insert the outcome you are trying to prove with the analogical reasoning).

Possible phrasing if the reasoning of the precedent cases is different:

The court in _______ (insert first precedent case name) reasoned _______ (insert the fact specific reasoning of the first precedent case on the specific legal issue the analogical reasoning is addressing). This reasoning applies to your client's case (use client's name) because _______ (explain why it applies). However, the court in _______ (insert second precedent case name) reasoned _______ (insert the fact specific reasoning of the second precedent case on the specific legal issue the analogical reasoning is addressing). This reasoning does not apply to your client's case (use client's name) because _______ (explain why it does not apply). Therefore, because the reasoning from (insert first precedent case name) applies to your client's case (use client's name) and the reasoning from (insert second precedent case name) does not apply to your client's case (use client's name), the outcome in your client's case (use client's name) will likely will be ______ (insert the outcome you are trying to prove with the analogical reasoning).

Component 8: Persuasively re-state the conclusion you want the reader to reach based on your analogical reasoning. This must connect to the argument provided by the analogical reasoning and to the conclusion stated in Component 1.

EXAMPLE MULTIPLE CASE ANALOGICAL REASONING:

TFF unlawfully used Ms. Anchor's photograph without her consent. TFF was required to obtain Ms. Anchor's consent to use her photograph because her photograph was used to further the company's commercial objectives, not to inform on a matter in the public interest. The use of Ms. Anchor's photograph is similar to the unauthorized use of a photograph in Downing and distinguishable from the authorized use of a photograph in Dora. In Downing, a clothing retailer used a famous surfer's photograph in its surf-themed clothing catalog. 265 F.3d 994. The court held that the photograph was only tenuously connected the public's interest in surfing because the retailer "did not explain that [the surfer] was a legend of the sport and incorrectly identifies where and when [the surfer's] photo was taken." Id. at 1003. Instead, the court held that the use of his photo only was used to sell clothing; therefore, its use required the surfer's consent. Id. Thus, where the use is commercial in nature, consent is required. Id.

Indeed, it is only if the connection between the use and the dissemination of information on matters in the public interest is clear that consent may be unnecessary. Dora v. Frontline Video, Inc., 15 Cal. App. 4th 536 (2nd Dist. 1993). For example, in Dora, consent to use a surfer's photograph in a surfing documentary was not required because the documentary was connected to the public's interest. Id. at 541. The court reasoned that because the "point of the program" was to inform the public about surfing and the people who impacted surf culture, the use of the surfer's photograph was connected to the public interest. 15 Cal. App. 4th at 543.

TFF's use of Ms. Anchor's photo was commercial in nature. Like in Downing, where the objective of the surf-themed catalog was to promote sales, TFF's primary business objective was to create and sell funny t-shirts for profit. The catalog used the surfer's photograph to capitalize on his fame and to "window-dress" the catalog, just like TFF used Ms. Anchor's photograph to capitalize on her highly publicized affair with the Mayor to sell t-shirts. Downing, 265 F.3d at 1003. Also, like the catalog's failure to properly identify the surfer and his relationship to the sport, TFF "did not explain" Ms. Anchor's situation with the Mayor and, therefore, did not connect the use of the photograph to the public interest. Id. Instead, TFF simply was trying to profit off of a highly publicized situation, like the catalog was trying to profit off the fame of the well-known surfer. Id. Furthermore, Ms. Anchor's is distinguishable from Dora because, in that case, the court reasoned that consent was unnecessary since the "point of the program" was to provide commentary on surfing. 15 Cal. App. 4th at 546. That reasoning does not apply here because the "point of the t-shirt" was to meet TFF's commercial objective of creating a humorous t-shirt

for profit, not to inform the public or provide social commentary on that topic. Because TFF's use of Ms. Anchor's photograph on its t-shirt was not connected to the public's interest, but instead used to make a profit, TFF was required to obtain Ms. Anchor's consent.

Case File Assignment:

Write an argument for your client's case using analogical reasoning based on the legal authority in the Case File and/or the legal authority assigned by your professor. To help you write an analogical reasoning argument, answer the following brainstorming questions:

1. Identify one specific issue you plan to address with analogical reasoning (or the specific issue assigned by your professor).

2. Identify the name of one precedent case you plan to use for the issue you selected above (or the case assigned by your professor).

3. Identify the specific holding of the precedent case on the legal issue you plan to argue with this analogical reasoning (NOTE: This must only be the holding specific to the legal issue you are addressing, not the overall holding of the precedent case.)

4. Describe the reasoning of the court from the precedent case on the legal issue you plan to argue with this analogical reasoning (NOTE: This must only be the reasoning specific to the legal issue you are addressing, not the overall reasoning of the precedent case.)

5. Make a list of the relevant facts from the precedent case on the legal issue you plan to argue with this analogical reasoning (NOTE: This must only be the facts specific to the legal issue you are addressing, not all of the facts from the precedent case.)

6. Make a list of the relevant facts from your client's case on the legal issue you plan to argue with this analogical reasoning (NOTE: This must be only the facts specific to the legal issue you are addressing, not all of the facts from your client's case).

7. Organize the facts of the precedent case and your client's case into the charts below:

Facts that are similar:

Your Client's Case	Precedent Case

Facts that are distinguishable:

Your Client's Case	Precedent Case

Using the information you filled into the charts above, decide whether you think your client's case and the precedent case are similar, distinguishable, or both. If they are similar, answer Questions 8–10 below. If they are distinguishable, answer Questions 11–13 below. If they are both similar and distinguishable, answer Questions 8–13 below.

8. Identify the fact(s) from your client's case and the precedent case to be compared as similar. (NOTE: This must only be the facts specific to the legal issue you are addressing, not all of the facts from the precedent case or your client's case.)

9. Explain why these facts are similar—use specific factual examples to prove the similarities.

10. Explain *why* these factual similarities support your legal analysis on the issue you are addressing. This is where you must directly apply the reasoning of the precedent case to the facts of your client's case. Specifically look at why and how the precedent case ruled as it did and why that same reasoning applies to your client's case.

11. Identify the fact(s) to be compared in your analysis as distinguishable. (NOTE: This must only be the facts specific to the legal issue you are addressing, not all of the facts from the precedent case or your client's case.)

12. Explain why these facts are distinguishable—use specific factual examples to prove the differences.

13. Explain *why* these factual differences support your legal analysis on the issue you are addressing. This is where you need to directly apply the reasoning of the precedent case to the facts of your client's case. Specifically look at why and how the precedent case ruled as it did and why that same reasoning does not apply to your client's case.

After answering these brainstorming questions, you should have a clear understanding of whether an analogical reasoning argument should be made in your client's case. You then must decide if the analogical reasoning will be based on a single case or multiple cases. If multiple cases are used to argue the same legal issue, then you must make these arguments at the same time, rather than as a separate analogical reasoning for each precedent case. Once you have decided if the analogical reasoning will be based on a single case or multiple cases, use one of the following formulas to write your analogical reasoning argument:

Analogical Reasoning Formula Using a Single Case:

Component 1: Persuasively state the legal conclusion you want the reader to reach based on your analogical reasoning (this is the overall thesis sentence for the analogical reasoning paragraph or paragraphs—case names should not be included in this sentence).

Component 2: Sentence stating, "In client's case (use client's name) is similar to/distinguishable from ______ (insert precedent case name) based on ______ (identify the specific issue this analogical reasoning is addressing)."

Component 3: Sentence stating, "In client's case (use client's name), (insert the specific facts about your client's case that will be compared—please note these are not all of the facts of the case but only the specific facts that will be compared)."

Component 4: Sentence stating, "This case is similar to/distinguishable from ______ (insert precedent case name). In ______ (insert precedent case name) where (insert detailed information about the facts, the holding, and the reasoning from the precedent case you are relying upon that are related to the specific issue to be compared)." Remember to describe the precedent case in a way that is favorable to your client's position.

Component 5: Explain, using *specific factual detail*, why the facts you are comparing are similar or distinguishable. This is where you need to provide specific fact-to-fact comparisons, using actual facts from your client's case and the precedent case. (i.e.—"Fact X in client's case is similar to/distinguishable from Fact Y in precedent case because ______"). Remember to make these factual comparisons in a way that is favorable to your client's position.

Component 6: Persuasively re-state the likely outcome of your client's case based on the similarities or differences you discussed in Component 5. This is a re-statement of the conclusion (Component 1) but with more detail and this likely is the beginning of a new paragraph.

Component 7: Explain *why* this is the likely outcome. This is where you must directly apply the reasoning from the precedent case to your client's case.

Possible phrasing:

The court in ______ (insert precedent case name) reasoned ______ (insert the fact specific reasoning of the precedent case on the specific legal issue the analogical reasoning is addressing). This reasoning applies to your client's case (use client's name) because ______ (explain why it applies). Therefore, because the reasoning from (insert precedent case name) applies to your client's case (use client's name), the outcome in your client's case (use client's name) is ______ (insert the outcome you are trying to prove with the analogical reasoning.)

Component 8: Persuasively re-state the conclusion you want the reader to reach based on your analogical reasoning. This must connect to the argument provided by the analogical reasoning and to the conclusion stated in Component 1.

Analogical Reasoning Formula Using Multiple Cases:

Component 1: Persuasively state legal conclusion you want the reader to reach based on your analogical reasoning (this is the overall thesis sentence for the analogical reasoning paragraph or paragraphs—case names should not be included in this sentence).

Component 2: Sentence stating, "Client's case (insert client's name) is similar to/distinguishable from ______ (insert first precedent case name) and/but similar to/distinguishable from ______ (insert second precedent case name) based on ______ (identify the specific issue this analogical reasoning is addressing)."

Component 3: Sentence stating, "In client's case (use client's name), (insert the specific facts about your client's case that will be compared—please note these are not all of the facts of the case but only the specific facts that will be compared)."

Component 4(a): Sentence stating, "This case is similar to/distinguishable from ______ (insert first precedent case name). In ______ (insert precedent case name) where (insert detailed information about the facts, the holding, and the reasoning from the precedent case you are relying upon that are related to the specific issue to be compared)." Remember to describe the precedent case in a way that is favorable to your client's position.

Component 4(b): Explain, using *specific factual detail*, why the facts you are comparing are similar/distinguishable. This is where you need to provide specific fact-to-fact comparisons, using actual facts from your client's case and the precedent case. (i.e.—"Fact X in client's case is similar to/distinguishable from Fact Y in precedent case because ______ "). Remember to make these factual comparisons in a way that is favorable to your client's position.

Component 5(a): Sentence stating, "This case is similar/distinguishable than ______ (insert second precedent case name). In (insert precedent case name) where (insert detailed information about the facts, the holding, and the reasoning from the precedent case you are relying upon that are related to the specific issue to be compared)." Remember to describe the precedent case in a way that is favorable to your client's position.

Component 5(b): Explain, using *specific factual detail*, why the facts you are comparing are similar/distinguishable. This is

where you need to provide specific fact-to-fact comparisons, using actual facts from your client's case and the precedent case. (i.e.—"Fact X in client's case is similar to/distinguishable from Fact Y in precedent case because ______"). Remember to make these factual comparisons in a way that is favorable to your client's position. [NOTE: you many need to use a transition to begin this sentence, such as "In addition," "Also," "However," or "On the other hand"]

Component 6: Persuasively re-state the likely outcome of your client's case based on the similarities/differences you discussed previously (see Components 4(b) and 5(b). This is a re-statement of the conclusion (Component 1) but with more detail and this likely is the beginning of a new paragraph.

Component 7: Explain *why* this is the likely outcome. This is where you must directly apply the reasoning from the precedent case to your client's case.

Possible phrasing if the reasoning of the precedent cases is the same:

The court in ______ (insert first and second precedent case names) reasoned ______ (insert the fact specific reasoning of the precedent cases on the specific legal issue the analogical reasoning is addressing). This reasoning applies to your client's case (use client's name) because ______ (explain why it applies). Therefore, because the reasoning from (insert precedent case names) applies to your client's case (use client's name), the outcome in your client's case (use client's name) will likely will be ______ (insert the outcome you are trying to prove with the analogical reasoning).

Possible phrasing if the reasoning of the precedent cases is different:

The court in ______ (insert first precedent case name) reasoned ______ (insert the fact specific reasoning of the first precedent case on the specific legal issue the analogical reasoning is addressing). This reasoning applies to your client's case (use client's name) because ______ (explain why it applies). However, the court in ______ (insert second precedent case name) reasoned ______ (insert the fact specific reasoning of the second precedent case on the specific legal issue the analogical reasoning is addressing). This reasoning does not apply to your client's case (use client's name) because

______ (explain why it does not apply). Therefore, because the reasoning from (insert first precedent case name) applies to your client's case (use client's name) and the reasoning from (insert second precedent case name) does not apply to your client's case, the outcome in your client's case (use client's name) will likely will be ______ (insert the outcome you are trying to prove with the analogical reasoning).

Component 8: Persuasively re-state the conclusion you want the reader to reach based on your analogical reasoning. This must connect to the argument provided by the analogical reasoning and to the conclusion stated in Component 1.

WORKSHEET NO. 7: POINT HEADINGS

Point headings provide the reader with structure and guidance. They allow the reader to obtain a broad overview of your argument and quickly locate the point he or she is most interested in reading without having to read the entire argument.

A point heading is substantively correct if it:

1. States the point heading affirmatively for your client;
2. Uses key words and phrases from the argument the point heading represents;
3. Uses specific facts and legal concepts from the argument the point heading represents; and
4. Summarizes the argument the point heading represents by using the following formula:
    a. The conclusion for the argument the point heading represents;
    b. Because (or a "because" equivalent);
    c. The rule justifying the legal conclusion + the key fact(s) from your client's case.

EXAMPLE POINT HEADINGS:

I. MS. ANCHOR HAS A VALID RIGHT OF PUBLICITY CLAIM AGAINST TFF BECAUSE IT KNOWINGLY USED HER PHOTOGRAPH FOR PROFIT WITHOUT HER CONSENT.

II. MS. ANCHOR HAS A VALID RIGHT OF PUBLICITY CLAIM AGAINST TFF BECAUSE TFF'S USE OF HER PHOTOGRAPH WAS NOT CONNECTED TO A MATTER IN THE PUBLIC INTEREST, BUT ONLY FOR COMMERCIAL GAIN.

III. MS. ANCHOR HAS A VALID RIGHT OF PUBLICITY CLAIM AGAINST TFF BECAUSE THE PHOTOGRAPHS ON THE T–SHIRT IMPLIED FALSE INFORMATION.

A point heading is technically correct if:

1. It is only one sentence;
2. The sentences wrap under each other so the left margin of the point heading lines up with the text of the point heading immediately above it;
3. It appropriately uses emphasizers (all caps, bold, italic, underline, etc.) to allow the point headings to stand out from the text of the argument but not distract the reader;
4. It does not have an A without a B or an I without an II; and

5. It does not have lone point headings at the end of the page (there must be at least 2 lines of text of the paragraph the point heading precedes at the bottom of the page; a point heading cannot be the last line on a page).

A series of point headings are technically correct if they:

1. Use parallel construction;
2. Use appropriate levels of point headings and sub-point headings; and
3. Provide the reader with an outline of the Argument section, when read together.

The formatting for point headings is proper if:

I. THE TEXT OF THE FIRST LEVEL POINT HEADING IS INDENTED A FULL TAB OVER AND ADDITIONAL LINES OF TEXT WRAP UNDER THE FIRST LINE OF TEXT.

   A. <u>The Text Of The Second Level Point Heading Is Indented So That The "A" Lines–Up Under The Text Of The First Level Point Heading; The Text Of This Heading Is A Full Tab Over From The "A;" And Additional Lines Of Text Wrap Under The First Line of Text.</u>

      1. The third level point heading is indented so that the "1" lines-up under the text of the second level point heading; the text of this heading is indented a full tab over from the "1;" and additional lines of text wrap under the first line of text.

Note: The type of emphasizers (all caps, initial caps, underlined, italics, etc.) used here are for demonstrative purposes only. You should use the types of emphasizers assigned by your professor.

Case File Assignment:

Write the point headings for your brief. To help you write the point headings, answer the following brainstorming questions for each argument you plan to emphasize with a point heading:

1. What is the conclusion reached by the argument the point heading represents?

2. What are the key words and phrases used in the argument the point heading represents?

3. What are the specific facts and legal concepts from the argument the point heading represents?

Using the answers to these brainstorming questions as your guide, write a point heading(s) for your argument. When writing a point heading, use the following formula:

> The conclusion for the argument/paragraph the point heading represents + because (or a "because" equivalent) + the rule justifying the legal conclusion + the key fact(s) from your client's case.

When writing the point heading, consider the following substantive and technical requirements:

1. State the point heading affirmatively for your client;
2. State the point heading in only one sentence;
3. Have the text of the point heading wrap so the left margin of the point heading lines-up;
4. Appropriately use emphasizers (bold, italic, underline, etc.) to allow the point headings to stand out from the text of the argument, but not distract the reader;
5. Do not have an A without a B or an I without an II; and
6. Do not have lone point headings at the end of the page (there must be at least 2 lines of text of the paragraph the point heading precedes at the bottom of the page; a point heading cannot be the last line on a page)

If you have a series of point headings, consider the following substantive and technical requirements:

1. State the point headings using parallel construction;
2. State the point headings using appropriate levels of point headings and sub-point headings; and
3. Collectively, when read together, the point headings should provide the reader with an outline of the Argument section.

WORKSHEET NO. 8: THE INTRODUCTION

The Introduction in a persuasive brief is the first thing the judge will read. Thus, it must provide a complete introduction to the case and use persuasive techniques to convince the judge from the beginning.

An Introduction is substantively complete if it includes:

1. The nature of the case;
2. The identity of the parties;
3. The procedural event that led to the filing of the brief;
4. The relief your client requests from the court in the brief; and
5. The primary legal points justifying that relief.

When presenting the substance of these five components, consider the following persuasive writing techniques and note that the above five components can be presented in any order:

1. Begin with your client's name and what your client requests;
2. Write the Introduction in the affirmative; do not directly restate your opponent's position or what your opponent wants (even if it is a responsive brief); and
3. Establish the theme of your argument early.

EXAMPLE INTRODUCTION:

Tasha V. Anchor, a well-known television reporter, has a valid right of publicity claim against T–Shirts For Fun (TFF) under the California statutory right of publicity. TFF knowingly used a photograph of Ms. Anchor on a t-shirt combined with a photograph of the Los Angeles Mayor as a miniature devil sitting on her shoulder. Ms. Anchor did not consent to this use of her photograph. Furthermore, TFF admits that it used the photograph primarily for commercial gain, not for social commentary, and admits that the image was designed to imply that Ms. Anchor was influenced by the Mayor to unethically report on his re-election campaign. Ms. Anchor denies this implication. Because TFF knowingly used Ms. Anchor's photograph on its t-shirt without her consent, did not connect the use of her photograph to a matter in the public interest, and provided false information about Ms. Anchor's reporting, TFF violated her right of publicity. Therefore, Ms. Anchor has stated a valid claim and TFF's motion to dismiss should be denied.

Case File Assignment:

Write the Introduction for your brief. To help you write the Introduction, answer the following brainstorming questions:

1. What is the nature of the case?

2. Who are the parties?

3. What is the procedural event that led to the filing of the brief?

4. What is the relief your client requests from the court in the brief?

5. What are the primary legal points justifying that relief?

Using the answers to these brainstorming questions as your guide, write the Introduction for your brief. Start by cutting and pasting your answers into paragraph form and then mold them into readable paragraphs.

When writing the Introduction, consider the following persuasive techniques:

1. Begin with your client's name and what your client requests from the court in filing the brief;
2. Write the Introduction in the affirmative; do not directly restate your opponent's position or what your opponent wants (even if it is a responsive brief); and
3. Establish the theme of your case or argument.

WORKSHEET NO. 9: PERSUASIVE STATEMENT OF FACTS

The four most important things to remember when writing a persuasive Statement of Facts are to: (1) include the legally significant facts; (2) organize the facts in an effective manner; (3) tell your client's story persuasively; and (4) represent the facts accurately.

The brainstorming process for a persuasive Statement of Facts is similar to the brainstorming process for an objective Facts section (See Worksheet No. 9 for Objective Writing). However, a persuasive Statement of Facts does not begin the same as an objective Facts section. As you recall, the first paragraph in an objective Facts section (See Worksheet No. 9 for Objective Writing) begins with foundational information to provide the reader with context for the memorandum. This same first paragraph is not required in a persuasive Statement of Facts because a persuasive brief begins with an Introduction, which provides the reader with all of this foundational information: the parties, their relationships, the setting, the procedural history, and the client's general problem or goal. Instead, a persuasive Statement of Facts needs to grab the reader's attention from the beginning by telling compelling story.

Therefore, the brainstorming process for a persuasive Statement of Facts is more focused on the substance and tone.

A persuasive Statement of Facts is substantively correct if it:

1. Includes the proper substance by:

    a. Including the legally significant facts. To determine the legally significant facts, review your Argument section and highlight all of the facts from your client's case that you relied upon. These are the legally significant facts. If you have not yet written your Argument section, determine the legally significant facts by asking yourself: what are the facts a court will consider in ruling on your client's case?

    b. Including the background facts necessary for the legally significant facts to make sense. To determine the necessary background facts, ask yourself: what context is needed for the legally significant facts to make sense, what else does the judge need to know to understand the story of your client's case, and what else is needed to establish the theme of your case?

    c. Including emotional facts that are needed to establish your theme or create empathy for your client.

    d. Describing the facts accurately.

    e. Omitting factual arguments, references to the law, legal conclusions, and factual conclusions.

2. Includes the proper persuasive tone by:

    a. Emphasizing favorable facts;

    b. Strategically including unfavorable facts (the facts the opposing party likely will rely upon) by burying them within favorable facts;

    c. Having a parallel tone and theme with the Argument section; and

    d. Using an appropriate and persuasive organization.

3. Has strategically selected an organization to most persuasively tell the story: chronological, topical, or a combination of chronological and topical. The organization you select must be a strategic choice based on the best approach to persuasively tell the reader the story of your client's case.

4. Provides closure to the persuasive Statement of Facts by not ending abruptly; connect to the theme of the case and end with significant relevant facts as readers will best remember information they read last.

EXAMPLE PERSUASIVE STATEMENT OF FACTS:

Tasha V. Anchor is a local television reporter for KTV-LA. She has had a successful career as a reporter for the last ten years. During that time, she has won numerous awards, including an Emmy for her journalism, co-hosted national shows, interviewed A-list celebrities, high-ranking politicians, and well-known authors, and reported live from the Democratic Headquarters in Los Angeles as Barack Obama was elected President.

Ms. Anchor recently began a relationship with the Mayor of Los Angeles, who has been legally separated from his wife for two years. Ms. Anchor and the Mayor have been in a committed relationship for approximately six months. Currently, Ms. Anchor hosts the morning show for KTV-LA called, "Good Morning So. Cal." and the Mayor is running for re-election. While both are busy with their careers, they try to make as much time as possible to spend with each other.

In the summer, news of their relationship was made public, which was followed by a frenzy of media attention. Ms. Anchor could barely leave her home without being hounded by paparazzi. The Mayor had to add additional security just to be able to get to work each day. The media ran stories alleging everything from Ms. Anchor being the Mayor's second cousin to the Mayor influencing Ms. Anchor's reporting on his re-election campaign.

Ms. Anchor denies these recent allegations, as she is not the Mayor's second cousin and she never reported on the Mayor's re-election campaign or on any matters that directly or indirectly relate to his position as Mayor. However, Ms. Anchor did conduct two short of interviews with the Mayor last October and November, but these interviews were on topics unrelated to his re-election campaign and the general manager for KTV-LA said "There is no concern as to Ms. Anchor's ethics whatsoever."

Soon after the relationship was made public, Ms. Anchor came across a t-shirt for sale in a Beverly Hills boutique with her photograph on it. The t-shirt featured her photograph combined with a photograph of a miniaturized Mayor, wearing a suit and devil horns, sitting on her left shoulder. Ms. Anchor did not consent to the use of her photograph and its use on the t-shirt is offensive to Ms. Anchor because it inappropriately implies that she unethically reported on the Mayor's re-election campaign or that he somehow controlled her reporting. Ms. Anchor vehemently denies both allegations.

The t-shirt was created and sold by T–Shirts for Fun (TFF), a company that designs, produces, and distributes t-shirts, which are pri-

marily meant to be humorous and provide commentary on public events. Despite the $29.95 received for each t-shirt, with over 100 sales, TFF claims the t-shirt at issue was only intended to provide subtle commentary on the possible conflict of interest created by Ms. Anchor's relationship with the Mayor. However, according to information posted on TFF's web site, it admits that the t-shirt is its "best seller" and that its business objective is more about making money than providing social commentary.

Seeking to prevent further manufacture and distribution of the t-shirt and for damages against TFF, Ms. Anchor filed a Complaint alleging TFF violated her statutory right of publicity.

Case File Assignment:

Write a persuasive Statement of Facts for your client's case. To help you write a persuasive Statement of Facts, answer the following brainstorming questions:

1. What is the theme or the story of your case?

2. Identify the relevant facts:

   a. What are the legally significant facts? Read your Argument section and highlight all of the facts from your client's case that you used to support your arguments. These are the legally significant facts and they must be included in your persuasive Statement of Facts. If you have not yet written your Argument section, then determine the legally significant facts by asking yourself: what are the facts the court will consider in ruling on your client's case?

   b. What background facts are necessary to provide context for the legally significant facts identified in response to Question 2(a) above, to tell your client's story, and to establish the theme of your case?

c. What emotional facts are needed to establish your theme or create empathy for your client?

d. What are the unfavorable facts? What are the facts the opposing party likely will rely upon?

3. Looking at your answers to these brainstorming questions and using your understanding your client's case, identify the organization that will most persuasively tell your client's story: Chronological? Topical? Combination of chronological and topical? The organization you select must be a strategic choice based on the best approach to persuasively tell your client's story.

Using the answers to these brainstorming questions as your guide, write a persuasive Statement of Facts for your client's case. Start by cutting and pasting your answers into paragraph form and then mold them into readable paragraphs.

When writing your persuasive Statement of Facts, consider the following:

1. The first paragraph must tell a compelling story and establish the theme of the case.
2. The overall substance and tone must:
    - Strategically select the most persuasive organization (avoid stream of consciousness writing);
    - Represent the record accurately;
    - Describe the facts persuasively;
    - Have a parallel tone and theme with the Argument section;

- Emphasize favorable facts and bury unfavorable facts (but not omit them);
- Omit factual arguments, references to the law, legal conclusions, and factual conclusions; and
- Maintain a persuasive tone.

3. The last paragraph must:
   - Connect to the theme of the case;
   - Conclude with significant relevant facts—readers will best remember information they read last; and
   - Avoid ending abruptly: create a transition between the Statement of Fact and Argument sections.

WORKSHEET NO. 10: CONCLUSION

The Conclusion in persuasive writing is similar to a Conclusion in objective writing. Like an objective Conclusion, the persuasive Conclusion summarizes the individual conclusions that you reached in your Argument section and reminds the court of the relief requested.

A persuasive Conclusion is complete if it includes:

1. The ultimate relief sought by your brief (NOTE: This must be consistent with the information provided in your Introduction);
2. Each rule applied to your client's case (the R in each persuasive paradigm included in your brief);
3. The conclusion for each rule applied in your client's case (the C in each persuasive paradigm included in your brief);
4. A summary of the reasoning that supports those conclusions (summarize the A sections in each persuasive paradigm included in your brief); and
5. A restatement of the ultimate relief sought by your brief.

Throughout each of these components, use a persuasive tone and incorporate the theme of your client's case.

EXAMPLE CONCLUSION:

Ms. Anchor's Complaint states a valid statutory right of publicity claim against TFF and TFF's motion to dismiss should be denied. A motion to dismiss should only be granted in extraordinary cases where the plaintiff can prove no set of facts in support of her claim. Ms. Anchor has alleged more than sufficient facts to prove her claim. First, under California Civil Code § 3344(a), use of another's photograph is unlawful unless there is consent. Ms. Anchor's Complaint sufficiently alleges that TFF knowingly used her photograph without her consent in violation of § 3344(a). Second, the only exception to this statutory consent requirement is if the defendant can show that the use of a photograph was in connection with a matter in the public interest; but, if the unauthorized use of a photograph is for commercial purposes, consent is required. Ms. Anchor's Complaint sufficiently alleges that TFF used her photograph for commercial purposes, not to provide social commentary. Third, if the defendant uses a celebrity's photograph in a manner that disseminates false information, the defendant violates the celebrity's right of publicity and the use is unprotected. Ms. Anchor's Complaint sufficiently alleges that TFF's use of her photograph on the t-shirt falsely implied that Ms. Anchor unethically reported on the Mayor's re-election campaign and that this false implication is exactly what the statute is designed to protect against. For these reasons, Ms. Anchor's Complaint properly states a right of publicity cause of action and TFF's motion to dismiss should be denied.

Case File Assignment:

Write the Conclusion for your brief. To help you write the Conclusion, answer the following brainstorming questions:

1. What is the ultimate relief sought by your brief? (NOTE: This must be consistent with the information provided in your Introduction)

2. Identify each rule applied to your client's case (the R in each persuasive paradigm included in your brief).

3. Identify the conclusion for each rule applied in your client's case (the C in each persuasive paradigm included in your brief).

4. Summarize the reasoning that supports the conclusions on each rule (summarize the A sections in each persuasive paradigm included in your brief).

5. Restate the ultimate relief sought by your brief.

Using the answers to these brainstorming questions as your guide, write the Conclusion for your brief. Start by cutting and pasting your answers into paragraph form and then mold them into readable paragraphs. When writing the Conclusion, maintain a persuasive tone, incorporate the theme of your client's case, have the organization of the Conclusion parallel the organization of the Argument section, and avoid simply repeating the Introduction.

CASE FILE NO. 2: FARMER JOHN v. FARMER FORD

WORKSHEET NO. 1: INTRODUCTION, FACTS, AND RELEVANT AUTHORITY

Introduction

Attorneys rarely research the law and write an analysis simply to learn the law. Instead, attorneys almost always research and write in response to the specific situation faced by a client. Therefore, before you turn to the attached statutes and cases, read the Office Memorandum on the next page to give yourself an understanding of your client's situation. The following Office Memorandum is an example of what you might receive when a supervising attorney asks you to work on a case.

After you have read the Office Memorandum, re-read the statutes and cases in the Case File. When re-reading the statutes and cases, begin to strategize on how to persuasively write a mediation brief arguing that Farmer Ford violated Rhode Island's spite fence statute with his refusal to remove the "planted" cars.

OFFICE MEMORANDUM

TO: Legal Intern
FROM: Supervising Attorney
DATE: September 1, YEAR
RE: Farmer John v. Farmer Ford; Spite fence mediation brief

Thank you for your hard work on the objective memorandum for our client, and my uncle, Farmer John. Based on your analysis, I am confident that we will prevail at mediation. In preparation for our mediation, I need you to write a persuasive mediation brief arguing that Farmer Ford violated Rhode Island's spite fence statute with his refusal to remove the "planted" cars. Please review the factual record below; these are the only facts available at this time.

Declaration of John Campbell

I, John Campbell, declare as follows:

1. I have personal knowledge of the facts stated herein and, if called upon, I could testify to those facts competently.
2. My name is John Campbell, but my friends call me Farmer John.
3. I own a farm in southern Rhode Island. This farm has been in my family for more than a century and it always has grown apples and sweet corn.
4. There are three other farms that border my farm. The farm on the northern side was sold three years ago to James Ford, who calls himself Farmer Ford. This farm has grown potatoes for more than a century, but it has not been owned by the same family. The owners come and go and it has not been a very profitable farm.
5. This farm has been bought and sold multiple times over the last fifty years, with Farmer Ford being its most recent owner.
6. The area I live in is a quiet farming community, where everybody knows everyone. And, for the most part, everyone gets along.
7. I have been friends with my neighboring farmers my whole life, except for Farmer Ford.
8. When Farmer Ford first moved in, he seemed nice enough. He wanted to grow potatoes, like all of the other owners. He came by a few times to get farming advice and borrow equipment. Myself and the other neighboring farmers helped him out because that is the kind of people we are.
9. That was how it was, up until recently. One morning, I looked out my window and saw Farmer Ford clearing his fields. All of the crops were just destroyed. No more potatoes. If you didn't know better, you never would have known that a farm ever existed on that land.

10. The next day, Farmer Ford started to build a structure out of old rusty scrap metal and then trucks started bringing old cars to his farm.

11. I asked Farmer Ford what he was doing. He told me that potatoes were not profitable for him or his farm anymore. He said decided to take advantage of the federal Cash for Clunkers program and turned his farm into an auto dismantling and junk yard.

12. Myself and the other farmers were very upset. We expressed our concerns about the noise, traffic, and pollution to Farmer Ford. There were large big rig trucks delivering junked cars on a weekly basis. He said, "It is my farm and I can do what I want."

13. I organized the neighbors to try to force Farmer Ford to stop his auto dismantling and junk yard business. We approached him and told him that he needed to do something to stop the noise, traffic, and pollution he created with his new business.

14. Farmer Ford responded by offering to have a fence built between his property and the other farms. He said he would pay for half of the cost of the fence.

15. I felt his offer was rude and offensive to us real farmers—farm land is supposed to be open and have a sense of community—and it was shocking that he only offered to pay for half of the fence.

16. Farmer Ford said never mind and that he would build his own fence. At first, we thought this was all over and we would not have to see Farmer Ford's auto dismantling and junk yard anymore.

17. The next morning, we awoke to Farmer Ford digging giant holes with a backhoe. He dug six large holes on the edge of his property that bordered my property. Farmer Ford then took six junked cars and planted them nose-first into the ground so that the cars were vertically "planted."

18. The six cars were standard sedans, which are 16 feet in length and 6 feet wide, and were planted about one foot apart from each other.

19. After "planting" the cars, Farmer Ford he asked us, "Aren't you happy now? You've got your stupid fence for free and I am growing crops again! This should be a good year to grow sedans, ha, ha!"

20. I told him that I would sue him if he did not remove his "Hillbilly Stonehenge" immediately.

21. Farmer Ford told us to calm down and that he planted the cars out of humor and as a temporary advertising gimmick for his new business. He said he planned to take it down after a few months.

22. We don't believe him. We think he did it to spite us because of our complaints and threats to sue.

I declare under penalty of perjury under the laws of the State of Rhode Island that the above is true and correct to the best of my recollection and understanding.

John Campbell

John Campbell

R.I. Gen. Laws 34–10–1

General Laws of Rhode Island

TITLE 34. PROPERTY
CHAPTER 10. FENCES

§ 34–10–1. Lawful fences defined

The following fences shall be adjudged to be lawful fences:

(1) A hedge with a ditch shall be three feet (3') high upon the bank of the ditch, well staked, at the distance of two feet and a half (2 1/2'), bound together at the top and sufficiently filled to prevent small stock from creeping through; and the bank of the ditch shall not be less than one foot (1') above the surface of the ground.

(2) A hedge without a ditch shall be four feet (4') high, staked, bound and filled, as a hedge with a ditch.

(3) A post-and-rail fence on the bank of a ditch shall be four (4) rails high, each well set in posts, and not less than four feet and a half (4 1/2') high.

(4) A stone wall fence shall be four feet (4') high, with a flat stone hanging over the top thereof or a good rail or pole thereon, well staked or secured with crotches or posts.

(5) A stone wall without flat stones, rails or posts on the top, shall be four feet and a half (4 1/2') high.

(6) A woven wire fence of wire not less than number nine, firmly fastened to posts not more than sixteen feet (16') apart, constructed of not less than eleven (11) horizontal wires, the top wire not less than fifty-four inches (54") from the ground, the bottom wire not more than two inches (2") from the ground and with stays or uprights not more than six inches (6") apart.

(7) All other kinds of fences not herein particularly described shall be four feet and a half (4 1/2') high.

§ 34–10–20. Spite fences

A fence or other structure in the nature of a fence which unnecessarily exceeds six feet (6') in height and is maliciously erected or maintained for the purpose of annoying the owners or occupants of adjoining property, shall be deemed a private nuisance, and any owner or occupant who is injured, either in the comfort or enjoyment of his or her estate thereby, may have an action to recover damages for the injury.

MUSUMECI et ux.

v.

LEONARDO et ux.

Supreme Court of Rhode Island

75 A.2d 175

July 13, 1950

CONDON

* * *

Fundamentally, the question raised by the appeal is whether a fence erected on one's own land with the intent to deprive an adjacent landowner of light and air is a private nuisance which equity will enjoin. Such a fence is popularly called a 'spite fence.' In this state, by virtue of General Laws 1938, chapter 645, § 20, a fence substantially of that character is deemed a private nuisance and one injured thereby is expressly given a right of **176 action at law for damages.

* * *

The evidence shows that respondents' land is higher than complainants' land. On the boundary there is a cement retaining wall which is about six feet from complainants' house and varies in height from five to seven feet. At its highest point it is about on a level with the top of the lower sash of the windows on the first floor and at its lowest point is about level with the bottom of such window sash. About two feet from this wall on their own land and parallel to the whole side of complainants' house facing the wall respondents have erected a board fence varying in height from five feet four inches to five feet six inches. Some of the posts, however, are as high as six feet, but none of the boarding is of that height. The fence is considerably higher than the top of the windows on the first floor. This admittedly blocks the view from such windows, darkens the rooms on that floor, and cuts off air.

Respondent Vincenzo Leonardo erected the fence as a result of an altercation with complainants' daughter, Mrs. Anna Fascitelli, in the summer of 1948 which arose in the following manner. It seems that on several occasions during that summer respondent while watering his garden had allowed water to go beyond into complainants' premises and through the open windows of Mrs. Fascitelli's apartment on the first floor which damaged her wallpaper and curtains and caused puddles on her rugs. She testified that she complained to him about this but that he ignored such complaints. As a result, ill feeling grew up between them, and finally Mrs. Fascitelli called respondent a vile name. Whereupon, according to Mrs. Fascitelli, the respondent said: '* * * I will fix you. I will build a fence so high I won't let you see no light and no sun any more.' The respondent, however, testified that he erected the fence to protect his interests and so that no water would go over the wall when he was watering his garden, and also to keep children out of his garden and off the wall.

It is obvious from the testimony presented by both sides that the fence itself does not exceed six feet in height nor does the wall and fence together, in our opinion, constitute a 'structure in the nature of a fence.' The wall was built by complainants and is apparently a necessary structure for the mutual benefit of the adjacent proprietors, as it is intended to preserve as nearly as possible the natural contour of the land by holding in place the upper proprietor's soil, thus preventing it from eroding and being cast upon the lower proprietor's land. In itself the wall is not a fence nor does it form any part of the actual board fence which respondents have erected on their own land. This being so, chap. 645, § 20, is not applicable as is clearly evident from its language which is as follows: 'A fence, or other structure in the nature of a fence, which unnecessarily exceeds 6 feet in height, and is maliciously erected or maintained for the purpose of annoying the owners or occupants of adjoining property, shall be deemed a private nuisance, and any such owner or occupant who is injured, either in the comfort or enjoyment of his estate thereby, may have an action of trespass on the case to recover damages for such injury.'

We agree, therefore, with complainants that this statute does not make available to them a remedy at law which would preclude them from relief in equity by injunction, if they are otherwise entitled to that equitable remedy. Hence if the trial justice's decision denying and dismissing**177 the bill of complaint were dependent for its correctness solely on the ground that complainants had a remedy at law by virtue of that section, it would be erroneous. However, we are of the opinion that it can be supported on other grounds.

First, the complainants' evidence does not show that respondents erected and now maintain their fence solely out of unmixed malice toward the complainants. Even the testimony of Mrs. Fascitelli herself tends to show that there was a good reason for some such barrier as the board fence to prevent water from entering her premises when respondent watered his garden. Whether it is effective for that purpose is not important here. The close proximity of the complainants' house to the wall, a matter of a mere six feet, plus the fact that the garden was more than five feet above the level of their lot made it likely that some water might escape from time to time to the complainants' lot below and occasionally enter the open windows of the first floor of their house. That is enough to show that the fence in question can and does perform a useful purpose regardless of the motive for its erection. So that even under the law as laid down in *Burke v. Smith*, 69 Mich. 380, 37 N.W. 838, 8 L.R.A. 184, relied on by complainants, this fence could not, on the evidence here, reasonably be said to be wholly malicious and, therefore, not enjoinable as a 'spite fence' within the meaning of that case.

The authorities cited by the complainants in addition to the Burke case hold that the maintenance of such fences may be enjoined if the alleged malice of the respondents is unmixed with an otherwise useful purpose or benefit to them which the fence will reasonably subserve. 133 A.L.R. 692, Anno. The *Burke case*, 69 Mich. at page 388, 37 N.W. at page 842, states the rule to be 'that no man has a legal right to make a malicious use of his property, *not for any benefit or advantage to himself*, but for the avowed purpose of damaging his neighbor.' (Italics ours.) See also 22 Am.Jur., Fences, § 43, where it is stated that 'Some authorities take the view that a fence erected maliciously and with no purpose other than to shut out light and air from a neighbor's window is a nuisance.' A similar statement of the law is to be found in Joyce, Law of Nuisance, § 37. Tested by those statements the fence in question here is not subject to injunction as a private nuisance.

The decree denying and dismissing the bill is correct, however, for another and stronger reason than those already stated. In this state a fence erected on one's own land for the purpose of shutting off light and air to an adjacent owner is not unlawful unless it violates G.L.1938, chap. 645, § 20. Hence the maintenance of such a fence cannot be enjoined in equity as a private nuisance. It is not a nuisance. In order to be such it would have to violate some right of the adjacent landowner. Under the common law as it is generally applied in America an adjacent proprietor has no right to light and air coming to him across the land of his neighbor. *Trustees Mathewson Street M. E. Church v. Shepard*, 22 R.I. 112, 46 A. 402.

The gravamen of the instant bill of complaint is that respondents have maliciously deprived them of light and air. But if complainants have no right to such light and air, of what does the alleged nuisance consist? They answer: the malice which motivated respondents in erecting the fence. In support of their position they argue that such malicious conduct is a clear violation of that ancient maxim of the law, *sic utere tuo ut alienum non laedas*. Their contention to this effect is borne out by the authorities which they cite, but we think it an unwarranted extension of the maxim. So use your own as not to injure another's property is, indeed, a sound and salutary principle for the promotion of justice, but it may not and should not be applied so as gratuitously to confer upon an adjacent property owner incorporeal rights incidental to his ownership of land which the law does not sanction.

A landowner has no right to the light and air coming to him across his neighbor's land. True, if the light and air be shut off damage may well result to his property for residential purposes, as is alleged here, but it is *damnum absque injuria*. It is damage **178 which the law does not recognize because there is no injury. Where there is no right, a deprivation works no injury. The motive with which the deprivation is caused may well be a wrong but it is a moral wrong too subtle for the law to recognize. And where such recognition is attempted the probabilities of working an injustice to the other landowner are real.

The municipal law regulates the conduct of men in their relations with each other and affords redress where the established civil right of one has been violated by another. Violations of ethics or morals which do not harm the public weal, it wisely leaves to the sanctions of the moral law. At that bar only can the motives of men be fully appraised and fairly judged. Positive law can only approach that ideal of perfect justice when it declares that one may not do what he will with his own to the injury of his neighbor. And so where one uses his property in such a manner as to cast noxious odors, smoke, or other deleterious substances over the land of his neighbor to his injury the law deems such conduct a nuisance in violation of the obligation formulated in that maxim.

This court has applied that concept where one used his property for otherwise legitimate purposes but in such a way that it constituted an annoyance to his neighbors and a potential danger to their property on account of the vibrations caused by the nature of the industrial work being done on his property. *Blomen v. N. Barstow Co.*, 35 R.I. 198, 85 A. 924, 44 L.R.A.,N.S., 1144. Complainants cite such case in support of their position here. The difficulty is that their case in no way resembles that case on its facts. The facts in evidence in the Blomen case properly called for the application of the maxim, as well-established rights belonging to the complainants there were being violated. In the case at bar complainants have no such rights.

Respondents cite a 'spite fence' case from Ohio in which this difference is expounded in considerable detail. *Letts v. Kessler*, 54 Ohio St. 73, 42 N.E. 765, 40 L.R.A. 177. Without adopting all that was there said we nevertheless approve the reasoning therein which distinguishes a case, such as the instant one, involving a deprivation of light and air from cases involving smoke, gas, noisome smells or noises. As that court well remarked in 54 Ohio St. at page 82, 42 N.E. at page 766: 'In such cases something is produced on one's own premises, and conveyed to the premises of another; but in this case nothing is sent, but the air and light are withheld.' See also *Rideout v. Knox*, 148 Mass. 368, 19 N.E. 390, 2 L.R.A. 81, 12 Am.St.Rep. 560; *Keats v. Hugo*, 115 Mass. 204, 15 Am.Rep. 76; *Giller v. West*, 162 Ind. 17, 69 N.E. 548.

The complainants' appeal is denied and dismissed, the decree appealed from is affirmed, and the cause is remanded to the superior court for further proceedings.

BOUTHILLIER

v.

STOLARZ

Superior Court of Rhode Island

Not Reported in A.2d

1999 WL 1334924 (R.I.Super.)

December 17, 1999

THUNBERG

*1 The plaintiffs, Susan R. and James D. Bouthillier have requested that this Court preliminarily enjoin defendant, Thomas Stolarz, from entering upon their property. The intrusion includes the placement of concrete blocks and fences as well as the installation of security cameras and lights upon property the plaintiffs contend is owned by them.

The Bouthilliers purchased their land, which sits upon a very private and rural two acre lot, in August of 1991. After moving in, Mr. Bouthillier went to introduce himself to his neighbor, defendant Stolarz. His neighbor, Mr. Bouthillier testified, resided in a very attractive gambrel amid well-maintained park-like grounds.

The plaintiffs contend that they, as well as their predecessors in title have observed a boundary line established by the defendant in 1980. In May of that year, the defendant placed huge boulders, as well as a row of ornamental arbor vitae along this line. Ever since the plaintiffs moved to the area in 1991, their conduct has been consistent with an understanding that the boulders and trees in a straight line mark the boundary. The plaintiffs cleared, mowed, mulched and stored firewood in a manner which reveals their recognition of the line in question as the true boundary.

All was well until 1997 when this controversy began to erupt. The result is the present state of the area with fences, concrete blocks, cameras and lights installed by the defendant on the plaintiffs' side of the arbor vitae/boulder boundary.

Plaintiff, James Bouthillier, has testified that the installation of these unsightly and invasive items has "wrecked his life." He and Mrs. Bouthillier are anxious and uncomfortable going to their own home at night, never knowing what to expect. The couple's residence has gone from living in "an oasis to hell." It must be noted that the 500 pound concrete blocks were not poured by the defendant until *after* this lawsuit was filed.

Plaintiff asserts that in 1976 a mistake occurred when a surveyor reversed the adjoining lots and placed a pipe at a width of 217 feet instead of 200 feet. Defendant testified that he placed the boulders 17 feet north of the boundary line because he was "trying to balance [his] lot." The evidence of what exists on defendant's property is as compelling as the evidence of what exists on the plaintiffs' property. Mr. Stolarz has done beautiful things with his property. He has designed and constructed a lovely home, thoughtfully placed in the center of his lot. He has created and maintained park-like surroundings with great care. He appears to be a meticulous man with a high appreciation for aesthetics and respect for his own property.

It is thus inconceivable to the Court that Mr. Stolarz would partake in the construction of this truly hideous concrete barrier and fence other than for sheer spite. The Court is certain that a man of his taste would be as repulsed as the plaintiffs are if he had to view this invasive eyesore in his comings and goings and while at his residence.

*2 Every property owner has the fundamental right to the fair use and enjoyment of his or her property. The defendant has interfered with the plaintiffs' property rights in a most vulgar and pernicious fashion.

The Court is satisfied by credible evidence that the plaintiffs have demonstrated a likelihood of success on the merits and that the presence of this egregious "spite fence" is causing them irreparable harm. Therefore, the Court orders that the wire fence, concrete barriers, lights and "security cameras" be removed forthwith. The boulders and arbor vitae are not to be disturbed. The Court does not deem it necessary to require the plaintiffs to post a bond and thus declines to do so.

DOWDELL

v.

BLOOMQUIST

Supreme Court of Rhode Island

847 A.2d 827

March 15, 2004

FLAHERTY

> "Tree at my window, window tree, My sash is lowered when night comes on; But let there never be curtain drawn Between you and me."
>
> —Robert Frost

In the matter before us, four western arborvitae trees are at the plaintiff's window. Sadly, however, the curtains between the neighboring parties have long since been drawn, forever dividing what was once an amicable relationship between them. The fate of the offending trees now hangs in the balance.

The plaintiff, Cheryl Dowdell, brought this action in Superior Court alleging that the defendant, Peter Bloomquist, planted four western arborvitae trees on his Charlestown property solely to exact revenge against her, to retaliate by blocking her view, and in violation of the spite fence statute, G.L.1956 34–10–20. [FN1] She sought legal and equitable relief. After considering the testimony and evidence presented at a nonjury trial, [FN2 Omitted] the presiding Superior Court justice found that the trees were planted to satisfy defendant's malicious intent, not his pretextual desire for privacy, and that defendant had violated 34–10–20. The trial justice granted plaintiff injunctive relief. We affirm the judgment of the trial justice. [FN3 Omitted]

> FN1. General Laws 1956 34–10–20 provides as follows:
>
> "Spite fences.—A fence or other structure in the nature of a fence which unnecessarily exceeds six feet (6') in height and is maliciously erected or maintained for the purpose of annoying the owners or occupants of adjoining property, shall be deemed a private nuisance, and any owner or occupant who is injured, either in the comfort or enjoyment of his or her estate thereby, may have an action to recover damages for the injury."

The facts pertinent to this appeal are as follows. The parties' homes are on adjoining lots in a subdivision of Charlestown, each approximately one acre in size. Dowdell's *829 home sits at a higher elevation than Bloomquist's and has a distant view of the ocean over the Bloomquist property. In June 2000, defendant acquired the home from his mother, Lorraine Bloomquist. Prior to that time, the Dowdell family had an amicable relationship with defendant's mother. Change was in the wind in the fall of 2000, however, when defendant petitioned for a zoning variance from the Charlestown zoning board seeking permission to build a second-story addition to his home. The plaintiff expressed concern about the petition, anxious that the addition would compromise her view of the Atlantic Ocean. For six months the parties argued before the Charlestown Zoning Board of Review as to the merits of the addition. As a result, the relationship between the neighbors became less than friendly. In March 2001, defendant began clearing land and digging holes to plant the disputed trees in a row between their homes. In April, defendant's counsel sent a letter to plaintiff warning him against trespass onto the Bloomquist property. In May, one day after the zoning board closed its hearing on defendant's variance request, [FN4 Omitted] defendant began planting the four western arborvitae trees that now stand in a row bordering the property line. [FN5] Although the forty-foot-high trees enabled little light to pass into Dowdell's second-and third-story picture windows, testimony at trial evidenced that the vegetation was not a bar to the unkind words between the neighbors.

FN5. The western arborvitae were planted directly behind a row of eastern arborvitae already existing on the Dowdell property near its boundary with the Bloomquist land. According to expert testimony at trial, the eastern arborvitae are smaller trees, growing to a height of eight to eleven feet. In contrast, the western arborvitae are capable of growing to a height of seventy feet. Although the Dowdell trees are in excess of six feet, there are no allegations that they were ever placed out of spite and these trees are not the subject of the instant matter. However, the trial justice noted that the Dowdell trees already offered sufficient privacy between the Dowdell and Bloomquist properties and cited this as one reason why he considered defendant's purported privacy motive to be a subterfuge for malicious intent.

After the trial justice heard four days of testimony and viewed the property, he made a finding that the row of trees were a fence, based on the language of § 34–10–1. [FN6] He further found that the objective of privacy claimed by defendant was "no more than a subterfuge for his clear intent to spite his neighbors by erecting a fence of totally out of proportion trees." Hence, the trial justice found that the trees constituted a spite fence in violation of 34–10–20. He noted testimony that plaintiff's real estate values had depreciated by as much as $100,000. Nonetheless, he found that money damages could not adequately compensate her and that equitable relief was more appropriate. Bloomquist was ordered "to cut the four Western Arborvitae to no more than 6' in height and keep them at that level or remove them entirely with no more Western Arborvitae to be planted." [FN7]

FN6. Section 34–10–1 includes in its definition of lawful fences "[a] hedge" of specified proportions. The trial justice concluded that the four arborvitae trees may be considered a hedge based on expert testimony at trial and that, therefore, the trees constitute a fence.

FN7. In employing the language ordering that "no more Western Arborvitae [are] to be planted," we assume that the trial justice is restricting the plantings along the property lines and in the nature of a fence.

*830 The defendant timely appealed to this Court. In his appeal, defendant asserts that the offending trees do not constitute a fence. Moreover, defendant contends that even if the trees were considered a fence, the trial justice erroneously granted relief in the face of testimony that the trees serve a useful purpose of privacy for defendant. To support that contention, defendant relies on *Musumeci v. Leonardo,* 77 R.I. 255, 259–60, 75 A.2d 175, 177–78 (1950), for the proposition that when a fence is erected for a useful purpose, despite spiteful motive, no relief may be granted. Moreover, defendant alleges that the trial justice lacked the authority to award injunctive relief based on the holding of *Musumeci* as well as the specific language of the spite fence statute, which states that one "may have an action to recover damages for the injury." Section 34–10–20. Additionally, defendant urges that the trial justice erred by granting relief that amounted to an easement for light or view where no such remedy exists at common law.

Not surprisingly, plaintiff defends the lower court ruling. She asserts that the trial justice had ample authority to award injunctive relief and correctly exercised this authority based on his well-supported finding that the four trees constituted nothing more than a fence erected out of spite.

The trial justice found a violation of the spite fence statute based on his careful and deliberate findings of fact and on his credibility assessment of the testimony at trial. We are mindful that factual findings "are entitled to great weight and will not be disturbed by this Court absent proof that they are clearly wrong or that the trial justice overlooked or misconceived material evidence." *Tavares v. Beck,* 814 A.2d 346, 350 (R.I.2003) (per curiam); *Perry v. Garey,* 799 A.2d 1018, 1022 (R.I.2002). We grant the same level of deference to a trial justice's determination of credibility. *See Bogosian v. Bederman,* 823 A.2d 1117, 1120 (R.I.2003). Based on this standard, we decline to disturb the trial justice's findings that the four arborvitae trees planted in a row constitute a fence and that defendant planted them with spiteful intentions. Based on the record before us, we cannot say that the trial justice was clearly wrong or that he overlooked or misconceived material evidence with respect to his findings of fact or credibility.

This is the first occasion this Court has had to address the issue of whether a row of trees may be considered a fence within the meaning of the spite fence statute, 34–10–20. We believe the trial justice properly referred to the definition of "lawful fences" found in § 34–10–1 to understand the simple meaning and legislative intent behind its use of the word "fence." Based upon the language of § 34–10–1, a fence clearly includes a hedge. And based upon the expert testimony relied on by the trial justice, a row of western arborvitae trees may constitute a hedge. However, even if the trees were not a hedge per se, the spite fence statute refers to "[a] fence or other structure in the nature of a fence." The trial justice considered the proximity of the four trees that touched one another, and the broad span of sixty feet across which they spread, and rationally interpreted that the trees were a fence. Although defendant argues that he presented expert testimony that the western arborvitae is not a hedge plant, we nonetheless believe that the trees, when taken as a whole, fall well within the statutory definition of a "structure in the nature of a fence." This may not be the most optimal species for the creation of a hedge owing to their enormous stature and girth. However, it is *831 specifically because of their towering presence, as well as their relative positioning on defendant's land, that we can consider the trees nothing less than a fence. We are not alone in this assessment. Recently, a California appellate court found a row of evergreen trees to be a fence within the meaning of the California spite fence statute. [FN8 Omitted] *Wilson v. Handley,* 97 Cal.App.4th 1301, 119 Cal.Rptr.2d 263 (2002). That court stated,

> "In light of this statutory purpose, a structure need not be built to prevent intrusion from without or straying from within to be a 'fence or other structure in the nature of a fence' within the meaning of the spite fence statute. Instead, the structure need only be built to separate or mark the boundary between adjoining parcels—albeit, in an unnecessarily high and annoying manner." Id. at 269.

We next consider defendant's contention that the trial justice erroneously discounted defendant's testimony that the trees were erected for the beneficial purpose of privacy. We recognize that some useful purpose for a fence may render the victim of one even maliciously erected without a remedy. In *Musumeci,* this Court determined that a fence served the useful purpose of preventing water from entering the premises of the first floor of the complainant's house. Hence, because the purpose of the fence was not wholly malicious, it was not enjoined as a private nuisance. *Musumeci,* 77 R.I. at 258–59, 75 A.2d at 177 (citing *Burke v. Smith,* 69 Mich. 380, 37 N.W. 838 (1888) (one of the first cases announcing the new American rule on spite fences, now considered to embody the prevailing modern view)). However, based on the turbulent history between the parties, the provocative statements made by defendant, the notice of trespass letter sent to plaintiff, and the size, timing, and placement of the trees, we cannot say that the trial justice was wrong to give defendant's testimony little weight and to find his claim that the fence was installed to enhance his privacy lacked credibility. In the circumstances of this case, we agree with the trial justice that defendant needed to provide more than just privacy as justification for the fence. This is especially true when a row of smaller arborvitae already stood between the homes. As the trial justice noted, "Accepting privacy alone would simply result in the statute being rendered meaningless and absurd." The very nature of a fence is such that privacy could always be given as the reason for erecting it. In an egregious case such as this, where evidence of malicious intent plainly outweighs the discounted benefit claimed by defendant, the court correctly found defendant's actions to violate the spite fence statute.

That said, the final issue to be determined is whether injunctive relief was an appropriate remedy for the aggrieved plaintiff. The defendant relies on *Musumeci* for the proposition that plaintiff is not entitled to injunctive relief because the loss of light and view that she alleges is not a private nuisance that equity will enjoin. Moreover, he maintains that the spite fence statute provides only for a monetary damages remedy. However, *832 upon careful review of the language of 34–10–20, this Court's discussion in *Musumeci,* and the law of private nuisance, we believe that injunctive relief is an available remedy for a violation of the spite fence statute. Consequently, we affirm the remedy ordered by the trial justice that the offending western arborvitae trees be topped off at six feet, or otherwise removed entirely.

The defendant mischaracterizes *Musumeci* as both relevant and conclusive authority on remedy in the instant case. In *Musumeci,* it was determined that a wall standing less than six feet tall and which served a useful purpose of blocking water run off onto the plaintiff's property was not a spite fence and therefore not governed by G.L.1938 ch. 645, 20, [FN9] the predecessor to the present spite fence statute, 34–10–20. The Court then said that "a fence erected on one's own land for the purpose of shutting off light and air to an adjacent owner is not unlawful unless it violates G.L.1938, chap. 645, 20." *Musumeci,* 77 R.I. at 259–60, 75 A.2d at 177. Having found no statutory violation, the Musumeci Court addressed the issue of whether an equitable remedy was available to the aggrieved party for the shutting off of light and air out of malice, notwithstanding the inapplicability of the spite fence statute. The Court held that absent a tangible violation to the adjacent landowner's rights, the fence could not be enjoined as a private nuisance because under the common law he has no right to light and air coming across the land. Hence, there was no nuisance. *Id.* at 260, 75 A.2d at 177–78. We distinguish *Musumeci* from the instant case based on the factual and legal distinctions at play in each case. Although *Musumeci* confirms that there is no common law right to light and air, it does not preclude equitable relief for erection of a spite fence. When the spite fence statute is violated, which was not the case in *Musumeci,* the offending action is deemed a "private nuisance." *See* 34–10–20. Under private nuisance law, equitable relief is an appropriate remedy. *See Harris v. Town of Lincoln,* 668 A.2d 321 (R.I.1995) (private nuisance of emission of noises, odors, and vibrations by sewer-processing facility pumping station onto neighboring residential property warranted injunctive relief, in addition to monetary damages); *Weida v. Ferry,* 493 A.2d 824 (R.I.1985) (noxious smells and flies emanating from dairy farm operations more suitably classified as a private nuisance rather than negligence action; case remanded for new trial with presumption that equitable relief would be an appropriate remedy had the farm not already ceased operations by this time); *DeNucci v. Pezza,* 114 R.I. 123, 329 A.2d 807 (1974) (injunctive relief properly granted upon trial justice's finding that noise from freight trucks hitching and unhitching in parking lot during early morning hours was unreasonable private nuisance interfering with the plaintiff's use and enjoyment of his residential property).

FN9. General Laws 1938 ch. 645, 20 closely mirrors the language of 34–10–20 and provided the following:

"A fence, or other structure in the nature of a fence, which unnecessarily exceeds 6 feet in height, and is maliciously erected or maintained for the purpose of annoying the owners or occupants of adjoining property, shall be deemed a private nuisance, and any such owner or occupant who is injured, either in the comfort or enjoyment of his estate thereby, may have an action of trespass on the case to recover damages for such injury."

We look to the case of Wilson for additional support that a spite fence that blocks light, air, or view is properly considered an actionable private nuisance because the statute defines it as such. In *833 *Wilson,* the court held that a row of trees blocking the plaintiff's view of Mt. Shasta may be considered a violation of the statute even though the fence interfered with nothing more than light and air. The court acknowledged that although interference with light and air was not considered a nuisance under the general definition of "nuisance," the spite fence statute never specified that the fence need interfere with more than light and air for it to be considered a nuisance. The court concluded that "we are not at liberty to read any such additional requirement into the statute." *Wilson,* 119 Cal.Rptr.2d at 270. We agree. What makes a spite fence a nuisance under 34–10–20 is not merely that it blocks the passage of light and view, but that it does so "unnecessarily" for the malicious purpose of "annoyance." This is a notable distinction.

Finally, defendant correctly asserts that the statute specifically allows for "an action to recover damages." Specifically, the statute states that one who is injured by a spite fence "*may* have an action to recover damages for the injury." Section 34–10–20. (Emphasis added.) However, contrary to defendant's assertion, we believe this language merely sanctions the additional remedy of damages, but does not exclude injunctive relief, which is a remedy logically rooted in the nature and purpose of the statute. To support this holding, we look to the remedial practice in other states that recognize the erection of a spite fence as actionable. Connecticut, Idaho, Indiana, Massachusetts, Montana, New Hampshire, and South Dakota all allow injunctive relief for violations of spite fence law. [FN10 Omitted] Especially illustrative is the law as it stands in Massachusetts, whose statute is strikingly similar to 34–10–20. The Massachusetts statute provides:

> "A fence or other structure in the nature of a fence which unnecessarily exceeds six feet in height and is maliciously erected or maintained for the purpose of annoying the owners or occupants of adjoining property shall be deemed a private nuisance. Any such owner or occupant injured * * * may have an action of tort for damages * * *." Mass. Gen. Laws Ann. ch. 49, 21 (West 1994).

In interpreting this law, the Supreme Judicial Court of Massachusetts recognized that despite the lack of explicit language, the court had the authority to order a spite fence to be "abated," in addition to damages and costs. *Rice v. Moorehouse,* 150 Mass. 482, 23 N.E. 229 (1890) (trial justice properly ordered abatement of so much of a spite fence as exceeded six feet in height). The Court relied on the law of nuisance as the basis for its decision, just as we do today.

Conclusion

For the reasons set forth above, we affirm the judgment of the Superior Court. The record shall be remanded to the Superior Court.

WORKSHEET NO. 2: THE PERSUASIVE RULE

Rule drafting in persuasive writing is different from rule drafting in objective writing. The main differences are in the organization, the breadth and depth of the rule, and the persuasive tone.

Before writing a persuasive rule, however, you should write the rule objectively first to ensure accuracy. Crafting an objective rule first will also offer perspective on the neutral rule the judge will consider when evaluating your persuasive rule. To write the rule objectively, use the approach explained in Worksheet No. 2 for Objective Writing, which is summarized below:

To determine rules of law from a single source or multiple sources of law, including the elements, definitions, and/or exceptions, answer the following brainstorming questions:

1. What is the rule?
2. What are the exceptions to the rule, if any?
3. What else will the court consider, if anything?

After answering these three questions, put your answers together in one or more sentences to write the rule. Once you have written a rule, evaluate it to ensure it is complete and appropriate in scope. To evaluate the rule(s), answer the following questions:

1. Is the rule too specific based on the legal authority and your client facts?
2. Is the rule too broad based on the legal authority and your client facts?
3. Does the rule include vague terms?
4. Is the rule circular?
5. If there is more than one rule, are the rules repetitive?

After answering the above questions, you should have a complete objective rule. Now you need to start thinking about how to write your objective rule persuasively. To help you do this, consider the following brainstorming questions:

1. Who is your client?
2. What outcome do you want for your client based on this rule?
3. What part of the rule do you want to emphasize for your client?
4. What part of the rule do you want to de-emphasize for your client?

Using the answers to these brainstorming questions as your guide, convert your objective rule into a persuasive rule. To write your persuasive rule, look at your objective rule, your answers to the above brainstorming questions, and the following considerations:

1. Begin the rule with the outcome you want for your client; that is, if you want an injunction to be granted begin by stating "An injunction will be granted when ..."
2. Begin the rule with your client's role in the litigation; that is, Plaintiff or Defendant. For example, "A plaintiff is entitled to an injunction when ..."
3. Include the favorable part of the rule at the beginning to provide emphasis.
4. Include unfavorable parts of the rule in the middle to bury them.
5. Emphasize the opposing party's requirements of proof (burdens, elements, evidence, etc.). For example, "For a defendant to prevail on his motion, he must prove five elements with substantial evidence." Or, "Defendant has the burden of proof."

Once you have written your rule persuasively, evaluate it for persuasive tone and presentation. To evaluate whether your rule is persuasively written for your client's case, answer the following questions:

1. Did you use active or passive voice? (Consider the benefits of each.)
2. Did you put your client's position in a point of emphasis in the rule?
3. If the rule is favorable, did you state it broadly?
4. If the rule is unfavorable, did you state it narrowly?
5. If there is an exception to the rule, did you include it in a way that is favorable to your client?

EXAMPLE OBJECTIVE RULE:

California Civil Code Section 3344(a) provides that the knowing use of another's photograph for commercial purposes without the person's prior consent is a violation of that person's right of publicity. Section 3344(d) provides an exception to the consent requirement contained in § 3344(a), which states that the use of a photograph in connection with "any news, public affairs, or sports broadcast or account, or any political campaign" does not require consent.

EXAMPLE PERSUASIVE RULE:

The knowing use of another's photograph for commercial purposes without the person's consent violates California Civil Code Section 3344(a). The only exception to the statutory consent requirement is if the defendant can prove that the use of a photograph was in connection with a matter in the public interest. Cal. Civ. Code § 3344(d).

Case File Assignment:

Write a persuasive rule for your client's case on the issue of what constitutes a spite fence using the legal authorities in the Case File. To help you write a persuasive rule, begin by writing an objective rule, or use the objective rule you wrote for Worksheet No. 2 for Objective Writing.

State your objective rule here:

Convert the objective rule into a persuasive rule. To help do this, answer the following brainstorming questions:

1. Who is your client?

2. What outcome do you want for your client based on this rule?

3. What part of the rule do you want to emphasize for your client?

4. What part of the rule do you want to de-emphasize for your client?

Using the answers to these brainstorming questions as your guide, convert your objective rule into a persuasive rule. To write your persuasive rule, look at your objective rule, your answers to the above brainstorming questions, and the following considerations:

1. Begin the rule with the outcome you want for your client; that is, if you want an injunction to be granted begin by stating "An injunction will be granted when …"
2. Begin the rule with your client's role in the litigation; that is, Plaintiff or Defendant. For example, "A plaintiff is entitled to an injunction when …"
3. Include the favorable part of the rule at the beginning to provide emphasis.
4. Include unfavorable parts of the rule in the middle to bury them.
5. Emphasize the opposing party's requirements of proof (burdens, elements, evidence, etc.). For example, "For a defendant to prevail on his motion, he must prove five elements with substantial evidence." Or, "Defendant has the burden of proof."

Once you have written the rule persuasively, evaluate it for persuasive tone and presentation. To evaluate whether your rule is persuasively written for your client, answer the following questions:

1. Did you use active or passive voice? (Consider the benefits of each.)
2. Did you put your client's position in a point of emphasis in the rule?
3. If the rule is favorable, did you state it broadly?
4. If the rule is unfavorable, did you state it narrowly?
5. If there is an exception to the rule, did you include it in a way that is favorable to your client?

WORKSHEET NO. 3: PARENTHETICALS

Parentheticals are a quick way to provide the reader with illustrations of a legal principle without having to include an objective case illustration. Writing parentheticals, however, can be tricky because you must include enough information for the reader to understand the significance of the precedent case and its connection to the legal principle the parenthetical is explaining, but not include so much information that you effectively have written an objective case illustration.

A parenthetical is substantively correct if it includes:

1. The legal principle or rule you plan to explain with the parenthetical;
2. The relevant facts from the precedent case that support the legal principle you plan to explain with the parenthetical; and
3. The key words and phrases from the precedent case that support the legal principle you plan to explain with the parenthetical.

A parenthetical is technically correct if it:

1. Asserts a legal principle prior to the parentheticals;
2. Follows the legal principle with a proper citation;
3. Has proper capitalization within the parenthetical—do not capitalize the first word of a parenthetical if it is only a word, phase, or clause; but do capitalize the first word of a parenthetical if it is a complete sentence;
4. Uses parallel construction for string parentheticals—if you use one form for one parenthetical, use that same form for all of the parentheticals in the string; and
5. Is kept short—if the information you want to provide cannot be provided in a phase, clause, or a single sentence, do not use a parenthetical.

Here are some examples that demonstrate parentheticals with "not enough" information and parentheticals with "enough" information. Please note the legal principle that precedes the parentheticals.

EXAMPLE PARENTHETICALS:

NOT ENOUGH INFORMATION IN THE PARENTHETICALS:

Although celebrities have the right to First Amendment protection from the unauthorized exploitation of their photographs under the right of publicity, the statutory cause of action specifically exempts from liability the use of a photograph in connection with a matter in the public interest. California Civil Code 3344(d) states that no prior consent is required for use of a photograph in the public interest, such as news, public affairs, or sports broadcast or account, or any political campaign. Public interest has been defined as "recent events or publications about people who, by their accomplishments, mode of living, professional standing or calling, create a legitimate and widespread attention to their activities." Dora v. Frontline Video, Inc., 15 Cal. App. 4th 536 (2nd Dist. 1993) (a 1987 surfing documentary); Gionfriddo v. Major League Baseball, 94 Cal. App. 4th 400 (1st Dist. 2001) (web cast of baseball statistics).

ENOUGH INFORMATION IN THE PARENTHETICALS:

Although celebrities have the right to First Amendment protection from the unauthorized exploitation of their photographs under the right of publicity, the statutory cause of action specifically exempts from liability the use of a photograph in connection with a matter in the public interest. California Civil Code 3344(d) states that no prior consent is required for use of a photograph in the public interest, such as news, public affairs, or sports broadcast or account, or any political campaign. Public interest has been defined as "recent events or publications about people who, by their accomplishments, mode of living, professional standing or calling, create a legitimate and widespread attention to their activities." Dora v. Frontline Video, Inc., 15 Cal. App. 4th 536 (2nd Dist. 1993) (a 1987 surfing documentary that included footage of a famous surfer was in the public interest and no prior consent was needed); Gionfriddo v. Major League Baseball, 94 Cal. App. 4th 400 (1st Dist. 2001) (web cast of baseball statistics that included a photograph of a famous baseball player was in the public interest and no prior consent was needed).

Case File Assignment:

Write a parenthetical(s) for your client's case using the legal authority in the Case File and/or the legal authority assigned by your professor. To help you write a parenthetical(s), answer the following brainstorming questions for each precedent case you plan to explain with a parenthetical:

1. What is the legal principle you plan to explain with a parenthetical(s)? Please note that this legal principle may precede more than one parenthetical (see examples above).

2. For each precedent case you plan to explain with a parenthetical, answer the following brainstorming questions:

    a. What is the proper citation for the precedent case you plan to explain with the parenthetical?

    b. What are the relevant facts from the precedent case that support the legal principle you plan to explain with the parenthetical?

    c. What is the legal conclusion from the precedent case that supports the legal principle you plan to explain with the parenthetical?

    d. What are the key words and phrases from the precedent case that support the legal principle you plan to explain with the parenthetical?

Using your answers to these brainstorming questions as your guide, you now are ready to write a parenthetical(s). Use one of the formulas below to organize your parenthetical(s). The order of the information contained inside the parentheticals can be reversed.

One Parenthetical:

Legal Principle. Cite (relevant facts + legal conclusion to support the legal principle, using the key words and phrases from the precedent case).

Multiple Parentheticals:

Legal Principle. Cite (relevant facts + legal conclusion to support the legal principle, using the key words and phrases from the precedent case); Cite (relevant facts + legal conclusion to support the legal principle, using the key words and phrases from the precedent case); Cite (relevant facts + legal conclusion to support the legal principle, using the key words and phrases from the precedent case).

When writing parenthetical(s), consider the following technical requirements:

1. Use proper capitalization within the parenthetical—do not capitalize the first word of a parenthetical if it is only a word, phase, or clause; but do capitalize the first word of a parenthetical if it is a complete sentence;

2. Use parallel construction for string parentheticals—if you use one form for one parenthetical use that same form for all of the parentheticals in the string; and

3. Keep it short—if the information you want to provide cannot be provided in a phase, clause, or a single sentence, do not use a parenthetical.

WORKSHEET NO. 4: DEDUCTIVE REASONING

Deductive reasoning justifies a result by directly applying a legal principle to the facts of your client's case. The result is the result simply because the law mandates it. There is no in-depth analysis, but rather a straightforward application of the legal principle to the facts of the client's case.

Deductive reasoning is substantively correct if it includes:

1. The legal principle or rule you are applying;
2. The legal conclusion you seek to establish by the application of the legal principle or rule; and
3. The relevant facts from your client's case needed to justify that legal conclusion.

*Please note that 2 and 3 can be reversed and that deductive reasoning is frequently paired with parentheticals.

EXAMPLE DEDUCTIVE REASONING:

It is illegal for anyone under the age of sixteen to operate a motor vehicle. (Citation omitted). The defendant illegally operated a motor vehicle because she was only thirteen years old at the time she drove her father's car.

EXAMPLE DEDUCTIVE REASONING WITH PARENTHETICALS:

Although celebrities have the right to First Amendment protection from the unauthorized exploitation of their photographs under the right of publicity, the statutory cause of action specifically exempts from liability the use of a photograph in connection with a matter in the public interest. California Civil Code 3344(d) states that no prior consent is required for use of a photograph in the public interest, such as news, public affairs, or sports broadcast or account, or any political campaign. Public interest has been defined as "recent events or publications about people who, by their accomplishments, mode of living, professional standing or calling, create a legitimate and widespread attention to their activities." Dora v. Frontline Video, Inc., 15 Cal. App. 4th 536 (2nd Dist. 1993) (a 1987 surfing documentary that included footage of a famous surfer was in the public interest and no prior consent was needed); Gionfriddo v. Major League Baseball, 94 Cal. App. 4th 400 (1st Dist. 2001) (web cast of baseball statistics that included a photograph of a famous baseball player in the public interest and no prior consent was needed). Because the use of Mr. Quarterback's photograph was used in connection with his fourth Superbowl victory in ten years, it is in the public interest and his consent was not required.

Case File Assignment:

Write an argument for your client's case using deductive reasoning based on the legal authority in the Case File and/or the legal authority assigned by your professor. To help you write a deductive reasoning argument, answer the following brainstorming questions:

1. What is the legal principle or rule that you want to apply to your client's case?

2. What is the legal conclusion you seek to establish by the application of the legal principle or rule?

3. What are the relevant facts from your client's case needed to justify that legal conclusion?

Using the answers to these brainstorming questions as your guide, write an argument using deductive reasoning. Start by cutting and pasting your answers into paragraph form and then mold them into a readable sentence or paragraph. Consider whether the deductive reasoning will follow a simple legal principle or a legal principle with parentheticals.

WORKSHEET NO. 5: POLICY-BASED REASONING

Policy-based reasoning in persuasive writing is not that different from policy-based reasoning in objective writing. The organization of the substance is the same; however, the presentation of the substance is different.

To write a persuasive policy-based argument, start by evaluating the policy-based argument objectively (as explained in Worksheet No. 5 for Objective Writing). To do this, consider:

1. The conclusion you will reach by applying the policy to your client's case. (You may need to answer this question after you have completed your analysis of the policy.)
2. The rule you are applying to your client's case.
3. The purpose underlying the rule identified in response to Question 2 above and the origin of that purpose. What greater societal purpose(s) was the court or legislature trying to protect in creating the rule? (NOTE: There may be more than one purpose. If there is more than one purpose, identify if the court seems to prefer one purpose over another.) Also, the purpose behind the rule should come from legal authority, such as legislative history, case authority, or well-established public opinion, not your personal opinion.
4. The potential outcomes for your client when applying the rule.
5. The potential outcomes for the other party when applying the rule.
6. How the outcomes identified in response to Questions 4 and 5 above are or are not served by the purpose(s) of the rule you identified in response to Question 3 above.
7. The outcome that best follows the purpose of the rule.

After evaluating these questions, you should have an objective understanding of whether the purpose(s) of the rule supports the arguments for your client's case. If it does, use the following formula to write a policy-based reasoning argument for your client's case. If it does not support the arguments for your client's case, do not include a policy-based argument.

A persuasive policy-based reasoning argument is substantively complete if it:

1. Begins the argument by stating the conclusion you want to argue by applying the purpose of the rule to your client's case. (This is the thesis sentence for this argument).
2. States the rule that is the basis of the policy-based reasoning argument.
3. Identifies and describes the purpose underlying the rule and the origin of that purpose. Remember, the purpose behind the rule must come from legal authority, such as legislative history, case authority,

or well-established public opinion, not your personal opinion. Also, if there is more than one purpose, explain which one the courts tend to use more.

4. States persuasively that the purpose underlying the rule applies to your client's case.
5. Explains with specific detail why the possible outcome(s) for your client furthers the purpose underlying the rule.
6. Concludes with a sentence that provides closure to the policy-based reasoning argument. This sentence must connect to the thesis sentence that began the policy-based reasoning argument.

> EXAMPLE POLICY–BASED REASONING ARGUMENT:
>
> Ms. Anchor's claim is supported by the purpose underlying the statute. While § 3344(d) protects information that is directly related to matters in the public interest, the legislature did not intend to protect false information that is presented as news. Eastwood, 149 Cal. App. 3d at 425. The Legislature stated that the public interest exception cannot be exercised so as to abuse the rights of individuals. Id. This policy applies to Ms. Anchor's case. Ms. Anchor denies that she ever reported on the Mayor's campaign and the general manager of her news station stated that "there are no concerns about Ms. Anchor's ethics whatsoever." Yet, TFF created a t-shirt that directly challenged Ms. Anchor's ethics. It is exactly this type of dissemination of false information the Legislature did not intend the public interest exception to protect. Id. Therefore, Ms. Anchor's right of publicity supported by the policy behind the statute and TFF's unauthorized use of her photograph is not protected.

Case File Assignment:

Write an argument for your client's case using policy-based reasoning based on the legal authority in the Case File and/or the legal authority assigned by your professor. To help you write a policy-based reasoning argument, answer the following brainstorming questions:

1. What is the conclusion you want to argue by applying the policy to your client's case? (You may need to answer this question last.)

2. What is the rule you are applying to your client's case?

3. What is the purpose underlying the rule identified in response to Question 2 above and the origin of that purpose? What greater societal purpose(s) was the court or legislature trying to protect in creating the rule? (NOTE: There may be more than one purpose. If there is more than one purpose, identify if the court seems to prefer one purpose over another.) Also, the purpose behind the rule should come from legal authority, such as legislative history, case authority, or well-established public opinion, not your personal opinion.

4. What are the potential outcomes for your client when applying the rule?

5. What are the potential outcomes for the other party when applying the rule?

6. How are the outcomes identified in response to Questions 4 and 5 above served or not served by the purpose(s) of the rule identified in response to Question 3 above?

7. Which outcome best follows the purpose(s) of the rule? Explain why.

After answering these brainstorming questions, you should have a clear understanding of whether the possible outcomes for your client do or do not serve the underlying purpose of the rule. If the purpose of the rule is served by your client's case, then use the following formula to write a policy-based reasoning argument. Each of these six parts must be included for a complete policy-based reasoning argument. This does not mean, however, that you need to have six sentences; a complete policy-based reasoning argument may be less than three sentences or as much as two full paragraphs.

1. Begin the paragraph(s) by stating the conclusion you want to argue by applying the purpose of the rule to your client's case. (This is the thesis sentence for this paragraph).
2. State the rule that is the basis of the policy-based reasoning argument.
3. Identify and describe the purpose underlying the rule and the origin of that purpose. Remember, the purpose behind the rule must come from legal authority, such as legislative history, case authority, or well-established public opinion. It is not your personal opinion on the purpose of the rule. Also, if there is more than one purpose, explain which one the courts tend to use more.
4. State persuasively that the purpose underlying the rule applies to your client's case.
5. Explain with specific detail why the possible outcome(s) for your client furthers the purpose underlying the rule.
6. Conclude with a sentence that provides closure to the policy-based reasoning argument. This sentence must connect to the thesis sentence that began the policy-based reasoning argument.

WORKSHEET NO. 6: ANALOGICAL REASONING

Analogical reasoning in persuasive writing is not that different from analogical reasoning in objective writing. The organization of the substance is essentially the same; however, to effectively persuade the reader, the content and presentation of the substance is different.

The two main differences between analogical reasoning in persuasive writing and objective writing are: (1) the depth of the substance provided and (2) the tone.

First, the depth of the substance provided is different in persuasive writing because there are no case illustrations or a traditional E section in persuasive writing as there is in objective writing. Instead, in persuasive writing the law is explained in the context of the analysis. Thus, the description of the precedent case in the persuasive analogical reasoning formula is more detailed than the description of the precedent case in the objective analogical reasoning formula.

Second, the tone must be more argumentative. Unlike objective writing, where the goal is to demonstrate to the reader all possible arguments and counter-arguments from a neutral perspective, in persuasive writing the goal is to persuade the reader to agree with your argument. Thus, in persuasive writing, you must state the arguments affirmatively and conclusively, begin with your strongest argument (or strongest analogy or distinction), and really prove the connection between the client's case and the precedent case(s).

To write analogical reasoning in persuasive writing, start by first evaluating the analogical reasoning argument objectively using the same brainstorming process used for analogical reasoning in objective writing (see Worksheet No. 6 for Objective Writing), which is provided below:

1. Identify one issue you plan to address with analogical reasoning.
2. Identify the name of one precedent case you plan to use for the issue you selected above.
3. Identify the specific holding of the precedent case on the legal issue you plan to argue with this analogical reasoning (NOTE: This must only be the holding specific to the legal issue you are addressing, not the overall holding of the precedent case).
4. Describe the reasoning of the precedent case on the legal issue you plan to argue with this analogical reasoning (NOTE: This must only be the reasoning specific to the legal issue you are addressing, not the overall reasoning of the precedent case).
5. Make a list of the relevant facts from the precedent case on the legal issue you plan to argue with this analogical reasoning (NOTE: This must only be the facts specific to the legal issue you are addressing, not all of the facts from the precedent case).

6. Make a list of the relevant facts from your client's case on the legal issue you plan to argue with this analogical reasoning (NOTE: This must only be the facts specific to the legal issue you are addressing, not all of the facts from your client's case).

7. Group the facts of the precedent case and your client's case into facts that are similar and facts that are distinguishable.

Depending on whether the facts are the similar or distinguishable or both, you may only need to consider some of the questions below. If the facts are similar, answer Questions 8–10. If the facts are distinguishable, answer Questions 11–13. If the facts are both similar and distinguishable, answer Questions 8–13.

8. Identify the fact(s) to be compared in your analysis as similar. (NOTE: This must only be the facts specific to the legal issue you are addressing, not all of the facts from the precedent case or your client's case.)

9. Explain why you think these facts are similar—use specific factual examples to demonstrate the similarities.

10. Explain *why* these factual similarities support your legal analysis on the issue you are addressing. This is where you must directly apply the reasoning of the precedent case to the facts of your client's case. Specifically look at why and how the precedent case ruled as it did and why that same reasoning applies to your client's case.

11. Identify the fact(s) to be compared in your analysis as distinguishable. (NOTE: This must only be the facts specific to the legal issue you are addressing and not all of the facts from the precedent case or your client's case.)

12. Explain why you think these facts are distinguishable—use specific factual examples to demonstrate the differences.

13. Explain *why* these factual differences support your legal analysis on the issue you are addressing. This is where you must directly apply the reasoning of the precedent case to the facts of your client's case. Specifically look at why and how the precedent case ruled as it did and why that same reasoning does not apply to your client's case.

After evaluating these brainstorming questions, you should have a clear understanding of whether an analogical reasoning argument should be made in your client's case. You then must decide if the analogical reasoning will be based on a single case or multiple cases. If multiple cases are used to argue the same legal issue, then you must make these arguments at the same time, rather than as a separate analogical reasoning for each precedent case. Once you have decided if the analogical reasoning will be based on a single case or multiple cases, use one of the following formulas to write your analogical reasoning argument:

Analogical Reasoning Formula Using a Single Case:

Component 1: Persuasively state the legal conclusion you want the reader to reach based on your analogical reasoning (this is the overall thesis sentence for the analogical reasoning paragraph or paragraphs—case names should not be included in this sentence).

Component 2: Sentence stating, "In client's case (use client's name) is similar to/distinguishable from _______ (insert precedent case name) based on _______ (identify the specific issue this analogical reasoning is addressing)."

Component 3: Sentence stating, "In client's case (use client's name), (insert the specific facts about your client's case that will be compared; these are not all of the facts of the case but only the specific facts that will be compared)."

Component 4: Sentence stating, "This case is similar to/distinguishable from _______ (insert precedent case name). In _______ (insert precedent case name) where (insert detailed information about the facts, the holding, and the reasoning from the precedent case you are relying upon that are related to the specific issue to be compared)." Remember to describe the precedent case in a way that is favorable to your client's position.

Component 5: Explain, using *specific factual detail*, why the facts you are comparing are similar or distinguishable. This is where you need to provide specific fact-to-fact comparisons, using actual facts from your client's case and the precedent case. (i.e.—"Fact X in client's case is similar to/distinguishable from Fact Y in precedent case because _______"). Remember to make these factual comparisons in a way that is favorable to your client's position.

Component 6: Persuasively re-state the likely outcome of your client's case based on the similarities or differences you discussed in Component 5. This is a re-statement of the conclusion (Component 1) but with more detail and this likely is the beginning of a new paragraph.

Component 7: Explain *why* this is the likely outcome. This is where you must directly apply the reasoning from the precedent case to your client's case.

Possible phrasing:

The court in _______ (insert precedent case name) reasoned _______ (insert the fact specific reasoning of the precedent case on the specific legal issue the analogical

reasoning is addressing). This reasoning applies to your client's case (use client's name) because ______ (explain why it applies). Therefore, because the reasoning from (insert precedent case name) applies to your client's case (use client's name), the outcome in your client's case (use client's name) is ______ (insert the outcome you are trying to prove with the analogical reasoning.)

Component 8: Persuasively re-state the conclusion you want the reader to reach based on your analogical reasoning. This must connect to the argument provided by the analogical reasoning and to the conclusion stated in Component 1.

EXAMPLE SINGLE CASE ANALOGICAL REASONING:

The implication that Ms. Anchor unethically reported on the Mayor's campaign is false and therefore unprotected. If the defendant uses a celebrity photograph in a manner that disseminates false information, the defendant violates the celebrity's right of publicity and the use is unprotected. Eastwood v. Super. Ct. of L.A. Co., 149 Cal. App. 3d 409 (2nd Dist. 1983). In Eastwood, for example, the court held Clint Eastwood's right of publicity was infringed when the National Enquirer published an article about Mr. Eastwood's alleged romantic involvement with two other celebrities; an article that was completely false. Id. at 414. Similarly, the implication that Ms. Anchor engaged in unethical reporting is also false. Ms. Anchor did not engage in any unethical reporting. Instead, and as alleged in her Complaint, Ms. Anchor never reported on the Mayor's re-election campaign and the general manager of her news station stated that "there are no concerns about Ms. Anchor's ethics whatsoever." The court in Eastwood reasoned that the veil of the public interest exception does not protect dissemination false information. Id. at 425. This reasoning applies to TFF's dissemination of false information regarding Ms. Anchor's reporting. Therefore, TFF's dissemination of false information is not protected.

Analogical Reasoning Formula Using Multiple Cases:

Component 1: Persuasively state legal conclusion you want the reader to reach based on your analogical reasoning (this is the overall thesis sentence for the analogical reasoning paragraph or paragraphs—case names should not be included in this sentence).

Component 2: Sentence stating, "Client's case (insert client's name) is similar to/distinguishable from ______ (insert first precedent case name) and/but similar to/distinguishable from ______ (insert second precedent case name) based on ______ (identify the specific issue this analogical reasoning is addressing)."

Component 3: Sentence stating, "In client's case (use client's name), (insert the specific facts about your client's case that will be compared; these are not all of the facts of the case but only the specific facts that will be compared)."

Component 4(a): Sentence stating, "This case is similar to/distinguishable from ______ (insert first precedent case name). In ______ (insert precedent case name) where (insert detailed information about the facts, the holding, and the reasoning from the precedent case you are relying upon that are related to the specific issue to be compared)." Remember to describe the precedent case in a way that is favorable to your client's position.

Component 4(b): Explain, using *specific factual detail*, why the facts you are comparing are similar/distinguishable. This is where you need to provide specific fact-to-fact comparisons, using actual facts from your client's case and the precedent case. (i.e.—"Fact X in client's case is similar to/distinguishable from Fact Y in precedent case because ______"). Remember to make these factual comparisons in a way that is favorable to your client's position.

Component 5(a): Sentence stating, "This case is similar/distinguishable than ______ (insert second precedent case name). In (insert precedent case name) where (insert detailed information about the facts, the holding, and the reasoning from the precedent case you are relying upon that are related to the specific issue to be compared)." Remember to describe the precedent case in a way that is favorable to your client's position.

Component 5(b): Explain, using *specific factual detail*, why the facts you are comparing are similar/distinguishable. This is where you need to provide specific fact-to-fact comparisons, using actual facts from your client's case and the precedent case. (i.e.—"Fact X in client's case is similar to/distinguishable from Fact Y in precedent case because ______ "). Remember to make these factual comparisons in a way that is favorable to your client's position. [NOTE: you many need to use a transition to begin this sentence, such as "In addition," "Also," "However," or "On the other hand".]

Component 6: Persuasively re-state the likely outcome of your client's case based on the similarities/differences you discussed previously (see Components 4(b) and 5(b)). This is a re-statement of the conclusion (Component 1) but with more detail and likely is the beginning of a new paragraph.

Component 7: Explain *why* this is the likely outcome. This is where you must directly apply the reasoning from the precedent case to your client's case.

Possible phrasing if the reasoning of the precedent cases is the same:

The court in ______ (insert first and second precedent case names) reasoned ______ (insert the fact specific reasoning of the precedent cases on the specific legal issue the analogical reasoning is addressing). This reasoning applies to your client's case (use client's name) because ______ (explain why it applies). Therefore, because the reasoning from (insert precedent case names) applies to your client's case (use client's name), the outcome in your client's case (use client's name) will likely will be ______ (insert the outcome you are trying to prove with the analogical reasoning).

Possible phrasing if the reasoning of the precedent cases is different:

The court in ______ (insert first precedent case name) reasoned ______ (insert the fact specific reasoning of the first precedent case on the specific legal issue the analogical reasoning is addressing). This reasoning applies to your client's case (use client's name) because ______ (explain why it applies). However, the court in ______ (insert second precedent case name) reasoned ______ (insert the fact specific reasoning of the second precedent case on the specific legal issue the analogical reasoning is addressing). This reasoning does not apply to your client's case (use client's name) because _______ (explain why it does not apply). Therefore, because the reasoning from (insert first precedent case name) applies to your client's case (use client's name) and the reasoning from (insert second precedent case name) does not apply to your client's case (use client's name), the outcome in your client's case (use client's name) will likely will be _______ (insert the outcome you are trying to prove with the analogical reasoning).

Component 8: Persuasively re-state the conclusion you want the reader to reach based on your analogical reasoning. This must connect to the argument provided by the analogical reasoning and to the conclusion stated in Component 1.

EXAMPLE MULTIPLE CASE ANALOGICAL REASONING:

TFF unlawfully used Ms. Anchor's photograph without her consent. TFF was required to obtain Ms. Anchor's consent to use her photograph because her photograph was used to further the company's commercial objectives, not to inform on a matter in the public interest. The use of Ms. Anchor's photograph is similar to the unauthorized use of a photograph in Downing and distinguishable from the authorized use of a photograph in Dora. In Downing, a clothing retailer used a famous surfer's photograph in its surf-themed clothing catalog. 265 F.3d 994. The court held that the photograph was only tenuously connected the public's interest in surfing because the retailer "did not explain that [the surfer] was a legend of the sport and incorrectly identifies where and when [the surfer's] photo was taken." Id. at 1003. Instead, the court held that the use of his photo only was used to sell clothing; therefore, its use required the surfer's consent. Id. Thus, where the use is commercial in nature, consent is required. Id.

Indeed, it is only if the connection between the use and the dissemination of information on matters in the public interest is clear that consent may be unnecessary. Dora v. Frontline Video, Inc., 15 Cal. App. 4th 536 (2nd Dist. 1993). For example, in Dora, consent to use a surfer's photograph in a surfing documentary was not required because the documentary was connected to the public's interest. Id. at 541. The court reasoned that because the "point of the program" was to inform the public about surfing and the people who impacted surf culture, the use of the surfer's photograph was connected to the public interest. 15 Cal. App. 4th at 543.

TFF's use of Ms. Anchor's photo was commercial in nature. Like in Downing, where the objective of the surf-themed catalog was to promote sales, TFF's primary business objective was to create and sell funny t-shirts for profit. The catalog used the surfer's photograph to capitalize on his fame and to "window-dress" the catalog, just like TFF used Ms. Anchor's photograph to capitalize on her highly publicized affair with the Mayor to sell t-shirts. Downing, 265 F.3d at 1003. Also, like the catalog's failure to properly identify the surfer and his relationship to the sport, TFF "did not explain" Ms. Anchor's situation with the Mayor and, therefore, did not connect the use of the photograph to the public interest. Id. Instead, TFF simply was trying to profit off of a highly publicized situation, like the catalog was trying to profit off the fame of the well-known surfer. Id. Furthermore, Ms. Anchor's is distinguishable from Dora because, in that case, the court reasoned that consent was unnecessary since the "point of the program" was to provide commentary on surfing. 15 Cal. App. 4th at 546. That reasoning does not apply here because the "point of the t-shirt" was to meet TFF's commercial objective of creating a humorous t-shirt

> for profit, not to inform the public or provide social commentary on that topic. Because TFF's use of Ms. Anchor's photograph on its t-shirt was not connected to the public's interest, but instead used to make a profit, TFF was required to obtain Ms. Anchor's consent.

Case File Assignment:

Write an argument for your client's case using analogical reasoning based on the legal authority in the Case File and/or the legal authority assigned by your professor. To help you write an analogical reasoning argument, answer the following brainstorming questions:

1. Identify one specific issue you plan to address with analogical reasoning (or the specific issue assigned by your professor).

2. Identify the name of one precedent case you plan to use for the issue you selected above (or the case assigned by your professor).

3. Identify the specific holding of the precedent case on the legal issue you plan to argue with this analogical reasoning (NOTE: This must only be the holding specific to the legal issue you are addressing, not the overall holding of the precedent case.)

4. Describe the reasoning of the court from the precedent case on the legal issue you plan to argue with this analogical reasoning (NOTE: This must only be the reasoning specific to the legal issue you are addressing, not the overall reasoning of the precedent case.)

5. Make a list of the relevant facts from the precedent case on the legal issue you plan to argue with this analogical reasoning (NOTE: This must only be the facts specific to the legal issue you are addressing, not all of the facts from the precedent case.)

6. Make a list of the relevant facts from your client's case on the legal issue you plan to argue with this analogical reasoning (NOTE: This must be only the facts specific to the legal issue you are addressing, not all of the facts from your client's case).

7. Organize the facts of the precedent case and your client's case into the charts below:

Facts that are similar:

Your Client's Case	Precedent Case

Facts that are distinguishable:

Your Client's Case	Precedent Case

Using the information you filled into the charts above, decide whether you think your client's case and the precedent case are similar, distinguishable, or both. If they are similar, answer Questions 8–10 below. If they are distinguishable, answer Questions 11–13 below. If they are both similar and distinguishable, answer Questions 8–13 below.

8. Identify the fact(s) from your client's case and the precedent case to be compared as similar. (NOTE: This must only be the facts specific to the legal issue you are addressing, not all of the facts from the precedent case or your client's case.)

9. Explain why these facts are similar—use specific factual examples to prove the similarities.

10. Explain *why* these factual similarities support your legal analysis on the issue you are addressing. This is where you must directly apply

the reasoning of the precedent case to the facts of your client's case. Specifically look at why and how the precedent case ruled as it did and why that same reasoning applies to your client's case.

11. Identify the fact(s) to be compared in your analysis as distinguishable. (NOTE: This must only be the facts specific to the legal issue you are addressing, not all of the facts from the precedent case or your client's case.)

12. Explain why these facts are distinguishable—use specific factual examples to prove the differences.

13. Explain *why* these factual differences support your legal analysis on the issue you are addressing. This is where you need to directly apply the reasoning of the precedent case to the facts of your client's case. Specifically look at why and how the precedent case ruled as it did and why that same reasoning does not apply to your client's case.

After answering these brainstorming questions, you should have a clear understanding of whether an analogical reasoning argument should be made in your client's case. You then must decide if the analogical reasoning will be based on a single case or multiple cases. If multiple cases are used to argue the same legal issue, then you must make these arguments at the same time, rather than as a separate analogical reasoning for each precedent case. Once you have decided if the analogical reasoning will be based on a single case or multiple cases, use one of the following formulas to write your analogical reasoning argument:

Analogical Reasoning Formula Using a Single Case:

Component 1: Persuasively state the legal conclusion you want the reader to reach based on your analogical reasoning (this is the overall thesis sentence for the analogical reasoning paragraph or paragraphs—case names should not be included in this sentence).

Component 2: Sentence stating, "In client's case (use client's name) is similar to/distinguishable from ______ (insert precedent case name) based on ______ (identify the specific issue this analogical reasoning is addressing)."

Component 3: Sentence stating, "In client's case (use client's name), (insert the specific facts about your client's case that will be compared—please note these are not all of the facts of the case but only the specific facts that will be compared)."

Component 4: Sentence stating, "This case is similar to/distinguishable from ______ (insert precedent case name). In ______ (insert precedent case name) where (insert detailed information about the facts, the holding, and the reasoning from the precedent case you are relying upon that are related to the specific issue to be compared)." Remember to describe the precedent case in a way that is favorable to your client's position.

Component 5: Explain, using *specific factual detail*, why the facts you are comparing are similar or distinguishable. This is where you need to provide specific fact-to-fact comparisons, using actual facts from your client's case and the precedent case. (i.e.—"Fact X in client's case is similar to/distinguishable from Fact Y in precedent case because ______"). Remember to make these factual comparisons in a way that is favorable to your client's position.

Component 6: Persuasively re-state the likely outcome of your client's case based on the similarities or differences you discussed in Component 5. This is a re-statement of the conclusion (Component 1) but with more detail and this likely is the beginning of a new paragraph.

Component 7: Explain *why* this is the likely outcome. This is where you must directly apply the reasoning from the precedent case to your client's case.

Possible phrasing:

The court in ______ (insert precedent case name) reasoned ______ (insert the fact specific reasoning of the precedent case on the specific legal issue the analogical reasoning is addressing). This reasoning applies to your client's case (use client's name) because ______ (explain why it applies). Therefore, because the reasoning from (insert precedent case name) applies to your client's case (use client's name), the outcome in your client's case (use client's name) is ______ (insert the outcome you are trying to prove with the analogical reasoning.)

Component 8: Persuasively re-state the conclusion you want the reader to reach based on your analogical reasoning. This must connect to the argument provided by the analogical reasoning and to the conclusion stated in Component 1.

Analogical Reasoning Formula Using Multiple Cases:

Component 1: Persuasively state legal conclusion you want the reader to reach based on your analogical reasoning (this is the overall thesis sentence for the analogical reasoning paragraph or paragraphs—case names should not be included in this sentence).

Component 2: Sentence stating, "Client's case (insert client's name) is similar to/distinguishable from ______ (insert first precedent case name) and/but similar to/distinguishable from ______ (insert second precedent case name) based on ______ (identify the specific issue this analogical reasoning is addressing)."

Component 3: Sentence stating, "In client's case (use client's name), (insert the specific facts about your client's case that will be compared—please note these are not all of the facts of the case but only the specific facts that will be compared)."

Component 4(a): Sentence stating, "This case is similar to/distinguishable from ______ (insert first precedent case name). In ______ (insert precedent case name) where (insert detailed information about the facts, the holding, and the reasoning from the precedent case you are relying upon that are related to the specific issue to be compared)." Remember to describe the precedent case in a way that is favorable to your client's position.

Component 4(b): Explain, using *specific factual detail*, why the facts you are comparing are similar/distinguishable. This is where you need to provide specific fact-to-fact comparisons, using actual facts from your client's case and the precedent case. (i.e.—"Fact X in client's case is similar to/distinguishable from Fact Y in precedent case because _______ "). Remember to make these factual comparisons in a way that is favorable to your client's position.

Component 5(a): Sentence stating, "This case is similar/distinguishable than _______ (insert second precedent case name). In (insert precedent case name) where (insert detailed information about the facts, the holding, and the reasoning from the precedent case you are relying upon that are related to the specific issue to be compared)." Remember to describe the precedent case in a way that is favorable to your client's position.

Component 5(b): Explain, using *specific factual detail*, why the facts you are comparing are similar/distinguishable. This is where you need to provide specific fact-to-fact comparisons, using actual facts from your client's case and the precedent case. (i.e.—"Fact X in client's case is similar to/distinguishable from Fact Y in precedent case because _______ "). Remember to make these factual comparisons in a way that is favorable to your client's position. [NOTE: you many need to use a transition to begin this sentence, such as "In addition," "Also," "However," or "On the other hand"]

Component 6: Persuasively re-state the likely outcome of your client's case based on the similarities/differences you discussed previously (see Components 4(b) and 5(b). This is a re-statement of the conclusion (Component 1) but with more detail and this likely is the beginning of a new paragraph.

Component 7: Explain *why* this is the likely outcome. This is where you must directly apply the reasoning from the precedent case to your client's case.

Possible phrasing if the reasoning of the precedent cases is the same:

The court in _______ (insert first and second precedent case names) reasoned _______ (insert the fact specific reasoning of the precedent cases on the specific legal issue the analogical reasoning is addressing). This reasoning applies to your client's case (use client's name) because _______ (explain why it applies). Therefore, because the reasoning from (insert precedent case names) applies to your client's case (use client's name), the outcome in your client's case (use client's name) will likely will be _______ (insert the outcome you are trying to prove with the analogical reasoning).

Possible phrasing if the reasoning of the precedent cases is different:

The court in _______ (insert first precedent case name) reasoned _______ (insert the fact specific reasoning of the first precedent case on the specific legal issue the analogical reasoning is addressing). This reasoning applies to your client's case (use client's name) because _______ (explain why it applies). However, the court in _______ (insert second precedent case name) reasoned _______ (insert the fact specific reasoning of the second precedent case on the specific legal issue the analogical reasoning is addressing). This reasoning does not apply to your client's case (use client's name) because _______ (explain why it does not apply). Therefore, because the reasoning from (insert first precedent case name) applies to your client's case (use client's name) and the reasoning from (insert second precedent case name) does not apply to your client's case, the outcome in your client's case (use client's name) will likely will be _______ (insert the outcome you are trying to prove with the analogical reasoning).

Component 8: Persuasively re-state the conclusion you want the reader to reach based on your analogical reasoning. This must connect to the argument provided by the analogical reasoning and to the conclusion stated in Component 1.

WORKSHEET NO. 7: POINT HEADINGS

Point headings provide the reader with structure and guidance. They allow the reader to obtain a broad overview of your argument and quickly locate the point he or she is most interested in reading without having to read the entire argument.

A point heading is substantively correct if it:

1. States the point heading affirmatively for your client;
2. Uses key words and phrases from the argument the point heading represents;
3. Uses specific facts and legal concepts from the argument the point heading represents; and
4. Summarizes the argument the point heading represents by using the following formula:
    a. The conclusion for the argument the point heading represents;
    b. Because (or a "because" equivalent);
    c. The rule justifying the legal conclusion + the key fact(s) from your client's case.

EXAMPLE POINT HEADINGS:

I. MS. ANCHOR HAS A VALID RIGHT OF PUBLICITY CLAIM AGAINST TFF BECAUSE IT KNOWINGLY USED HER PHOTOGRAPH FOR PROFIT WITHOUT HER CONSENT.

II. MS. ANCHOR HAS A VALID RIGHT OF PUBLICITY CLAIM AGAINST TFF BECAUSE TFF'S USE OF HER PHOTOGRAPH WAS NOT CONNECTED TO A MATTER IN THE PUBLIC INTEREST, BUT ONLY FOR COMMERCIAL GAIN.

III. MS. ANCHOR HAS A VALID RIGHT OF PUBLICITY CLAIM AGAINST TFF BECAUSE THE PHOTOGRAPHS ON THE T-SHIRT IMPLIED FALSE INFORMATION.

A point heading is technically correct if:

1. It is only one sentence;
2. The sentences wrap under each other so the left margin of the point heading lines up with the text of the point heading immediately above it;
3. It appropriately uses emphasizers (all caps, bold, italic, underline, etc.) to allow the point headings to stand out from the text of the argument but not distract the reader;
4. It does not have an A without a B or an I without an II; and

5. It does not have lone point headings at the end of the page (there must be at least 2 lines of text of the paragraph the point heading precedes at the bottom of the page; a point heading cannot be the last line on a page).

A series of point headings are technically correct if they:

1. Use parallel construction;
2. Use appropriate levels of point headings and sub-point headings; and
3. Provide the reader with an outline of the Argument section, when read together.

The formatting for point headings is proper if:

I. THE TEXT OF THE FIRST LEVEL POINT HEADING IS INDENTED A FULL TAB OVER AND ADDITIONAL LINES OF TEXT WRAP UNDER THE FIRST LINE OF TEXT.

A. <u>The Text Of The Second Level Point Heading Is Indented So That The "A" Lines–Up Under The Text Of The First Level Point Heading; The Text Of This Heading Is A Full Tab Over From The "A;" And Additional Lines Of Text Wrap Under The First Line of Text.</u>

1. The third level point heading is indented so that the "1" lines-up under the text of the second level point heading; the text of this heading is indented a full tab over from the "1;" and additional lines of text wrap under the first line of text.

Note: The type of emphasizers (all caps, initial caps, underlined, italics, etc.) used here are for demonstrative purposes only. You should use the types of emphasizers assigned by your professor.

Case File Assignment:

Write the point headings for your brief. To help you write the point headings, answer the following brainstorming questions for each argument you plan to emphasize with a point heading:

1. What is the conclusion reached by the argument the point heading represents?

2. What are the key words and phrases used in the argument the point heading represents?

3. What are the specific facts and legal concepts from the argument the point heading represents?

Using the answers to these brainstorming questions as your guide, write a point heading(s) for your argument. When writing a point heading, use the following formula:

> The conclusion for the argument/paragraph the point heading represents + because (or a "because" equivalent) + the rule justifying the legal conclusion + the key fact(s) from your client's case.

When writing the point heading, consider the following substantive and technical requirements:

1. State the point heading affirmatively for your client;
2. State the point heading in only one sentence;
3. Have the text of the point heading wrap so the left margin of the point heading lines-up;
4. Appropriately use emphasizers (bold, italic, underline, etc.) to allow the point headings to stand out from the text of the argument, but not distract the reader;
5. Do not have an A without a B or an I without an II; and
6. Do not have lone point headings at the end of the page (there must be at least 2 lines of text of the paragraph the point heading precedes at the bottom of the page; a point heading cannot be the last line on a page)

If you have a series of point headings, consider the following substantive and technical requirements:

1. State the point headings using parallel construction;
2. State the point headings using appropriate levels of point headings and sub-point headings; and
3. Collectively, when read together, the point headings should provide the reader with an outline of the Argument section.

WORKSHEET NO. 8: THE INTRODUCTION

The Introduction in a persuasive brief is the first thing the judge will read. Thus, it must provide a complete introduction to the case and use persuasive techniques to convince the judge from the beginning.

An Introduction is substantively complete if it includes:

1. The nature of the case;
2. The identity of the parties;
3. The procedural event that led to the filing of the brief;
4. The relief your client requests from the court in the brief; and
5. The primary legal points justifying that relief.

When presenting the substance of these five components, consider the following persuasive writing techniques and note that the above five components can be presented in any order:

1. Begin with your client's name and what your client requests;
2. Write the Introduction in the affirmative; do not directly restate your opponent's position or what your opponent wants (even if it is a responsive brief); and
3. Establish the theme of your argument early.

EXAMPLE INTRODUCTION:

Tasha V. Anchor, a well-known television reporter, has a valid right of publicity claim against T–Shirts For Fun (TFF) under the California statutory right of publicity. TFF knowingly used a photograph of Ms. Anchor on a t-shirt combined with a photograph of the Los Angeles Mayor as a miniature devil sitting on her shoulder. Ms. Anchor did not consent to this use of her photograph. Furthermore, TFF admits that it used the photograph primarily for commercial gain, not for social commentary, and admits that the image was designed to imply that Ms. Anchor was influenced by the Mayor to unethically report on his re-election campaign. Ms. Anchor denies this implication. Because TFF knowingly used Ms. Anchor's photograph on its t-shirt without her consent, did not connect the use of her photograph to a matter in the public interest, and provided false information about Ms. Anchor's reporting, TFF violated her right of publicity. Therefore, Ms. Anchor has stated a valid claim and TFF's motion to dismiss should be denied.

Case File Assignment:

Write the Introduction for your brief. To help you write the Introduction, answer the following brainstorming questions:

1. What is the nature of the case?

2. Who are the parties?

3. What is the procedural event that led to the filing of the brief?

4. What is the relief your client requests from the court in the brief?

5. What are the primary legal points justifying that relief?

Using the answers to these brainstorming questions as your guide, write the Introduction for your brief. Start by cutting and pasting your answers into paragraph form and then mold them into readable paragraphs.

When writing the Introduction, consider the following persuasive techniques:

1. Begin with your client's name and what your client requests from the court in filing the brief;
2. Write the Introduction in the affirmative; do not directly restate your opponent's position or what your opponent wants (even if it is a responsive brief); and
3. Establish the theme of your case or argument.

WORKSHEET NO. 9: PERSUASIVE STATEMENT OF FACTS

The four most important things to remember when writing a persuasive Statement of Facts are to: (1) include the legally significant facts; (2) organize the facts in an effective manner; (3) tell your client's story persuasively; and (4) represent the facts accurately.

The brainstorming process for a persuasive Statement of Facts is similar to the brainstorming process for an objective Facts section (See Worksheet No. 9 for Objective Writing). However, a persuasive Statement of Facts does not begin the same as an objective Facts section. As you recall, the first paragraph in an objective Facts section (See Worksheet No. 9 for Objective Writing) begins with foundational information to provide the reader with context for the memorandum. This same first paragraph is not required in a persuasive Statement of Facts because a persuasive brief begins with an Introduction, which provides the reader with all of this foundational information: the parties, their relationships, the setting, the procedural history, and the client's general problem or goal. Instead, a persuasive Statement of Facts needs to grab the reader's attention from the beginning by telling compelling story.

Therefore, the brainstorming process for a persuasive Statement of Facts is more focused on the substance and tone.

A persuasive Statement of Facts is substantively correct if it:

1. Includes the proper substance by:

    a. Including the legally significant facts. To determine the legally significant facts, review your Argument section and highlight all of the facts from your client's case that you relied upon. These are the legally significant facts. If you have not yet written your Argument section, determine the legally significant facts by asking yourself: what are the facts a court will consider in ruling on your client's case?

    b. Including the background facts necessary for the legally significant facts to make sense. To determine the necessary background facts, ask yourself: what context is needed for the legally significant facts to make sense, what else does the judge need to know to understand the story of your client's case, and what else is needed to establish the theme of your case?

    c. Including emotional facts that are needed to establish your theme or create empathy for your client.

    d. Describing the facts accurately.

    e. Omitting factual arguments, references to the law, legal conclusions, and factual conclusions.

2. Includes the proper persuasive tone by:

   a. Emphasizing favorable facts;

   b. Strategically including unfavorable facts (the facts the opposing party likely will rely upon) by burying them within favorable facts;

   c. Having a parallel tone and theme with the Argument section; and

   d. Using an appropriate and persuasive organization.

3. Has a strategically selected an organization to most persuasively tell the story: chronological, topical, or a combination of chronological and topical. The organization you select must be a strategic choice based on the best approach to persuasively tell the reader the story of your client's case.

4. Provides closure to the persuasive Statement of Facts by not ending abruptly; connect to the theme of the case and end with significant relevant facts as readers will best remember information they read last.

EXAMPLE PERSUASIVE STATEMENT OF FACTS:

Tasha V. Anchor is a local television reporter for KTV-LA. She has had a successful career as a reporter for the last ten years. During that time, she has won numerous awards, including an Emmy for her journalism, co-hosted national shows, interviewed A-list celebrities, high-ranking politicians, and well-known authors, and reported live from the Democratic Headquarters in Los Angeles as Barack Obama was elected President.

Ms. Anchor recently began a relationship with the Mayor of Los Angeles, who has been legally separated from his wife for two years. Ms. Anchor and the Mayor have been in a committed relationship for approximately six months. Currently, Ms. Anchor hosts the morning show for KTV-LA called, "Good Morning So. Cal." and the Mayor is running for re-election. While both are busy with their careers, they try to make as much time as possible to spend with each other.

In the summer, news of their relationship was made public, which was followed by a frenzy of media attention. Ms. Anchor could barely leave her home without being hounded by paparazzi. The Mayor had to add additional security just to be able to get to work each day. The media ran stories alleging everything from Ms. Anchor being the Mayor's second cousin to the Mayor influencing Ms. Anchor's reporting on his re-election campaign.

Ms. Anchor denies these recent allegations, as she is not the Mayor's second cousin and she never reported on the Mayor's re-election campaign or on any matters that directly or indirectly relate to his position as Mayor. However, Ms. Anchor did conduct two short of interviews with the Mayor last October and November, but these interviews were on topics unrelated to his re-election campaign and the general manager for KTV-LA said "There is no concern as to Ms. Anchor's ethics whatsoever."

Soon after the relationship was made public, Ms. Anchor came across a t-shirt for sale in a Beverly Hills boutique with her photograph on it. The t-shirt featured her photograph combined with a photograph of a miniaturized Mayor, wearing a suit and devil horns, sitting on her left shoulder. Ms. Anchor did not consent to the use of her photograph and its use on the t-shirt is offensive to Ms. Anchor because it inappropriately implies that she unethically reported on the Mayor's re-election campaign or that he somehow controlled her reporting. Ms. Anchor vehemently denies both allegations.

The t-shirt was created and sold by T–Shirts for Fun (TFF), a company that designs, produces, and distributes t-shirts, which are pri-

marily meant to be humorous and provide commentary on public events. Despite the $29.95 received for each t-shirt, with over 100 sales, TFF claims the t-shirt at issue was only intended to provide subtle commentary on the possible conflict of interest created by Ms. Anchor's relationship with the Mayor. However, according to information posted on TFF's web site, it admits that the t-shirt is its "best seller" and that its business objective is more about making money than providing social commentary.

Seeking to prevent further manufacture and distribution of the t-shirt and for damages against TFF, Ms. Anchor filed a Complaint alleging TFF violated her statutory right of publicity.

Case File Assignment:

Write a persuasive Statement of Facts for your client's case. To help you write a persuasive Statement of Facts, answer the following brainstorming questions:

1. What is the theme or the story of your case?

2. Identify the relevant facts:

   a. What are the legally significant facts? Read your Argument section and highlight all of the facts from your client's case that you used to support your arguments. These are the legally significant facts and they must be included in your persuasive Statement of Facts. If you have not yet written your Argument section, then determine the legally significant facts by asking yourself: what are the facts the court will consider in ruling on your client's case?

   b. What background facts are necessary to provide context for the legally significant facts identified in response to Question 2(a) above, to tell your client's story, and to establish the theme of your case?

c. What emotional facts are needed to establish your theme or create empathy for your client?

d. What are the unfavorable facts? What are the facts the opposing party likely will rely upon?

3. Looking at your answers to these brainstorming questions and using your understanding your client's case, identify the organization that will most persuasively tell your client's story: Chronological? Topical? Combination of chronological and topical? The organization you select must be a strategic choice based on the best approach to persuasively tell your client's story.

Using the answers to these brainstorming questions as your guide, write a persuasive Statement of Facts for your client's case. Start by cutting and pasting your answers into paragraph form and then mold them into readable paragraphs.

When writing your persuasive Statement of Facts, consider the following:

1. The first paragraph must tell a compelling story and establish the theme of the case.

2. The overall substance and tone must:

    - Strategically select the most persuasive organization (avoid stream of consciousness writing);
    - Represent the record accurately;
    - Describe the facts persuasively;
    - Have a parallel tone and theme with the Argument section;

- Emphasize favorable facts and bury unfavorable facts (but not omit them);
- Omit factual arguments, references to the law, legal conclusions, and factual conclusions; and
- Maintain a persuasive tone.

3. The last paragraph must:
   - Connect to the theme of the case;
   - Conclude with significant relevant facts—readers will best remember information they read last; and
   - Avoid ending abruptly: create a transition between the Statement of Fact and Argument sections.

WORKSHEET NO. 10: CONCLUSION

The Conclusion in persuasive writing is similar to a Conclusion in objective writing. Like an objective Conclusion, the persuasive Conclusion summarizes the individual conclusions that you reached in your Argument section and reminds the court of the relief requested.

A persuasive Conclusion is complete if it includes:

1. The ultimate relief sought by your brief (NOTE: This must be consistent with the information provided in your Introduction);
2. Each rule applied to your client's case (the R in each persuasive paradigm included in your brief);
3. The conclusion for each rule applied in your client's case (the C in each persuasive paradigm included in your brief);
4. A summary of the reasoning that supports those conclusions (summarize the A sections in each persuasive paradigm included in your brief); and
5. A restatement of the ultimate relief sought by your brief.

Throughout each of these components, use a persuasive tone and incorporate the theme of your client's case.

EXAMPLE CONCLUSION:

Ms. Anchor's Complaint states a valid statutory right of publicity claim against TFF and TFF's motion to dismiss should be denied. A motion to dismiss should only be granted in extraordinary cases where the plaintiff can prove no set of facts in support of her claim. Ms. Anchor has alleged more than sufficient facts to prove her claim. First, under California Civil Code § 3344(a), use of another's photograph is unlawful unless there is consent. Ms. Anchor's Complaint sufficiently alleges that TFF knowingly used her photograph without her consent in violation of § 3344(a). Second, the only exception to this statutory consent requirement is if the defendant can show that the use of a photograph was in connection with a matter in the public interest; but, if the unauthorized use of a photograph is for commercial purposes, consent is required. Ms. Anchor's Complaint sufficiently alleges that TFF used her photograph for commercial purposes, not to provide social commentary. Third, if the defendant uses a celebrity's photograph in a manner that disseminates false information, the defendant violates the celebrity's right of publicity and the use is unprotected. Ms. Anchor's Complaint sufficiently alleges that TFF's use of her photograph on the t-shirt falsely implied that Ms. Anchor unethically reported on the Mayor's re-election campaign and that this false implication is exactly what the statute is designed to protect against. For these reasons, Ms. Anchor's Complaint properly states a right of publicity cause of action and TFF's motion to dismiss should be denied.

Case File Assignment:

Write the Conclusion for your brief. To help you write the Conclusion, answer the following brainstorming questions:

1. What is the ultimate relief sought by your brief? (NOTE: This must be consistent with the information provided in your Introduction.)

2. Identify each rule applied to your client's case (the R in each persuasive paradigm included in your brief).

3. Identify the conclusion for each rule applied in your client's case (the C in each persuasive paradigm included in your brief).

4. Summarize the reasoning that supports the conclusions on each rule (summarize the A sections in each persuasive paradigm included in your brief).

5. Restate the ultimate relief sought by your brief.

Using the answers to these brainstorming questions as your guide, write the Conclusion for your brief. Start by cutting and pasting your answers into paragraph form and then mold them into readable paragraphs. When writing the Conclusion, maintain a persuasive tone, incorporate the theme of your client's case, have the organization of the Conclusion parallel the organization of the Argument section, and avoid simply repeating the Introduction.

CASE FILE NO. 3: CELEBRITY v. FULLBACK STEAKHOUSES, INC.

WORKSHEET NO. 1: INTRODUCTION, FACTS, AND RELEVANT AUTHORITY

Introduction

Attorneys rarely research the law and write an analysis simply to learn the law. Instead, attorneys almost always research and write in response to the specific situation faced by a client. Therefore, before you turn to the attached statutes and cases, read the Office Memorandum on the next page to give yourself an understanding of your client's situation. The Office Memorandum is an example of what you might receive when a supervising attorney asks you to work on a case.

After you have read the Office Memorandum, re-read the statutes and cases in the Case File. When re-reading the statutes and cases, begin to strategize on how to persuasively write a motion to dismiss Plaintiff's misappropriation of likeness claim based on New York's statutory right of privacy.

OFFICE MEMORANDUM

TO: Legal Intern

FROM: Supervising Attorney

DATE: September 1, YEAR

RE: Celebrity v. Fullback Steakhouse; Misappropriation of likeness

---

Thank you for your hard work on the objective memorandum for our client, John Ritchie, the CEO of Fullback Steakhouses, Inc. (Fullback). Based on your analysis, I am confident that we can prevail on a motion to dismiss Suzie Celebrity's misappropriation of likeness claim under New York law, which I need you to write. Please review the Complaint below; these are the only facts available at this time.

Payton Henderson, Esq.
Attorney to the Stars
5000 Park Avenue
New York, New York

Attorney for Plaintiff

Suzie Celebrity,	
Plaintiff	
vs.	Complaint for Damages Case No.: No. 12–3–456789–1
Fullback Steakhouses, Inc. and John Ritchie, CEO of Fullback Steakhouses, Inc.,	
Defendants.	

Plaintiff Suzie Celebrity sues Defendants Fullback Steakhouses, Inc. and John Ritchie, CEO of Fullback Steakhouses, as follows:

COMMON ALLEGATIONS

1. Suzie Celebrity is a resident of New York. She is a well-known socialite in New York. She has appeared on multiple reality shows, is paid for her appearances at events, and she is one of the most "Googled" celebrities.

2. Ms. Celebrity has signature look of blonde hair, large sun glasses, over-sized purse, stiletto heals, and she always is carrying a small dog in a small pink carrier.

3. Ms. Celebrity also is known for the catch-phrase "spicy," which she has trademarked.

4. Fullback Steakhouses, Inc. is a chain of sports bars located and incorporated in New York.

5. John Ritchie is the CEO of Fullback Steakhouses, Inc. and a resident of New York.

FIRST CAUSE OF ACTION
(Misappropriation of Likeness)

6. In August YEAR, Fullback began running an animated television commercial, featuring a cartoon robot wearing a blonde wig, carrying a small dog in a small pink carrier, that says "spicy" in the advertisement.

7. In the commercial, a robot waiter dressed as a referee brings plate of Buffalo wings to table where a blonde robot is sitting with a group of friends. The blonde robot is very thin, has blonde hair, and a Chihuahua in a pink purse. The robot waiter sets down plates of Buffalo wings on the table and says, "Be careful, they are spicy." One of the robot friends asks, "What's spicy?"

8. The blonde robot puts a Buffalo wing it in her mouth, says, "Mmm, spicy," and winks at the camera. This was not Ms. Celebrity's voice.

9. Although her name is not included anywhere in the commercial, the blonde robot is intended to resemble Ms. Celebrity and imply that Ms. Celebrity endorses Fullback.

10. Ms. Celebrity did not authorize Fullback to use her likeness.

11. Fullback's use of Ms. Celebrity's likeness violates New York's statutory right of privacy.

WHEREFORE, Suzie Celebrity demands judgment against Defendants granting the following relief:

1. Injunctive relief;
2. Compensatory damages;
3. Punitive damages, to the full extent permitted by law;
4. An award of interest, costs and attorney's fees; and
5. Such other relief as the court deems appropriate.

Payton Henderson

Payton Henderson, Esq.
Attorney for Plaintiff

McKinney's Consolidated Laws of New York
Civil Rights Law
Chapter 6 of the Consolidated Laws
Article 5 Right of Privacy

§ 50. Right of privacy

A person, firm or corporation that uses for advertising purposes, or for the purposes of trade, the name, portrait or picture of any living person without having first obtained the written consent of such person, or if a minor of his or her parent or guardian, is guilty of a misdemeanor.

§ 51. Action for injunction and for damages

Any person whose name, portrait, picture or voice is used within this state for advertising purposes or for the purposes of trade without the written consent first obtained as above provided may maintain an equitable action in the supreme court of this state against the person, firm or corporation so using his name, portrait, picture or voice, to prevent and restrain the use thereof; and may also sue and recover damages for any injuries sustained by reason of such use and if the defendant shall have knowingly used such person's name, portrait, picture or voice in such manner as is forbidden or declared to be unlawful by section fifty of this article, the jury, in its discretion, may award exemplary damages. But nothing contained in this article shall be so construed as to prevent any person, firm or corporation from selling or otherwise transferring any material containing such name, portrait, picture or voice in whatever medium to any user of such name, portrait, picture or voice, or to any third party for sale or transfer directly or indirectly to such a user, for use in a manner lawful under this article; nothing contained in this article shall be so construed as to prevent any person, firm or corporation, practicing the profession of photography, from exhibiting in or about his or its establishment specimens of the work of such establishment, unless the same is continued by such person, firm or corporation after written notice objecting thereto has been given by the person portrayed; and nothing contained in this article shall be so construed as to prevent any person, firm or corporation from using the name, portrait, picture or voice of any manufacturer or dealer in connection with the goods, wares and merchandise manufactured, produced or dealt in by him which he has sold or disposed of with such name, portrait, picture or voice used in connection therewith; or from using the name, portrait, picture or voice of any author, composer or artist in connection with his literary, musical or artistic productions which he has sold or disposed of with such name, portrait, picture or voice used in connection therewith. Nothing contained in this section shall be construed to prohibit the copyright owner of a sound recording from disposing of, dealing in, licensing or selling that sound recording to any party, if the right to dispose of, deal in, license or sell such sound recording has been conferred by contract or other written document by such living person or the holder of such right. Nothing contained in the foregoing sentence shall be deemed to abrogate or otherwise limit any rights or remedies otherwise conferred by federal law or state law.

Jacqueline Kennedy ONASSIS, Plaintiff

v.

CHRISTIAN DIOR–NEW YORK, INC., Lansdowne Advertising, Inc., Richard Avedon, Barbara Reynolds and Ron Smith Celebrity Look–Alikes, Defendants

Supreme Court, New York County, New York, Special Term, Part I

472 N.Y.S.2d 254

January 11, 1984

GREENFIELD

This case poses for judicial resolution the question of whether the use for commercial purposes of a "look-alike" of a well-known personality violates the right of privacy legislatively granted by enactment of Civil Rights Law §§ 50 and 51. Put another way, can one person enjoin the use of someone else's face? The questions appear not to have been definitively answered before.

Plaintiff, Jacqueline Kennedy Onassis, former First Lady of the United States, widow of President John F. Kennedy, one of the world's most powerful men, and of Aristotle Onassis, one of the world's wealthiest men, but a well-known personality in her own right, moves for a preliminary injunction under the Civil Rights Law to restrain defendants, all of whom were associated with an advertising campaign to promote the products and the image of Christian Dior–New York, Inc., from using or distributing a certain advertisement, and for associated relief. She alleges simply in her complaint that defendants have knowingly caused the preparation and publication of an advertisement for Dior products which includes her likeness in the form of a photograph of look-alike Barbara Reynolds; that Reynolds' picture causes her to be identified with the ad to which she has not given her consent; that this was a violation of her rights of privacy and that it caused her irreparable injury.

Defendant Christian Dior–New York, Inc. is the corporate entity which controls advertising and publicity for the 35 United States licensees who sell varied lines of merchandise under the coveted Dior label. **257

* * *

So it was that J. Walter Thompson's Lansdowne Division, in conjunction with noted photographer Richard Avedon, hit upon the idea of a running series of ads featuring a trio known as the Diors (one female and two males), who were characterized by an article in Newsweek Magazine as idle rich, suggestively decadent, and aggressively chic. Indeed, it was suggested that this *menage a trois,* putatively inspired by the characters portrayed by Noel Coward, Alfred Lunt and Lynn Fontanne in Coward's 1933 play "Design for Living", would become the most notorious personae in advertising since Brooke Shields refused to let anything come between her and her Calvins (for the uninitiated, blue jeans advertised under designer Calvin Klein's label). To emphasize the impression of the unconventional, the copy for one ad had read, "When the Diors got away from it all, they brought with them nothing except 'The Decline of the West' and one toothbrush." Evidently, to stir comment, the relationship portrayed in the ad campaign was meant to be ambiguous, "to specify nothing but suggest everything." The 16 sequential ads would depict this steadfast trio in varying situations leading to the marriage of two (but not the exclusion of the third), birth of a baby, and their ascent to Heaven (subject to resurrection on demand).

Thus, the Diors, and by association their products, would be perceived as chic, sophisticated, elite, unconventional, quirky, audacious, elegant, and unorthodox. The advertisement for the wedding, which is the one challenged here, is headed "Christian Dior: Sportswear for Women and Clothing for Men." Portrayed in the ad are the happy Dior trio attended by their ostensible intimates, all ecstatically beaming-Gene Shalit, the T.V. personality, model Shari Belafonte, actress Ruth Gordon, and Barbara Reynolds, a secretary who bears a remarkable resemblance to plaintiff Jacqueline Onassis.

* * *

Of course, what stamps it as "legendary" is the presence of this eclectic group, a frothy mix, the most legendary of which would clearly be Jacqueline Kennedy Onassis, shown discreetly behind Gordon and Shalit, obviously delighted to be in attendance at this "event."

That the person behind Gordon and Shalit bore a striking resemblance to the plaintiff was no mere happenstance. Defendants knew there was little or no likelihood that Mrs. Onassis would ever consent to be depicted in this kind of advertising campaign for Dior. She has asserted in her affidavit, and it is well-known, that she has never permitted her name or picture to be used in connection with the promotion of commercial products. Her name has been used sparingly only in connection with certain public services, civic, art and educational projects which she has supported. Accordingly, Lansdowne and Avedon, once the content of the picture and the make-up of the wedding party having been determined, contacted defendant Ron Smith Celebrity Look–Alikes to provide someone who could pass for Jacqueline Kennedy Onassis. That agency, which specializes in locating and providing persons who bear a close resemblance to well-known personalities on request (and for a fee), came up with defendant Barbara Reynolds, regularly an appointments secretary to a congressman, who, with appropriate coiffure and appointments looks remarkably like Mrs. Onassis, and has made this resemblance an adjunct to her career.

The ad was run in September and October of 1983 in several upscale publications including Esquire, Harper's Bazaar, The New Yorker, and the New York Times **258 Magazine. It received widespread circulation, and apparently was the subject of considerable comment, as was the entire series. Dior reportedly committed 2.5 million dollars to the campaign, and boasted that as a result, sales went through the roof. In opposition to the application for an injunction, defendants urge, among other things, that it is unnecessary because the ad has already appeared, and it is not scheduled for republication. However, they declined to enter into any formal stipulation to that effect, and trade papers are abuzz with speculation about the resurrection and reincarnation of the campaign, with possible television showings to reach an even wider audience. Moreover, the case presents an important question under the privacy law, and it is appropriate that it be judicially resolved. *Matter of Baumann & Son Buses Inc.,* 46 N.Y.2d 1061, 1063, 416 N.Y.S.2d 788, 390 N.E.2d 295; *Le Drugstore Etats Unis v. N.Y. State Board of Pharmacy,* 33 N.Y.2d 298, 301, 352 N.Y.S.2d 188, 307 N.E.2d 249.

Section 50 of the New York Civil Rights Law provides:

> "A person, firm or corporation that uses for advertising purposes, or for the purposes of trade, the name, portrait or picture of any living person without having first obtained the written consent of such person ... is guilty of a misdemeanor."

Having defined the offense, and declaring it to be criminal, § 51 of the Civil Rights Law goes on to provide civil remedies for violation as well, including injunction and damages.

> "Any person whose name, portrait or picture is used within this state for advertising purposes or for the purposes of trade without the written consent first obtained as above provided may maintain an equitable action in the supreme court of this state against the person, firm or corporation so using his name, portrait or picture, to prevent and restrain the use thereof; and may also sue and recover damages for any injuries sustained by reason of such use and if the defendant shall have knowingly used such person's name, portrait or picture in such manner as is forbidden or declared to be unlawful by section fifty of this article, the jury, in its discretion, may award exemplary damages...."

* * *

Is there a violation? Defendants, urging a strict and literal compliance with the statute, say that there is not.

* * *

Plaintiff's name appears nowhere in the advertisement. Nevertheless, the picture of a well-known personality, used in an ad and instantly recognizable, will still serve as a badge of approval for that commercial product. It is designed to "catch the eye and focus it on the advertisement." *Negri v. Schering Corp.,* 333 F.Supp. 101, 105. That is why the use of a person's "portrait or picture" without consent is also proscribed.**259 Just what is comprehended by the term "portrait or picture?"

In *Negri v. Schering Corp.,* supra, plaintiff, the well-known movie actress of the 1920's, Pola Negri, objected to the publication of an advertisement in 1969 showing a scene from one of her early movies with words issuing from her mouth in the balloon caption suggesting the use of the anti-histamine drug Pola-ramine. To defendant's contention that the picture did not really show plaintiff as she was then, the Southern District court, applying New York Law, held that as long as the ad portrayed a recognizable likeness it was actionable, declaring, "If a picture so used is a clear and identifiable likeness of a living person, her or she is entitled to recover damages suffered by reason of such use * * *." (id. p. 105).

In *Ali v. Playgirl, Inc.,* 447 F.Supp. 723, the portrait or picture was not an actual photo, but a composite photo-drawing depicting a naked black man in a boxing ring, with the recognizable facial features of the former world's heavyweight champion. The Southern District court, again applying New York law, held that the phrase "portrait or picture" as used in § 51 of the Civil Rights Law is not restricted to actual photographs, but comprises any representations which are recognizable as likenesses of the complaining individual. In that case, the picture represented something short of actuality—somewhere between representational art and a cartoon.

In *Loftus v. Greenwich Lithographing Co. Inc.,* 192 App.Div. 251, 182 N.Y.S. 428 the objection again was not to an actual picture of the plaintiff, but to an advertising poster for a movie called "Shame", which showed a sketch of a female figure in a costume plaintiff had popularized in a Ziegfeld production. The court rejected defendant's contention that the poster was not an actual depiction of plaintiff. Despite changes that were made as between plaintiff's actual picture and defendant's drawing, the court found it evident that the drawing took plaintiff's appearance as its starting point, and declared that slight changes or deviations would not thwart the application of the wholesome provisions of the Civil Rights Law.

In *Young v. Greneker Studios, Inc.,* 175 Misc. 1027, 26 N.Y.S.2d 357, this court extended the literal definition of portrait or picture to include a manikin or sculpture for which plaintiff was the model. The words "portrait or picture" were construed to be broad enough to cover any likeness or representation of the plaintiff, whether two or three dimensional. On the other hand, conveying the likeness of a person, not graphically, but through sound, by means of the imitation of a distinctive voice does not come within the prohibition of the statute (possibly an oversight, since the possibility of reproducing and disseminating the sound of a voice was not contemplated in 1903 when the §§ 50 and 51 of the Civil Rights Law were first enacted). See *Lahr v. Adell Chemical Co., Inc.,* 1 Cir., 300 F.2d 256, 258. This is not because the portrayal of plaintiff's distinctive vocal delivery was by an imitator, but because a voice was not construed as the equivalent of a name or picture, and the picture used was that of a duck.

The Court of Appeals, 70 years ago, in *Binns v. Vitagraph Co. of America,* 210 N.Y. 51, 103 N.E. 1108, dealt with the question of whether the use of the picture of another person suggestive of the plaintiff is a prohibited use of a plaintiff's portrait or picture. The plaintiff was a wireless operator on a sinking ship, whose radioed distress signal, "COD", resulted in the rescue of hundreds of passengers, and made him a hero. Defendant, attempting to capitalize on the widespread public interest in the story, did a photoplay based on the event (what we would today call a "docudrama"). A professional actor was employed to portray the plaintiff, and was photographed playing the part. The court declared, "A picture within the meaning of the statute is not necessarily a photograph of the living person, but includes any representation of such person. The picture ... was intended to be, and it was, a representation of the plaintiff." **260 id, p. 57, 103 N.E. 1108. The court expressly rejected the contention of the defendant that all it used "was an actual picture of a person made up to look like and impersonate the plaintiff." While we might take a different view today as to whether a depiction of a newsworthy event (see *Murray v. New York Magazine Co.,* 27 N.Y.2d 406, 318 N.Y.S.2d 474, 267 N.E.2d 256) or a dramatized re-enactment or even a satirical portrayal is a commercial statement or protected comment (*University of Notre Dame v. Twentieth Century Fox Film Corp.,* 22 A.D.2d 452, 256 N.Y.S.2d 301, aff'd. 15 N.Y.2d 940, 259 N.Y.S.2d 832, 207 N.E.2d 508) the court was clear that the photographic portrayal by one person to simulate another without consent was forbidden by the statute.

Defendants urge as controlling *Lombardo v. Doyle, Dane & Bernbach, Inc.,* 58 A.D.2d 620, 396 N.Y.S.2d 661, in which there was a dismissal of an invasion of privacy action (by a vote of 3–2) against a television commercial which showed an actor conducting a band at a New Year's Eve party playing "Auld Lang Syne", similar to the way plaintiff bandleader had done for decades, and with which he was associated in the public mind. However, there the majority of court was refusing to equate a person's style or characteristics or musical arrangements with a "name, portrait or picture" where plaintiff's name was not mentioned and the actor did not physically resemble the plaintiff. Similarly, in *Shaw v. Time & Life Records,* 38 N.Y.2d 201, 379 N.Y.S.2d 390, 341 N.E.2d 817, plaintiff bandleader was denied the right to make claim under §§ 50 and 51 of the Civil Rights Law against defendant for simulating the "sound" and style of arrangements of his swing era band. And in *Toscani v. Hersey,* 271 App. Div. 445, 65 N.Y.S.2d 814, where the plaintiff was portrayed in the book and play "A Bell for Adano", but under a different and fictionalized name, the court held that a work inspired by the acts, events and experiences of a living person is not an unauthorized use of his "name, portrait or picture."

The principle to be distilled from a study of the statute and of the cases construing it is that all persons, of whatever station in life, from the relatively unknown to the world famous, are to be secured against rapacious commercial exploitation. While the statute may not, by its terms, cover voice or movement, characteristics or style, it is intended to protect the essence of the person, his or her identity or *persona* from being unwillingly or unknowingly misappropriated for the profit of another.

* * *

Today, the visual have superseded the verbal arts, and news photography, television, and motion pictures can accord instant world-wide recognition to a face. For some people, even without their American Express Cards, the face is total identification, more than a signature or a coat of arms. (Cf. *Orsini v. Eastern Wine Corp.,* 190 Misc. 235, 73 N.Y.S.2d 426 aff'd. 273 App.Div. 947, 78 N.Y.S.2d 224). The unauthorized use of a person's signature would not pass muster under the statute because it was claimed merely to be a facsimile. Is a picture or portrait intended to look like someone not that person's picture if it is similarly a facsimile or a simulation?

* * *

The statute is in the disjunctive. There need not be, as defendants suggest, a coupling of name *and* picture. The essence of what is prohibited, as the statute, the cases, and the dictionary definitions make clear, is the exploitation of one's identity as that is conveyed verbally or graphically. A photograph may be a depiction only of the person before the lens, but a "portrait or picture" gives wider scope, to encompass a representation which conveys the essence and likeness of an individual, not only actuality, but the close and purposeful resemblance to reality. That is how it was defined in *Binns v. Vitagraph Co. of America,* supra, as any representation, including the picture of another, which was intended to be, and did, in fact, convey the idea that it was the plaintiff.

We are dealing here with actuality and appearance, where illusion often heightens reality and all is not quite what it seems. Is the illusionist to be free to step aside, having reaped the benefits of his creation, and permitted to disclaim the very impression he sought to create? If we were to permit it, we would be sanctioning an obvious loophole to evade the statute. If a person is unwilling to give his or her endorsement to help sell a product, either at an offered price or at any price, no matter-hire a double and the same effect is achieved. The essential purpose of the statute must be carried out by giving it a common sense reading which bars easy evasion. If we truly value the right of privacy in a world of exploitation, where every mark of distinctiveness becomes grist for the mills of publicity, then we must give it more than lip service and grudging recognition. Let the word go forth-there is no free ride. The commercial hitchhiker seeking to travel on the fame of another will have to learn to pay the fare or stand on his own two feet.

There are many aspects of identity. A person may be known not only by objective indicia-name, face, and social security number, but by other characteristics as well-voice, movement, style, coiffure, typical phrases, as well as by his or her history and accomplishments. Thus far, the legislature has accorded protection only to those aspects of identity embodied in name and face. Imitators are free to simulate voice or hair-do, or characteristic clothing or accessories, and writers to comment on and actors to re-enact events. No one is free to trade on another's name or appearance and claim immunity because what he is using is similar to but not identical with the original.

* * *

The fact that even as between people who resemble one another, there are variances and points of dissimilarity is of no moment. It is the over-all impression being made that counts. The statute necessarily contemplates that a depiction may not be precise, for the words "portrait or picture" comprehend a sketch, a cartoon, or a caricature which selectively omit some features and accentuate others. There are then points of resemblance and points of difference and distortion, but if done well there is instant recognition. What difference if a sketch is used instead of a look-alike model in connection with a commercial promotion? The end result is the same-trading on the name or features of another and the unwarranted commercial exploitation of a person who has not consented to be commercially exploited.

* * *

In essence, this court finds on the undisputed facts, that plaintiff's identity was impermissibly misappropriated for the purposes of trade and advertising, and that it makes no difference if the picture used to establish that identity was genuine or counterfeit.

* * *

Plaintiff's statutory right to privacy has been trampled upon, and that is **264 all that need be shown. The motion is granted; the cross-motion is denied.

Robert BURCK d/b/a The Naked Cowboy, Plaintiff

v.

MARS, INCORPORATED and Chute Gerdeman, Inc., Defendants

United States District Court,
S.D. New York

571 F.Supp.2d 446

June 23, 2008

CHIN

This is the case of The Naked Cowboy versus The Blue M & M.

Plaintiff Robert Burck is a "street entertainer" who performs in New York City's Times Square as The Naked Cowboy, wearing only a white cowboy hat, cowboy boots, and underpants, and carrying a guitar strategically placed to give the illusion of nudity. He has registered trademarks to "The Naked Cowboy" name and likeness.

Beginning in April 2007, defendants Mars, Incorporated ("Mars") and Chute Gerdeman, Inc. ("Chute") began running an animated cartoon advertisement on two oversized video billboards in Times Square, featuring a blue M & M dressed "exactly like The Naked Cowboy," wearing only a white cowboy hat, cowboy boots, and underpants, and carrying a guitar.

In this case, Burck sues defendants for compensatory and punitive damages. He alleges that defendants have violated his "right to publicity" under New York law and infringed his trademarks under federal law by using his likeness, persona, and image for commercial purposes without his written permission and by falsely suggesting that he has endorsed M & M candy.

Three motions are before the Court: Chute moves pursuant to Fed.R.Civ.P. 12(b)(6) to dismiss the complaint; Mars moves pursuant to Fed.R.Civ.P. 12(c) for judgment on the pleadings; and Burck moves pursuant to Fed.R. Civ.P. 12(f) to strike certain of defendants' affirmative defenses.

For the reasons that follow, Burck's motion is denied and defendants' motions are denied in part and granted in part. Burck's right to privacy claim (denominated as a right of publicity claim) is dismissed, for the New York statute protects*449 the name, portrait, or picture of a "living person," not a character created or a role performed by a living person. Burck may proceed, however, with his false endorsement claim, for he plausibly alleges that consumers seeing defendants' advertisements would conclude-incorrectly-that he had endorsed M & M candy.

BACKGROUND

A. *The Facts*

As alleged in the complaint and set forth in the exhibits incorporated therein by reference, the facts are as follows:

For the past ten years, Burck "has performed as a street entertainer in New York City's Times Square under the persona known as The Naked Cowboy," wearing only "a white cowboy hat, white cowboy boots, white underpants, and an acoustic guitar." (Compl.¶ ¶ 5, 6). His street performances "have become a fixture of New York City culture, as well as one of the top tourist attractions" in Times Square. (*Id.* ¶ 7).

The Naked Cowboy has become "a prominent and well-known persona," and Burck has registered trademarks to The Naked Cowboy name and likeness. (*Id.* ¶ ¶ 20, 21). In addition to performing in Times Square, Burck has appeared as The Naked Cowboy in various television shows, movies, and video games. (*Id.* ¶ ¶ 10–19). He has also licensed his name and likeness to companies for endorsements and advertisements. (*Id.* ¶ 22). For instance, he appeared in a Chevrolet commercial that debuted during Super Bowl XLI. (*Id.* ¶ 23).

Mars sells candies and chocolate products, including the world-famous M & M's. (*Id.* ¶ 33). Mars retained Chute, an advertising and design agency, to create a video for two electronic billboards in Times Square and a mural for its M & M World store located in Times Square. (*Id.* ¶ ¶ 32, 33).

The video (an animated cartoon) featured "a blue 'M & M' dressed up exactly like The Naked Cowboy-white underwear, white cowboy hat, white cowboy boots, and white guitar." (*Id.* ¶ 26; *see* DX C).[FN1] In addition to the M & M Cowboy character, the video showed other M & Ms as famous New York figures, such as the Statue of Liberty and King Kong, as well as everyday New Yorkers and tourists engaging in typical New York activities such as hailing a cab and riding a carriage through Central Park. Beginning in April 2007 (Compl. ¶ 29), the video "played on a continuous loop every few minutes over a nine-month period" (Tr. at 22).

FN1. References to "DX" are to defendants' exhibits submitted at the oral argument on June 11, 2008. These exhibits are referred to in the complaint and are deemed incorporated therein by reference. (*See* Transcript of Proceedings of June 11, 2008 ("Tr.") at 4).

The mural inside the M & M World store was a snapshot of the heart of Times Square, transformed into an animated world populated by M & M characters. (Compl. ¶ 30; *see* DX B1). Neon lights, oversized billboards advertising Broadway shows, and familiar landmarks, such as the Cup Noodles sign, filled the scene. Many of the signs and billboards in the mural were altered to incorporate the M & M logo or candy themes, such as replacing "STOMP" (the name of a show) with the word "CHOMP" and substituting a red M & M in place of the red heart in the logo" I NY." In the middle of the mural, in the midst of a cluster of billboards, was a small billboard featuring a yellow M & M wearing The Naked Cowboy's signature costume. (DX B1).

Defendants did not request, nor did they receive, permission from Burck to use a *450 likeness of The Naked Cowboy for the M & M Cowboy characters. (Compl. ¶ 25).

* * *

DISCUSSION

I start with defendants' motions, addressing first Burck's right of privacy claim under New York law and second his trademark infringement claim under the Lanham Act. I then turn to Burck's motion to strike certain affirmative defenses.

* * *

2. *The Right of Privacy Claim*

a. *The Statute*

The right to privacy has been recognized by statute in New York for more than a century. *See Groden v. Random House, Inc.,* 61 F.3d 1045, 1048 (2d Cir.1995). The New York legislature enacted sections 50 and 51 of the Civil Rights Law to protect against "nonconsensual commercial appropriations of the name, portrait or picture of a living person." *Finger v. Omni Publ'ns. Int'l, Ltd.,* 77 N.Y.2d 138, 141, 564 N.Y.S.2d 1014, 566 N.E.2d 141 (1990); *see also Arrington v. New York Times Co.,* 55 N.Y.2d 433, 439, 449 N.Y.S.2d 941, 434 N.E.2d 1319 (1982). There is no common law right to privacy or publicity in New York, and thus sections 50 and 51 provide the only remedy for such claims. *Groden,* 61 F.3d at 1049.

*451 Section 50 of the New York Civil Rights Law makes it a misdemeanor to use "for advertising purposes, or for the purposes of trade, the name, portrait or picture of any living person without having first obtained the written consent of such person." N.Y. Civ. Rights Law § 50 (McKinney 1992). Section 51 creates a cause of action for the invasion of the "right of privacy" granted by section 50. *See Zacchini v. Scripps–Howard Broad. Co.,* 433 U.S. 562, 571 n. 6, 97 S.Ct. 2849, 53 L.Ed.2d 965 (1977). Section 51 provides:

> Any person whose name, portrait, picture or voice is used within this state for advertising purposes or for the purposes of trade without the written consent first obtained as above provided [in section 50] may maintain an equitable action … to prevent and restrain the use thereof; and may also sue and recover damages for any injuries sustained by reason of such use.

N.Y. Civ. Rights Law § 51 (McKinney Supp.2008). To maintain a civil action under section 51, a plaintiff must show that the defendant (1) used his name, portrait, picture, or voice, (2) for advertising or trade purposes, (3) without his written consent. *Allen v. Nat'l Video, Inc.,* 610 F.Supp. 612, 621 (S.D.N.Y.1985).

Sections 50 and 51 are limited in their reach because of the First Amendment. They do not apply, for example, to "reports of newsworthy events or matters of public interest." *Messenger v. Gruner + Jahr Printing & Publ'g,* 94 N.Y.2d 436, 441, 706 N.Y.S.2d 52, 727 N.E.2d 549 (2000). Likewise, they do not apply to works of art. *Hoepker v. Kruger,* 200 F.Supp.2d 340, 349 (S.D.N.Y.2002). For example, the use of a town justice's picture without his permission was held not to violate section 50 where it was used as part of a painting that was a caricature and parody. *Altbach v. Kulon,* 302 A.D.2d 655, 657, 754 N.Y.S.2d 709 (3d Dep't 2003). Similarly, "entertainment broadcasts" that involve, for example, humor and comedy are forms of expression that may also be protected by the First Amendment, although not categorically. *See Geary v. Goldstein,* 831 F.Supp. 269, 273 (S.D.N.Y.1993) (quoting *Frank v. Nat'l Broad. Co.,* 119 A.D.2d 252, 257, 506 N.Y.S.2d 869 (2d Dep't 1986)).

Over the years there has been much litigation over what constitutes a person's "portrait" or "picture" for purposes of sections 50 and 51. It is settled that "any recognizable likeness, not just an actual photograph, may qualify as a 'portrait or picture.' " *Allen,* 610 F.Supp. at 622 (citing *Ali v. Playgirl, Inc.,* 447 F.Supp. 723, 726 (S.D.N.Y.1978)). *Ali* involved a composite photograph and drawing of a naked African–American man in a boxing ring, with facial features recognizable as those of Muhammad Ali. 447 F.Supp. at 726. The court held that this was a portrait or picture of the former world heavyweight boxing champion. *Id.* Similarly, in *Young v. Greneker Studios,* 175 Misc. 1027, 26 N.Y.S.2d 357 (N.Y.Sup.Ct.1941), the court held that a manikin that was modeled on the plaintiff was a portrait or picture of her. *Id.* at 1027–28, 26 N.Y.S.2d 357. The court explained that "[t]he words 'picture' and 'portrait' are broad enough to include any representation [of a living person], whether by photograph, painting or sculpture." *Id.* at 1028, 26 N.Y.S.2d 357.

The use in advertisements of "look-alikes"—models who look like celebrities-has generated lawsuits. The Supreme Court, New York County, held that the use in an advertisement of a model who looked like Jacqueline Kennedy Onassis violated sections 50 and 51. *452 *Onassis v. Christian Dior–New York, Inc.,* 122 Misc.2d 603, 472 N.Y.S.2d 254 (N.Y.Sup.Ct.1984). The court held that "a representation which conveys the essence and likeness of an individual, ... which was intended to be, and did, in fact, convey the idea that it was the plaintiff" was a picture or portrait for purposes of the Civil Rights Law. *Id.* at 611, 472 N.Y.S.2d 254.

In contrast, in *Allen v. National Video, Inc.,* a case involving the use in an advertisement of a Woody Allen look-alike, Judge Motley declined to apply section 51, concluding that she would have to reach a "somewhat strained construction" of the statute to hold that it governed. 610 F.Supp. at 624.

The court framed the question as whether "the mixture of fantasy and reality [in the advertisement] suggested almost unavoidably the actual presence of the real-life celebrity," that is, whether "the photograph in question ... create [d], as a matter of law, the illusion of Woody Allen's actual presence in the advertisement." *Id.* at 623–24. The court concluded that the claim was more appropriately analyzed as a Lanham Act claim. *Id.* at 624.

Judge Motley recognized in *Allen* that "[t]he privacy law does not prohibit one from evoking certain aspects of another's personality." *Id.* at 623 (citing *Lombardo v. Doyle, Dane & Bernbach, Inc.,* 58 A.D.2d 620, 396 N.Y.S.2d 661 (2d Dep't 1977)). Indeed, she held that "[m]erely suggesting certain characteristics of the plaintiff, without literally using his or her name, portrait, or picture, is not actionable under the statute." 610 F.Supp. at 621.

In *Lombardo,* the court rejected a claim under section 51 by the conductor Guy Lombardo based on a commercial showing an actor conducting a band playing "Auld Lang Syne" at a New Year's Eve party much as Lombardo had done for decades. The court held that "it is clear that the Civil Rights Law is to be strictly construed and is not to be applied so as to prohibit the portrayal of an individual's personality or style of performance." 58 A.D.2d at 622, 396 N.Y.S.2d 661.

b. *Application*

There is no dispute as to the second and third elements of Burck's claim under section 51. Defendants concede that the video and mural were used, at least in part, for commercial purposes and that Burck did not give permission, written or otherwise, to defendants to use The Naked Cowboy likeness. (Tr. at 5–6). As to the first element, it is also undisputed that defendants did not invoke the name "Robert Burck" or the name of his character "The Naked Cowboy." Nor did they use Burck's voice. Rather, the sole issue is whether defendants used Burck's "portrait" or "picture."

I conclude that defendants did not.

First, defendants did not use an actual photograph or picture of Burck himself, nor did they use a recognizable likeness or representation of him. *See Allen,* 610 F.Supp. at 622. Obviously, no viewer would have thought that the M & M Cowboy characters were actually Burck or were intended to be him. *See Onassis,* 122 Misc.2d at 611, 472 N.Y.S.2d 254. The M & M Cowboy characters are not portraits or pictures of Burck, and thus defendants did not use a portrait or picture of Burck.

Second, defendants did evoke certain aspects of the character created by Burck, and they copied The Naked Cowboy's costume, but these actions were not prohibited by sections 50 and 51. Merely evoking certain aspects of another's character or role does not violate sections 50 and 51. *See Allen,* 610 F.Supp. at 623 ("The privacy law does not prohibit one from evoking certain aspects of another's personali*453 ty...."); *Lombardo,* 58 A.D.2d at 622, 396 N.Y.S.2d 661.

The plain language of the Civil Rights Law makes it clear that the statutory right to privacy does not extend to fictitious characters adopted or created by celebrities. Section 51 protects "any person," and section 50 limits the statutory protection to "any living person." *See Messenger v. Gruner + Jahr Printing & Publ'g,* 208 F.3d 122, 125 (2d Cir.2000). The Naked Cowboy is not a living person, but a character Burck takes on when performing. The privacy statutes were not intended to protect a trademarked, costumed character publicly performed by a person.

The case law supports the conclusion that the M & M Cowboy characters depicted in the video and mural are merely personifications that do not fall within the literal meaning of "portrait" or "picture" of a person. In *White v. Samsung Elecs. Am., Inc.,* 971 F.2d 1395 (9th Cir.1992), Vanna White, the hostess of the popular game show "Wheel of Fortune," sued defendants for, among other things, violating her right to privacy under California's privacy statute, which is substantively similar to the New York privacy statute. FN2 (Omitted) Defendants had produced an advertisement using a robot dressed in a wig, gown, and jewelry that resembled White's hair and dress. The Ninth Circuit affirmed the lower court's dismissal of her right of privacy claim on the ground that "a robot with mechanical features [was] not, for example, a manikin molded to White's precise features." *Id.* at 1397. It thus concluded that the "caricature or impressionistic resemblance" was not a "likeness" FN3 (Omitted) within the meaning of the statute.[FN4] The M & M characters dressed to look like The Naked Cowboy here are comparable to the robot made to look like Vanna White.

FN4. The Ninth Circuit did allow White to proceed with her right to publicity claim under California common law, which the court concluded was "not so confined" as the statutory right of privacy. New York, however, does not recognize an analogous common law right to publicity. *See Allen,* 610 F.Supp. at 621.

Burck argues that his "persona" as The Naked Cowboy qualifies as a "portrait" or "picture" within the meaning of section 51. But the statutory right of privacy was not intended to protect the "property interest of the celebrity in his or her public identity." *Allen,* 610 F.Supp. at 621. Instead, sections 50 and 51 were "primarily designed to compensate for the hurt feelings of private people who find their identities usurped for another's commercial gain." *Id.* This statutory purpose is reflected in the title of Article 5 of the New York Civil Rights law, "Right of Privacy." Although public figures do not forfeit their right of privacy, *see Onassis,* 122 Misc.2d at 614, 472 N.Y.S.2d 254, aspects of their public personas not captured in their physical features or voice are not protected under the privacy statute, *see Allen,* 610 F.Supp. at 623 (under section 51, "the commercial use complained of [must] amount to a 'portrait or picture' of an individual, not merely the suggestion of some aspect of a person's public persona").

As discussed above, the "look-alike cases" are also instructive, for they emphasize*454 the point that although a representation of "any recognizable likeness, not just an actual photograph, may qualify as a 'portrait or picture,' " *id.* at 622, that likeness must be a "close and purposeful resemblance to reality" of the actual person, *Onassis,* 122 Misc.2d at 611–12, 472 N.Y.S.2d at 261. In *Onassis,* the court found that the advertisement created the overall impression that plaintiff herself was in the advertisement. The court in *Allen* distinguished *Onassis* and found that Allen's look-alike was not a portrait or picture as required by section 51. The court explained that the " 'illusion' created in *Onassis* was that plaintiff had actually appeared in the advertisement," and thus the advertisement was, "as a matter of law, a portrait of Jacqueline Onassis." *Allen,* 610 F.Supp. at 623. In contrast, there were "several physical differences" between the Allen look-alike and Allen himself, such as defendant's larger eyebrows, wider face, and more uneven complexion, and thus the court concluded that the advertisement did not use Allen's portrait or picture. *Id.* at 624. Here, of course, there was no "illusion" that Burck was actually in defendants' advertisements.

Citing *Loftus v. Greenwich Lithographing Co.,* 192 A.D. 251, 182 N.Y.S. 428 (1st Dep't 1920), Burck contends that section 51 prohibits images even where the only recognizable likeness to the plaintiff is his or her signature costume. In *Loftus,* the plaintiff was an actress who was photographed in a "red costume representing a rose." *Id.* at 252, 182 N.Y.S. 428. This costume was never worn by any person other than the plaintiff, and she was "readily recognized from the photograph, and particularly from the costume." *Id.* To promote a film, the defendant produced a poster that featured a female figure with an identical costume. Although the main identifying feature in the infringing poster was the costume, the basis of the court's decision was that the female figure in the poster was such "an accurate likeness of the plaintiff" that it was "perfectly evident that [the infringer] had and used a copy of [plaintiff's] photograph, and that he copied the features of the plaintiff." *Id.* at 254, 256, 182 N.Y.S. 428. In other words, the poster in *Loftus* violated section 51 not because it depicted a unique costume, but because it attempted to create a "portrait or picture" of the actress herself.

Here, there was no attempt to create a portrait or picture of Burck himself. Rather, the purportedly infringing images were M & M characters wearing Burck's signature outfit. The images were not portraits or pictures of Burck as The Naked Cowboy, but of M & Ms dressed as The Naked Cowboy. Thus, they do not violate sections 50 and 51, and accordingly, Burck's right of privacy claim is dismissed.

* * *

*458 *CONCLUSION*

For the reasons set forth above, Burck's motion is denied and defendants' motions are denied in part and granted in part. Chute's motion to dismiss and Mars's motion for judgment on the pleading are granted with respect to the right to privacy claim …

SO ORDERED.

WORKSHEET NO. 2: THE PERSUASIVE RULE

Rule drafting in persuasive writing is different from rule drafting in objective writing. The main differences are in the organization, the breadth and depth of the rule, and the persuasive tone.

Before writing a persuasive rule, however, you should write the rule objectively first to ensure accuracy. Crafting an objective rule first will also offer perspective on the neutral rule the judge will consider when evaluating your persuasive rule. To write the rule objectively, use the approach explained in Worksheet No. 2 for Objective Writing, which is summarized below:

To determine rules of law from a single source or multiple sources of law, including the elements, definitions, and/or exceptions, answer the following brainstorming questions:

1. What is the rule?
2. What are the exceptions to the rule, if any?
3. What else will the court consider, if anything?

After answering these three questions, put your answers together in one or more sentences to write the rule. Once you have written a rule, evaluate it to ensure it is complete and appropriate in scope. To evaluate the rule(s), answer the following questions:

1. Is the rule too specific based on the legal authority and your client facts?
2. Is the rule too broad based on the legal authority and your client facts?
3. Does the rule include vague terms?
4. Is the rule circular?
5. If there is more than one rule, are the rules repetitive?

After answering the above questions, you should have a complete objective rule. Now you need to start thinking about how to write your objective rule persuasively. To help you do this, consider the following brainstorming questions:

1. Who is your client?
2. What outcome do you want for your client based on this rule?
3. What part of the rule do you want to emphasize for your client?
4. What part of the rule do you want to de-emphasize for your client?

Using the answers to these brainstorming questions as your guide, convert your objective rule into a persuasive rule. To write your persuasive rule, look at your objective rule, your answers to the above brainstorming questions, and the following considerations:

1. Begin the rule with the outcome you want for your client; that is, if you want an injunction to be granted begin by stating "An injunction will be granted when ..."
2. Begin the rule with your client's role in the litigation; that is, Plaintiff or Defendant. For example, "A plaintiff is entitled to an injunction when ..."
3. Include the favorable part of the rule at the beginning to provide emphasis.
4. Include unfavorable parts of the rule in the middle to bury them.
5. Emphasize the opposing party's requirements of proof (burdens, elements, evidence, etc.). For example, "For a defendant to prevail on his motion, he must prove five elements with substantial evidence." Or, "Defendant has the burden of proof."

Once you have written your rule persuasively, evaluate it for persuasive tone and presentation. To evaluate whether your rule is persuasively written for your client's case, answer the following questions:

1. Did you use active or passive voice? (Consider the benefits of each.)
2. Did you put your client's position in a point of emphasis in the rule?
3. If the rule is favorable, did you state it broadly?
4. If the rule is unfavorable, did you state it narrowly?
5. If there is an exception to the rule, did you include it in a way that is favorable to your client?

EXAMPLE OBJECTIVE RULE:
California Civil Code Section 3344(a) provides that the knowing use of another's photograph for commercial purposes without the person's prior consent is a violation of that person's right of publicity. Section 3344(d) provides an exception to the consent requirement contained in § 3344(a), which states that the use of a photograph in connection with "any news, public affairs, or sports broadcast or account, or any political campaign" does not require consent.

EXAMPLE PERSUASIVE RULE:
The knowing use of another's photograph for commercial purposes without the person's consent violates California Civil Code Section 3344(a). The only exception to the statutory consent requirement is if the defendant can prove that the use of a photograph was in connection with a matter in the public interest. Cal. Civ. Code § 3344(d).

Case File Assignment:

Write a persuasive rule for your client's case on the issue of misappropriation of likeness using the legal authorities in the Case File. To help you write a persuasive rule, begin by writing an objective rule, or use the objective rule you wrote for Worksheet No. 2 for Objective Writing.

State your objective rule here:

Convert the objective rule into a persuasive rule. To help do this, answer the following brainstorming questions:

1. Who is your client?

2. What outcome do you want for your client based on this rule?

3. What part of the rule do you want to emphasize for your client?

4. What part of the rule do you want to de-emphasize for your client?

Using the answers to these brainstorming questions as your guide, convert your objective rule into a persuasive rule. To write your persuasive rule, look at your objective rule, your answers to the above brainstorming questions, and the following considerations:

1. Begin the rule with the outcome you want for your client; that is, if you want an injunction to be granted begin by stating "An injunction will be granted when ..."
2. Begin the rule with your client's role in the litigation; that is, Plaintiff or Defendant. For example, "A plaintiff is entitled to an injunction when ..."
3. Include the favorable part of the rule at the beginning to provide emphasis.
4. Include unfavorable parts of the rule in the middle to bury them.
5. Emphasize the opposing party's requirements of proof (burdens, elements, evidence, etc.). For example, "For a defendant to prevail on his motion, he must prove five elements with substantial evidence." Or, "Defendant has the burden of proof."

Once you have written the rule persuasively, evaluate it for persuasive tone and presentation. To evaluate whether your rule is persuasively written for your client, answer the following questions:

1. Did you use active or passive voice? (Consider the benefits of each.)
2. Did you put your client's position in a point of emphasis in the rule?
3. If the rule is favorable, did you state it broadly?
4. If the rule is unfavorable, did you state it narrowly?
5. If there is an exception to the rule, did you include it in a way that is favorable to your client?

WORKSHEET NO. 3: PARENTHETICALS

Parentheticals are a quick way to provide the reader with illustrations of a legal principle without having to include an objective case illustration. Writing parentheticals, however, can be tricky because you must include enough information for the reader to understand the significance of the precedent case and its connection to the legal principle the parenthetical is explaining, but not include so much information that you effectively have written an objective case illustration.

A parenthetical is substantively correct if it includes:

1. The legal principle or rule you plan to explain with the parenthetical;
2. The relevant facts from the precedent case that support the legal principle you plan to explain with the parenthetical; and
3. The key words and phrases from the precedent case that support the legal principle you plan to explain with the parenthetical.

A parenthetical is technically correct if it:

1. Asserts a legal principle prior to the parentheticals;
2. Follows the legal principle with a proper citation;
3. Has proper capitalization within the parenthetical—do not capitalize the first word of a parenthetical if it is only a word, phase, or clause; but do capitalize the first word of a parenthetical if it is a complete sentence;
4. Uses parallel construction for string parentheticals—if you use one form for one parenthetical, use that same form for all of the parentheticals in the string; and
5. Is kept short—if the information you want to provide cannot be provided in a phase, clause, or a single sentence, do not use a parenthetical.

Here are some examples that demonstrate parentheticals with not enough information and parentheticals with enough information. Please note the legal principle that precedes the parentheticals.

EXAMPLE PARENTHETICALS:

NOT ENOUGH INFORMATION IN THE PARENTHETICALS:
Although celebrities have the right to First Amendment protection from the unauthorized exploitation of their photographs under the right of publicity, the statutory cause of action specifically exempts from liability the use of a photograph in connection with a matter in the public interest. California Civil Code 3344(d) states that no prior consent is required for use of a photograph in the public interest, such as news, public affairs, or sports broadcast or account, or any political campaign. Public interest has been defined as "recent events or publications about people who, by their accomplishments, mode of living, professional standing or calling, create a legitimate and widespread attention to their activities." Dora v. Frontline Video, Inc., 15 Cal. App. 4th 536 (2nd Dist. 1993) (a 1987 surfing documentary); Gionfriddo v. Major League Baseball, 94 Cal. App. 4th 400 (1st Dist. 2001) (web cast of baseball statistics).

ENOUGH INFORMATION IN THE PARENTHETICALS:
Although celebrities have the right to First Amendment protection from the unauthorized exploitation of their photographs under the right of publicity, the statutory cause of action specifically exempts from liability the use of a photograph in connection with a matter in the public interest. California Civil Code 3344(d) states that no prior consent is required for use of a photograph in the public interest, such as news, public affairs, or sports broadcast or account, or any political campaign. Public interest has been defined as "recent events or publications about people who, by their accomplishments, mode of living, professional standing or calling, create a legitimate and widespread attention to their activities." Dora v. Frontline Video, Inc., 15 Cal. App. 4th 536 (2nd Dist. 1993) (a 1987 surfing documentary that included footage of a famous surfer was in the public interest and no prior consent was needed); Gionfriddo v. Major League Baseball, 94 Cal. App. 4th 400 (1st Dist. 2001) (web cast of baseball statistics that included a photograph of a famous baseball player was in the public interest and no prior consent was needed).

Case File Assignment:

Write a parenthetical(s) for your client's case using the legal authority in the Case File and/or the legal authority assigned by your professor. To help you write a parenthetical(s), answer the following brainstorming questions for each precedent case you plan to explain with a parenthetical:

1. What is the legal principle you plan to explain with a parenthetical(s)? Please note that this legal principle may precede more than one parenthetical (see examples above).

2. For each precedent case you plan to explain with a parenthetical, answer the following brainstorming questions:

   a. What is the proper citation for the precedent case you plan to explain with the parenthetical?

   b. What are the relevant facts from the precedent case that support the legal principle you plan to explain with the parenthetical?

   c. What is the legal conclusion from the precedent case that supports the legal principle you plan to explain with the parenthetical?

   d. What are the key words and phrases from the precedent case that support the legal principle you plan to explain with the parenthetical?

Using your answers to these brainstorming questions as your guide, you now are ready to write a parenthetical(s). Use one of the formulas below to organize your parenthetical(s). The order of the information contained inside the parentheticals can be reversed.

One Parenthetical:

Legal Principle. Cite (relevant facts + legal conclusion to support the legal principle, using the key words and phrases from the precedent case).

Multiple Parentheticals:

Legal Principle. Cite (relevant facts + legal conclusion to support the legal principle, using the key words and phrases from the precedent case); Cite (relevant facts + legal conclusion to support the legal principle, using the key words and phrases from the precedent case); Cite (relevant facts + legal conclusion to support the legal principle, using the key words and phrases from the precedent case).

When writing parenthetical(s), consider the following technical requirements:

1. Use proper capitalization within the parenthetical—do not capitalize the first word of a parenthetical if it is only a word, phase, or clause; but do capitalize the first word of a parenthetical if it is a complete sentence;

2. Use parallel construction for string parentheticals—if you use one form for one parenthetical use that same form for all of the parentheticals in the string; and

3. Keep it short—if the information you want to provide cannot be provided in a phase, clause, or a single sentence, do not use a parenthetical.

WORKSHEET NO. 4: DEDUCTIVE REASONING

Deductive reasoning justifies a result by directly applying a legal principle to the facts of your client's case. The result is the result simply because the law mandates it. There is no in-depth analysis, but rather a straightforward application of the legal principle to the facts of the client's case.

Deductive reasoning is substantively correct if it includes:

1. The legal principle or rule you are applying;
2. The legal conclusion you seek to establish by the application of the legal principle or rule; and
3. The relevant facts from your client's case needed to justify that legal conclusion.

*Please note that 2 and 3 can be reversed and that deductive reasoning is frequently paired with parentheticals.

EXAMPLE DEDUCTIVE REASONING:

It is illegal for anyone under the age of sixteen to operate a motor vehicle. (Citation omitted). The defendant illegally operated a motor vehicle because she was only thirteen years old at the time she drove her father's car.

EXAMPLE DEDUCTIVE REASONING WITH PARENTHETICALS:

Although celebrities have the right to First Amendment protection from the unauthorized exploitation of their photographs under the right of publicity, the statutory cause of action specifically exempts from liability the use of a photograph in connection with a matter in the public interest. California Civil Code 3344(d) states that no prior consent is required for use of a photograph in the public interest, such as news, public affairs, or sports broadcast or account, or any political campaign. Public interest has been defined as "recent events or publications about people who, by their accomplishments, mode of living, professional standing or calling, create a legitimate and widespread attention to their activities." Dora v. Frontline Video, Inc., 15 Cal. App. 4th 536 (2nd Dist. 1993) (a 1987 surfing documentary that included footage of a famous surfer was in the public interest and no prior consent was needed); Gionfriddo v. Major League Baseball, 94 Cal. App. 4th 400 (1st Dist. 2001) (web cast of baseball statistics that included a photograph of a famous baseball player in the public interest and no prior consent was needed). Because the use of Mr. Quarterback's photograph was used in connection with his fourth Superbowl victory in ten years, it is in the public interest and his consent was not required.

Case File Assignment:

Write an argument for your client's case using deductive reasoning based on the legal authority in the Case File and/or the legal authority assigned by your professor. To help you write a deductive reasoning argument, answer the following brainstorming questions:

1. What is the legal principle or rule that you want to apply to your client's case?

2. What is the legal conclusion you seek to establish by the application of the legal principle or rule?

3. What are the relevant facts from your client's case needed to justify that legal conclusion?

Using the answers to these brainstorming questions as your guide, write an argument using deductive reasoning. Start by cutting and pasting your answers into paragraph form and then mold them into a readable sentence or paragraph. Consider whether the deductive reasoning will follow a simple legal principle or a legal principle with parentheticals.

WORKSHEET NO. 5: POLICY–BASED REASONING

Policy-based reasoning in persuasive writing is not that different from policy-based reasoning in objective writing. The organization of the substance is the same; however, the presentation of the substance is different.

To write a persuasive policy-based argument, start by evaluating the policy-based argument objectively (as explained in Worksheet No. 5 for Objective Writing). To do this, consider:

1. The conclusion you will reach by applying the policy to your client's case. (You may need to answer this question after you have completed your analysis of the policy.)

2. The rule you are applying to your client's case.

3. The purpose underlying the rule identified in response to Question 2 above and the origin of that purpose. What greater societal purpose(s) was the court or legislature trying to protect in creating the rule? (NOTE: There may be more than one purpose. If there is more than one purpose, identify if the court seems to prefer one purpose over another.) Also, the purpose behind the rule should come from legal authority, such as legislative history, case authority, or well-established public opinion, not your personal opinion.

4. The potential outcomes for your client when applying the rule.

5. The potential outcomes for the other party when applying the rule.

6. How the outcomes identified in response to Questions 4 and 5 above are or are not served by the purpose(s) of the rule you identified in response to Question 3 above.

7. The outcome that best follows the purpose of the rule.

After evaluating these questions, you should have an objective understanding of whether the purpose(s) of the rule supports the arguments for your client's case. If it does, use the following formula to write a policy-based reasoning argument for your client's case. If it does not support the arguments for your client's case, do not include a policy-based argument.

A persuasive policy-based reasoning argument is substantively complete if it:

1. Begins the argument by stating the conclusion you want to argue by applying the purpose of the rule to your client's case. (This is the thesis sentence for this argument).

2. States the rule that is the basis of the policy-based reasoning argument.

3. Identifies and describes the purpose underlying the rule and the origin of that purpose. Remember, the purpose behind the rule must

come from legal authority, such as legislative history, case authority, or well-established public opinion, not your personal opinion. Also, if there is more than one purpose, explain which one the courts tend to use more.

4. States persuasively that the purpose underlying the rule applies to your client's case.
5. Explains with specific detail why the possible outcome(s) for your client furthers the purpose underlying the rule.
6. Concludes with a sentence that provides closure to the policy-based reasoning argument. This sentence must connect to the thesis sentence that began the policy-based reasoning argument.

> EXAMPLE POLICY–BASED REASONING ARGUMENT:
>
> Ms. Anchor's claim is supported by the purpose underlying the statute. While § 3344(d) protects information that is directly related to matters in the public interest, the legislature did not intend to protect false information that is presented as news. Eastwood, 149 Cal. App. 3d at 425. The Legislature stated that the public interest exception cannot be exercised so as to abuse the rights of individuals. Id. This policy applies to Ms. Anchor's case. Ms. Anchor denies that she ever reported on the Mayor's campaign and the general manager of her news station stated that "there are no concerns about Ms. Anchor's ethics whatsoever." Yet, TFF created a t-shirt that directly challenged Ms. Anchor's ethics. It is exactly this type of dissemination of false information the Legislature did not intend the public interest exception to protect. Id. Therefore, Ms. Anchor's right of publicity supported by the policy behind the statute and TFF's unauthorized use of her photograph is not protected.

Case File Assignment:

Write an argument for your client's case using policy-based reasoning based on the legal authority in the Case File and/or the legal authority assigned by your professor. To help you write a policy-based reasoning argument, answer the following brainstorming questions:

1. What is the conclusion you want to argue by applying the policy to your client's case? (You may need to answer this question last.)

2. What is the rule you are applying to your client's case?

3. What is the purpose underlying the rule identified in response to Question 2 above and the origin of that purpose? What greater societal purpose(s) was the court or legislature trying to protect in creating the rule? (NOTE: There may be more than one purpose. If there is more than one purpose, identify if the court seems to prefer one purpose over another.) Also, the purpose behind the rule should come from legal authority, such as legislative history, case authority, or well-established public opinion, not your personal opinion.

4. What are the potential outcomes for your client when applying the rule?

5. What are the potential outcomes for the other party when applying the rule?

6. How are the outcomes identified in response to Questions 4 and 5 above served or not served by the purpose(s) of the rule identified in response to Question 3 above?

7. Which outcome best follows the purpose(s) of the rule? Explain why.

After answering these brainstorming questions, you should have a clear understanding of whether the possible outcomes for your client do or do not serve the underlying purpose of the rule. If the purpose of the rule is served by your client's case, then use the following formula to write a policy-based reasoning argument. Each of these six parts must be included for a complete policy-based reasoning argument. This does not mean, however, that you need to have six sentences; a complete policy-based reasoning argument may be less than three sentences or as much as two full paragraphs.

1. Begin the paragraph(s) by stating the conclusion you want to argue by applying the purpose of the rule to your client's case. (This is the thesis sentence for this paragraph).
2. State the rule that is the basis of the policy-based reasoning argument.
3. Identify and describe the purpose underlying the rule and the origin of that purpose. Remember, the purpose behind the rule must come from legal authority, such as legislative history, case authority, or well-established public opinion. It is not your personal opinion on the purpose of the rule. Also, if there is more than one purpose, explain which one the courts tend to use more.
4. State persuasively that the purpose underlying the rule applies to your client's case.
5. Explain with specific detail why the possible outcome(s) for your client furthers the purpose underlying the rule.
6. Conclude with a sentence that provides closure to the policy-based reasoning argument. This sentence must connect to the thesis sentence that began the policy-based reasoning argument.

WORKSHEET NO. 6: ANALOGICAL REASONING

Analogical reasoning in persuasive writing is not that different from analogical reasoning in objective writing. The organization of the substance is essentially the same; however, to effectively persuade the reader, the content and presentation of the substance is different.

The two main differences between analogical reasoning in persuasive writing and objective writing are: (1) the depth of the substance provided and (2) the tone.

First, the depth of the substance provided is different in persuasive writing because there are no case illustrations or a traditional E section in persuasive writing as there is in objective writing. Instead, in persuasive writing the law is explained in the context of the analysis. Thus, the description of the precedent case in the persuasive analogical reasoning formula is more detailed than the description of the precedent case in the objective analogical reasoning formula.

Second, the tone must be more argumentative. Unlike objective writing, where the goal is to demonstrate to the reader all possible arguments and counter-arguments from a neutral perspective, in persuasive writing the goal is to persuade the reader to agree with your argument. Thus, in persuasive writing, you must state the arguments affirmatively and conclusively, begin with your strongest argument (or strongest analogy or distinction), and really prove the connection between the client's case and the precedent case(s).

To write analogical reasoning in persuasive writing, start by first evaluating the analogical reasoning argument objectively using the same brainstorming process used for analogical reasoning in objective writing (see Worksheet No. 6 for Objective Writing), which is provided below:

1. Identify one issue you plan to address with analogical reasoning.
2. Identify the name of one precedent case you plan to use for the issue you selected above.
3. Identify the specific holding of the precedent case on the legal issue you plan to argue with this analogical reasoning (NOTE: This must only be the holding specific to the legal issue you are addressing, not the overall holding of the precedent case).
4. Describe the reasoning of the precedent case on the legal issue you plan to argue with this analogical reasoning (NOTE: This must only be the reasoning specific to the legal issue you are addressing, not the overall reasoning of the precedent case).
5. Make a list of the relevant facts from the precedent case on the legal issue you plan to argue with this analogical reasoning (NOTE: This must only be the facts specific to the legal issue you are addressing, not all of the facts from the precedent case).

6. Make a list of the relevant facts from your client's case on the legal issue you plan to argue with this analogical reasoning (NOTE: This must only be the facts specific to the legal issue you are addressing, not all of the facts from your client's case).

7. Group the facts of the precedent case and your client's case into facts that are similar and facts that are distinguishable.

Depending on whether the facts are the similar or distinguishable or both, you may only need to consider some of the questions below. If the facts are similar, answer Questions 8–10. If the facts are distinguishable, answer Questions 11–13. If the facts are both similar and distinguishable, answer Questions 8–13.

8. Identify the fact(s) to be compared in your analysis as similar. (NOTE: This must only be the facts specific to the legal issue you are addressing, not all of the facts from the precedent case or your client's case.)

9. Explain why you think these facts are similar—use specific factual examples to demonstrate the similarities.

10. Explain *why* these factual similarities support your legal analysis on the issue you are addressing. This is where you must directly apply the reasoning of the precedent case to the facts of your client's case. Specifically look at why and how the precedent case ruled as it did and why that same reasoning applies to your client's case.

11. Identify the fact(s) to be compared in your analysis as distinguishable. (NOTE: This must only be the facts specific to the legal issue you are addressing and not all of the facts from the precedent case or your client's case.)

12. Explain why you think these facts are distinguishable—use specific factual examples to demonstrate the differences.

13. Explain *why* these factual differences support your legal analysis on the issue you are addressing. This is where you must directly apply the reasoning of the precedent case to the facts of your client's case. Specifically look at why and how the precedent case ruled as it did and why that same reasoning does not apply to your client's case.

After evaluating these brainstorming questions, you should have a clear understanding of whether an analogical reasoning argument should be made in your client's case. You then must decide if the analogical reasoning will be based on a single case or multiple cases. If multiple cases are used to argue the same legal issue, then you must make these arguments at the same time, rather than as a separate analogical reasoning for each precedent case. Once you have decided if the analogical reasoning will be based on a single case or multiple cases, use one of the following formulas to write your analogical reasoning argument:

Analogical Reasoning Formula Using a Single Case:

Component 1:	Persuasively state the legal conclusion you want the reader to reach based on your analogical reasoning (this is the overall thesis sentence for the analogical reasoning paragraph or paragraphs—case names should not be included in this sentence).
Component 2:	Sentence stating, "In client's case (use client's name) is similar to/distinguishable from ______ (insert precedent case name) based on ______ (identify the specific issue this analogical reasoning is addressing)."
Component 3:	Sentence stating, "In client's case (use client's name), (insert the specific facts about your client's case that will be compared; these are not all of the facts of the case but only the specific facts that will be compared)."
Component 4:	Sentence stating, "This case is similar to/distinguishable from ______ (insert precedent case name). In ______ (insert precedent case name) where (insert detailed information about the facts, the holding, and the reasoning from the precedent case you are relying upon that are related to the specific issue to be compared)." Remember to describe the precedent case in a way that is favorable to your client's position.
Component 5:	Explain, using *specific factual detail*, why the facts you are comparing are similar or distinguishable. This is where you need to provide specific fact-to-fact comparisons, using actual facts from your client's case and the precedent case. (i.e.—"Fact X in client's case is similar to/distinguishable from Fact Y in precedent case because ______ "). Remember to make these factual comparisons in a way that is favorable to your client's position.
Component 6:	Persuasively re-state the likely outcome of your client's case based on the similarities or differences you discussed in Component 5. This is a re-statement of the conclusion (Component 1) but with more detail and this likely is the beginning of a new paragraph.
Component 7:	Explain *why* this is the likely outcome. This is where you must directly apply the reasoning from the precedent case to your client's case. *Possible phrasing:* The court in ______ (insert precedent case name) reasoned ______ (insert the fact specific reasoning of the precedent case on the specific legal issue the analogical

reasoning is addressing). This reasoning applies to your client's case (use client's name) because ______ (explain why it applies). Therefore, because the reasoning from (insert precedent case name) applies to your client's case (use client's name), the outcome in your client's case (use client's name) is ______ (insert the outcome you are trying to prove with the analogical reasoning.)

Component 8: Persuasively re-state the conclusion you want the reader to reach based on your analogical reasoning. This must connect to the argument provided by the analogical reasoning and to the conclusion stated in Component 1.

EXAMPLE SINGLE CASE ANALOGICAL REASONING:

The implication that Ms. Anchor unethically reported on the Mayor's campaign is false and therefore unprotected. If the defendant uses a celebrity photograph in a manner that disseminates false information, the defendant violates the celebrity's right of publicity and the use is unprotected. Eastwood v. Super. Ct. of L.A. Co., 149 Cal. App. 3d 409 (2nd Dist. 1983). In Eastwood, for example, the court held Clint Eastwood's right of publicity was infringed when the National Enquirer published an article about Mr. Eastwood's alleged romantic involvement with two other celebrities; an article that was completely false. Id. at 414. Similarly, the implication that Ms. Anchor engaged in unethical reporting is also false. Ms. Anchor did not engage in any unethical reporting. Instead, and as alleged in her Complaint, Ms. Anchor never reported on the Mayor's re-election campaign and the general manager of her news station stated that "there are no concerns about Ms. Anchor's ethics whatsoever." The court in Eastwood reasoned that the veil of the public interest exception does not protect dissemination false information. Id. at 425. This reasoning applies to TFF's dissemination of false information regarding Ms. Anchor's reporting. Therefore, TFF's dissemination of false information is not protected.

Analogical Reasoning Formula Using Multiple Cases:

Component 1: Persuasively state legal conclusion you want the reader to reach based on your analogical reasoning (this is the overall thesis sentence for the analogical reasoning paragraph or paragraphs—case names should not be included in this sentence).

Component 2: Sentence stating, "Client's case (insert client's name) is similar to/distinguishable from ______ (insert first precedent case name) and/but similar to/distinguishable from ______ (insert second precedent case name) based on ______ (identify the specific issue this analogical reasoning is addressing)."

Component 3: Sentence stating, "In client's case (use client's name), (insert the specific facts about your client's case that will be compared; these are not all of the facts of the case but only the specific facts that will be compared)."

Component 4(a): Sentence stating, "This case is similar to/distinguishable from ______ (insert first precedent case name). In ______ (insert precedent case name) where (insert detailed information about the facts, the holding, and the reasoning from the precedent case you are relying upon that are related to the specific issue to be compared)." Remember to describe the precedent case in a way that is favorable to your client's position.

Component 4(b): Explain, using *specific factual detail*, why the facts you are comparing are similar/distinguishable. This is where you need to provide specific fact-to-fact comparisons, using actual facts from your client's case and the precedent case. (i.e.—"Fact X in client's case is similar to/distinguishable from Fact Y in precedent case because ______"). Remember to make these factual comparisons in a way that is favorable to your client's position.

Component 5(a): Sentence stating, "This case is similar/distinguishable than ______ (insert second precedent case name). In (insert precedent case name) where (insert detailed information about the facts, the holding, and the reasoning from the precedent case you are relying upon that are related to the specific issue to be compared)." Remember to describe the precedent case in a way that is favorable to your client's position.

Component 5(b): Explain, using *specific factual detail*, why the facts you are comparing are similar/distinguishable. This is where you need to provide specific fact-to-fact comparisons, using actual facts from your client's case and the precedent case. (i.e.—"Fact X in client's case is similar to/distinguishable from Fact Y in precedent case because ______ "). Remember to make these factual comparisons in a way that is favorable to your client's position. [NOTE: you many need to use a transition to begin this sentence, such as "In addition," "Also," "However," or "On the other hand".]

Component 6: Persuasively re-state the likely outcome of your client's case based on the similarities/differences you discussed previously (see Components 4(b) and 5(b)). This is a re-statement of the conclusion (Component 1) but with more detail and likely is the beginning of a new paragraph.

Component 7: Explain *why* this is the likely outcome. This is where you must directly apply the reasoning from the precedent case to your client's case.

Possible phrasing if the reasoning of the precedent cases is the same:

The court in ______ (insert first and second precedent case names) reasoned ______ (insert the fact specific reasoning of the precedent cases on the specific legal issue the analogical reasoning is addressing). This reasoning applies to your client's case (use client's name) because ______ (explain why it applies). Therefore, because the reasoning from (insert precedent case names) applies to your client's case (use client's name), the outcome in your client's case (use client's name) will likely will be ______ (insert the outcome you are trying to prove with the analogical reasoning).

Possible phrasing if the reasoning of the precedent cases is different:

The court in ______ (insert first precedent case name) reasoned ______ (insert the fact specific reasoning of the first precedent case on the specific legal issue the analogical reasoning is addressing). This reasoning applies to your client's case (use client's name) because ______ (explain why it applies). However, the court in ______ (insert second precedent case name) reasoned ______ (insert the fact specific reasoning of the second precedent case on the specific legal issue the analogical reasoning is addressing). This reasoning does not apply to your client's case (use client's name) because ______ (explain why it does not apply). Therefore, because the reasoning from (insert first precedent case name) applies to your client's case (use client's name) and the reasoning from (insert second precedent case name) does not apply to your client's case (use client's name), the outcome in your client's case (use client's name) will likely will be ______ (insert the outcome you are trying to prove with the analogical reasoning).

Component 8: Persuasively re-state the conclusion you want the reader to reach based on your analogical reasoning. This must connect to the argument provided by the analogical reasoning and to the conclusion stated in Component 1.

EXAMPLE MULTIPLE CASE ANALOGICAL REASONING:

TFF unlawfully used Ms. Anchor's photograph without her consent. TFF was required to obtain Ms. Anchor's consent to use her photograph because her photograph was used to further the company's commercial objectives, not to inform on a matter in the public interest. The use of Ms. Anchor's photograph is similar to the unauthorized use of a photograph in Downing and distinguishable from the authorized use of a photograph in Dora. In Downing, a clothing retailer used a famous surfer's photograph in its surf-themed clothing catalog. 265 F.3d 994. The court held that the photograph was only tenuously connected the public's interest in surfing because the retailer "did not explain that [the surfer] was a legend of the sport and incorrectly identifies where and when [the surfer's] photo was taken." Id. at 1003. Instead, the court held that the use of his photo only was used to sell clothing; therefore, its use required the surfer's consent. Id. Thus, where the use is commercial in nature, consent is required. Id.

Indeed, it is only if the connection between the use and the dissemination of information on matters in the public interest is clear that consent may be unnecessary. Dora v. Frontline Video, Inc., 15 Cal. App. 4th 536 (2nd Dist. 1993). For example, in Dora, consent to use a surfer's photograph in a surfing documentary was not required because the documentary was connected to the public's interest. Id. at 541. The court reasoned that because the "point of the program" was to inform the public about surfing and the people who impacted surf culture, the use of the surfer's photograph was connected to the public interest. 15 Cal. App. 4th at 543.

TFF's use of Ms. Anchor's photo was commercial in nature. Like in Downing, where the objective of the surf-themed catalog was to promote sales, TFF's primary business objective was to create and sell funny t-shirts for profit. The catalog used the surfer's photograph to capitalize on his fame and to "window-dress" the catalog, just like TFF used Ms. Anchor's photograph to capitalize on her highly publicized affair with the Mayor to sell t-shirts. Downing, 265 F.3d at 1003. Also, like the catalog's failure to properly identify the surfer and his relationship to the sport, TFF "did not explain" Ms. Anchor's situation with the Mayor and, therefore, did not connect the use of the photograph to the public interest. Id. Instead, TFF simply was trying to profit off of a highly publicized situation, like the catalog was trying to profit off the fame of the well-known surfer. Id. Furthermore, Ms. Anchor's is distinguishable from Dora because, in that case, the court reasoned that consent was unnecessary since the "point of the program" was to provide commentary on surfing. 15 Cal. App. 4th at 546. That reasoning does not apply here because the "point of the t-shirt" was to meet TFF's commercial objective of creating a humorous t-shirt

for profit, not to inform the public or provide social commentary on that topic. Because TFF's use of Ms. Anchor's photograph on its t-shirt was not connected to the public's interest, but instead used to make a profit, TFF was required to obtain Ms. Anchor's consent.

Case File Assignment:

Write an argument for your client's case using analogical reasoning based on the legal authority in the Case File and/or the legal authority assigned by your professor. To help you write an analogical reasoning argument, answer the following brainstorming questions:

1. Identify one specific issue you plan to address with analogical reasoning (or the specific issue assigned by your professor).

2. Identify the name of one precedent case you plan to use for the issue you selected above (or the case assigned by your professor).

3. Identify the specific holding of the precedent case on the legal issue you plan to argue with this analogical reasoning (NOTE: This must only be the holding specific to the legal issue you are addressing, not the overall holding of the precedent case.)

4. Describe the reasoning of the court from the precedent case on the legal issue you plan to argue with this analogical reasoning (NOTE: This must only be the reasoning specific to the legal issue you are addressing, not the overall reasoning of the precedent case.)

5. Make a list of the relevant facts from the precedent case on the legal issue you plan to argue with this analogical reasoning (NOTE: This must only be the facts specific to the legal issue you are addressing, not all of the facts from the precedent case.)

6. Make a list of the relevant facts from your client's case on the legal issue you plan to argue with this analogical reasoning (NOTE: This must be only the facts specific to the legal issue you are addressing, not all of the facts from your client's case).

7. Organize the facts of the precedent case and your client's case into the charts below:

Facts that are similar:

Your Client's Case	Precedent Case

Facts that are distinguishable:

Your Client's Case	Precedent Case

Using the information you filled into the charts above, decide whether you think your client's case and the precedent case are similar, distinguishable, or both. If they are similar, answer Questions 8–10 below. If they are distinguishable, answer Questions 11–13 below. If they are both similar and distinguishable, answer Questions 8–13 below.

8. Identify the fact(s) from your client's case and the precedent case to be compared as similar. (NOTE: This must only be the facts specific to the legal issue you are addressing, not all of the facts from the precedent case or your client's case.)

9. Explain why these facts are similar—use specific factual examples to prove the similarities.

10. Explain *why* these factual similarities support your legal analysis on the issue you are addressing. This is where you must directly apply the reasoning of the precedent case to the facts of your client's case. Specifically look at why and how the precedent case ruled as it did and why that same reasoning applies to your client's case.

11. Identify the fact(s) to be compared in your analysis as distinguishable. (NOTE: This must only be the facts specific to the legal issue you are addressing, not all of the facts from the precedent case or your client's case.)

12. Explain why these facts are distinguishable—use specific factual examples to prove the differences.

13. Explain *why* these factual differences support your legal analysis on the issue you are addressing. This is where you need to directly apply the reasoning of the precedent case to the facts of your client's case. Specifically look at why and how the precedent case ruled as it did and why that same reasoning does not apply to your client's case.

After answering these brainstorming questions, you should have a clear understanding of whether an analogical reasoning argument should be made in your client's case. You then must decide if the analogical reasoning will be based on a single case or multiple cases. If multiple cases are used to argue the same legal issue, then you must make these arguments at the same time, rather than as a separate analogical reasoning for each precedent case. Once you have decided if the analogical reasoning will be based on a single case or multiple cases, use one of the following formulas to write your analogical reasoning argument:

Analogical Reasoning Formula Using a Single Case:

Component 1: Persuasively state the legal conclusion you want the reader to reach based on your analogical reasoning (this is the overall thesis sentence for the analogical reasoning paragraph or paragraphs—case names should not be included in this sentence).

Component 2: Sentence stating, "In client's case (use client's name) is similar to/distinguishable from _______ (insert precedent case name) based on _______ (identify the specific issue this analogical reasoning is addressing)."

Component 3: Sentence stating, "In client's case (use client's name), (insert the specific facts about your client's case that will be compared—please note these are not all of the facts of the case but only the specific facts that will be compared)."

Component 4: Sentence stating, "This case is similar to/distinguishable from _______ (insert precedent case name). In _______ (insert precedent case name) where (insert detailed information about the facts, the holding, and the reasoning from the precedent case you are relying upon that are related to the specific issue to be compared)." Remember to describe the precedent case in a way that is favorable to your client's position.

Component 5: Explain, using *specific factual detail*, why the facts you are comparing are similar or distinguishable. This is where you need to provide specific fact-to-fact comparisons, using actual facts from your client's case and the precedent case. (i.e.—"Fact X in client's case is similar to/distinguishable from Fact Y in precedent case because _______ "). Remember to make these factual comparisons in a way that is favorable to your client's position.

Component 6: Persuasively re-state the likely outcome of your client's case based on the similarities or differences you discussed in Component 5. This is a re-statement of the conclusion (Component 1) but with more detail and this likely is the beginning of a new paragraph.

Component 7: Explain *why* this is the likely outcome. This is where you must directly apply the reasoning from the precedent case to your client's case.

Possible phrasing:

The court in _______ (insert precedent case name) reasoned _______ (insert the fact specific reasoning of the precedent case on the specific legal issue the analogical reasoning is addressing). This reasoning applies to your client's case (use client's name) because ______ (explain why it applies). Therefore, because the reasoning from (insert precedent case name) applies to your client's case (use client's name), the outcome in your client's case (use client's name) is ______ (insert the outcome you are trying to prove with the analogical reasoning.)

Component 8: Persuasively re-state the conclusion you want the reader to reach based on your analogical reasoning. This must connect to the argument provided by the analogical reasoning and to the conclusion stated in Component 1.

<u>Analogical Reasoning Formula Using Multiple Cases:</u>

Component 1: Persuasively state legal conclusion you want the reader to reach based on your analogical reasoning (this is the overall thesis sentence for the analogical reasoning paragraph or paragraphs—case names should not be included in this sentence).

Component 2: Sentence stating, "Client's case (insert client's name) is similar to/distinguishable from ______ (insert first precedent case name) and/but similar to/distinguishable from ______ (insert second precedent case name) based on ______ (identify the specific issue this analogical reasoning is addressing)."

Component 3: Sentence stating, "In client's case (use client's name), (insert the specific facts about your client's case that will be compared—please note these are not all of the facts of the case but only the specific facts that will be compared)."

Component 4(a): Sentence stating, "This case is similar to/distinguishable from ______ (insert first precedent case name). In ______ (insert precedent case name) where (insert detailed information about the facts, the holding, and the reasoning from the precedent case you are relying upon that are related to the specific issue to be compared)." Remember to describe the precedent case in a way that is favorable to your client's position.

Component 4(b): Explain, using *specific factual detail*, why the facts you are comparing are similar/distinguishable. This is where you need to provide specific fact-to-fact comparisons, using actual facts from your client's case and the precedent case. (i.e.—"Fact X in client's case is similar to/distinguishable from Fact Y in precedent case because ______ "). Remember to make these factual comparisons in a way that is favorable to your client's position.

Component 5(a): Sentence stating, "This case is similar/distinguishable than ______ (insert second precedent case name). In (insert precedent case name) where (insert detailed information about the facts, the holding, and the reasoning from the precedent case you are relying upon that are related to the specific issue to be compared)." Remember to describe the precedent case in a way that is favorable to your client's position.

Component 5(b): Explain, using *specific factual detail*, why the facts you are comparing are similar/distinguishable. This is where you need to provide specific fact-to-fact comparisons, using actual facts from your client's case and the precedent case. (i.e.—"Fact X in client's case is similar to/distinguishable from Fact Y in precedent case because ______ "). Remember to make these factual comparisons in a way that is favorable to your client's position. [NOTE: you many need to use a transition to begin this sentence, such as "In addition," "Also," "However," or "On the other hand"]

Component 6: Persuasively re-state the likely outcome of your client's case based on the similarities/differences you discussed previously (see Components 4(b) and 5(b)). This is a re-statement of the conclusion (Component 1) but with more detail and this likely is the beginning of a new paragraph.

Component 7: Explain *why* this is the likely outcome. This is where you must directly apply the reasoning from the precedent case to your client's case.

Possible phrasing if the reasoning of the precedent cases is the same:

The court in ______ (insert first and second precedent case names) reasoned ______ (insert the fact specific reasoning of the precedent cases on the specific legal issue the analogical reasoning is addressing). This reasoning applies to your client's case (use client's name) because ______ (explain why it applies). Therefore, because the reasoning from (insert precedent case names) applies to your client's case (use client's name), the outcome in your client's case (use client's name) will likely will be ______ (insert the outcome you are trying to prove with the analogical reasoning).

Possible phrasing if the reasoning of the precedent cases is different:

The court in ______ (insert first precedent case name) reasoned ______ (insert the fact specific reasoning of the first precedent case on the specific legal issue the analogical reasoning is addressing). This reasoning applies to your client's case (use client's name) because ______ (explain why it applies). However, the court in ______ (insert second precedent case name) reasoned ______ (insert the fact specific reasoning of the second precedent case on the specific legal issue the analogical reasoning is addressing). This reasoning does not apply to your client's case (use client's name) because ______ (explain why it does not apply). Therefore, because the reasoning from (insert first precedent case name) applies to your client's case (use client's name) and the reasoning from (insert second precedent case name) does not apply to your client's case, the outcome in your client's case (use client's name) will likely will be ______ (insert the outcome you are trying to prove with the analogical reasoning).

Component 8: Persuasively re-state the conclusion you want the reader to reach based on your analogical reasoning. This must connect to the argument provided by the analogical reasoning and to the conclusion stated in Component 1.

WORKSHEET NO. 7: POINT HEADINGS

Point headings provide the reader with structure and guidance. They allow the reader to obtain a broad overview of your argument and quickly locate the point he or she is most interested in reading without having to read the entire argument.

A point heading is substantively correct if it:

1. States the point heading affirmatively for your client;
2. Uses key words and phrases from the argument the point heading represents;
3. Uses specific facts and legal concepts from the argument the point heading represents; and
4. Summarizes the argument the point heading represents by using the following formula:
    a. The conclusion for the argument the point heading represents;
    b. Because (or a because equivalent);
    c. The rule justifying the legal conclusion + the key fact(s) from your client's case.

> EXAMPLE POINT HEADINGS:
>
> I. MS. ANCHOR HAS A VALID RIGHT OF PUBLICITY CLAIM AGAINST TFF BECAUSE IT KNOWINGLY USED HER PHOTOGRAPH FOR PROFIT WITHOUT HER CONSENT.
>
> II. MS. ANCHOR HAS A VALID RIGHT OF PUBLICITY CLAIM AGAINST TFF BECAUSE TFF'S USE OF HER PHOTOGRAPH WAS NOT CONNECTED TO A MATTER IN THE PUBLIC INTEREST, BUT ONLY FOR COMMERCIAL GAIN.
>
> III. MS. ANCHOR HAS A VALID RIGHT OF PUBLICITY CLAIM AGAINST TFF BECAUSE THE PHOTOGRAPHS ON THE T–SHIRT IMPLIED FALSE INFORMATION.

A point heading is technically correct if:

1. It is only one sentence;
2. The sentences wrap under each other so the left margin of the point heading lines up with the text of the point heading immediately above it;
3. It appropriately uses emphasizers (all caps, bold, italic, underline, etc.) to allow the point headings to stand out from the text of the argument but not distract the reader;
4. It does not have an A without a B or an I without an II; and

5. It does not have lone point headings at the end of the page (there must be at least 2 lines of text of the paragraph the point heading precedes at the bottom of the page; a point heading cannot be the last line on a page).

A series of point headings are technically correct if they:

1. Use parallel construction;
2. Use appropriate levels of point headings and sub-point headings; and
3. Provide the reader with an outline of the Argument section, when read together.

The formatting for point headings is proper if:

I. THE TEXT OF THE FIRST LEVEL POINT HEADING IS INDENTED A FULL TAB OVER AND ADDITIONAL LINES OF TEXT WRAP UNDER THE FIRST LINE OF TEXT.

   A. <u>The Text Of The Second Level Point Heading Is Indented So That The "A" Lines–Up Under The Text Of The First Level Point Heading; The Text Of This Heading Is A Full Tab Over From The "A;" And Additional Lines Of Text Wrap Under The First Line of Text.</u>

      1. The third level point heading is indented so that the "1" lines-up under the text of the second level point heading; the text of this heading is indented a full tab over from the "1;" and additional lines of text wrap under the first line of text.

Note: The type of emphasizers (all caps, initial caps, underlined, italics, etc.) used here are for demonstrative purposes only. You should use the types of emphasizers assigned by your professor.

Case File Assignment:

Write the point headings for your brief. To help you write the point headings, answer the following brainstorming questions for each argument you plan to emphasize with a point heading:

1. What is the conclusion reached by the argument the point heading represents?

2. What are the key words and phrases used in the argument the point heading represents?

3. What are the specific facts and legal concepts from the argument the point heading represents?

Using the answers to these brainstorming questions as your guide, write a point heading(s) for your argument. When writing a point heading, use the following formula:

> The conclusion for the argument/paragraph the point heading represents + because (or a "because" equivalent) + the rule justifying the legal conclusion + the key fact(s) from your client's case.

When writing the point heading, consider the following substantive and technical requirements:

1. State the point heading affirmatively for your client;
2. State the point heading in only one sentence;
3. Have the text of the point heading wrap so the left margin of the point heading lines-up;
4. Appropriately use emphasizers (bold, italic, underline, etc.) to allow the point headings to stand out from the text of the argument, but not distract the reader;
5. Do not have an A without a B or an I without an II; and
6. Do not have lone point headings at the end of the page (there must be at least 2 lines of text of the paragraph the point heading precedes at the bottom of the page; a point heading cannot be the last line on a page).

If you have a series of point headings, consider the following substantive and technical requirements:

1. State the point headings using parallel construction;
2. State the point headings using appropriate levels of point headings and sub-point headings; and
3. Collectively, when read together, the point headings should provide the reader with an outline of the Argument section.

WORKSHEET NO. 8: THE INTRODUCTION

The Introduction in a persuasive brief is the first thing the judge will read. Thus, it must provide a complete introduction to the case and use persuasive techniques to convince the judge from the beginning.

An Introduction is substantively complete if it includes:

1. The nature of the case;
2. The identity of the parties;
3. The procedural event that led to the filing of the brief;
4. The relief your client requests from the court in the brief; and
5. The primary legal points justifying that relief.

When presenting the substance of these five components, consider the following persuasive writing techniques and note that the above five components can be presented in any order:

1. Begin with your client's name and what your client requests;
2. Write the Introduction in the affirmative; do not directly restate your opponent's position or what your opponent wants (even if it is a responsive brief); and
3. Establish the theme of your argument early.

EXAMPLE INTRODUCTION:

Tasha V. Anchor, a well-known television reporter, has a valid right of publicity claim against T–Shirts For Fun (TFF) under the California statutory right of publicity. TFF knowingly used a photograph of Ms. Anchor on a t-shirt combined with a photograph of the Los Angeles Mayor as a miniature devil sitting on her shoulder. Ms. Anchor did not consent to this use of her photograph. Furthermore, TFF admits that it used the photograph primarily for commercial gain, not for social commentary, and admits that the image was designed to imply that Ms. Anchor was influenced by the Mayor to unethically report on his re-election campaign. Ms. Anchor denies this implication. Because TFF knowingly used Ms. Anchor's photograph on its t-shirt without her consent, did not connect the use of her photograph to a matter in the public interest, and provided false information about Ms. Anchor's reporting, TFF violated her right of publicity. Therefore, Ms. Anchor has stated a valid claim and TFF's motion to dismiss should be denied.

Case File Assignment:

Write the Introduction for your brief. To help you write the Introduction, answer the following brainstorming questions:

1. What is the nature of the case?

2. Who are the parties?

3. What is the procedural event that led to the filing of the brief?

4. What is the relief your client requests from the court in the brief?

5. What are the primary legal points justifying that relief?

Using the answers to these brainstorming questions as your guide, write the Introduction for your brief. Start by cutting and pasting your answers into paragraph form and then mold them into readable paragraphs.

When writing the Introduction, consider the following persuasive techniques:

1. Begin with your client's name and what your client requests from the court in filing the brief;
2. Write the Introduction in the affirmative; do not directly restate your opponent's position or what your opponent wants (even if it is a responsive brief); and
3. Establish the theme of your case or argument.

WORKSHEET NO. 9: PERSUASIVE STATEMENT OF FACTS

The four most important things to remember when writing a persuasive Statement of Facts are to: (1) include the legally significant facts; (2) organize the facts in an effective manner; (3) tell your client's story persuasively; and (4) represent the facts accurately.

The brainstorming process for a persuasive Statement of Facts is similar to the brainstorming process for an objective Facts section (See Worksheet No. 9 for Objective Writing). However, a persuasive Statement of Facts does not begin the same as an objective Facts section. As you recall, the first paragraph in an objective Facts section (See Worksheet No. 9 for Objective Writing) begins with foundational information to provide the reader with context for the memorandum. This same first paragraph is not required in a persuasive Statement of Facts because a persuasive brief begins with an Introduction, which provides the reader with all of this foundational information: the parties, their relationships, the setting, the procedural history, and the client's general problem or goal. Instead, a persuasive Statement of Facts needs to grab the reader's attention from the beginning by telling compelling story.

Therefore, the brainstorming process for a persuasive Statement of Facts is more focused on the substance and tone.

A persuasive Statement of Facts is substantively correct if it:

1. Includes the proper substance by:

    a. Including the legally significant facts. To determine the legally significant facts, review your Argument section and highlight all of the facts from your client's case that you relied upon. These are the legally significant facts. If you have not yet written your Argument section, determine the legally significant facts by asking yourself: what are the facts a court will consider in ruling on your client's case?

    b. Including the background facts necessary for the legally significant facts to make sense. To determine the necessary background facts, ask yourself: what context is needed for the legally significant facts to make sense, what else does the judge need to know to understand the story of your client's case, and what else is needed to establish the theme of your case?

    c. Including emotional facts that are needed to establish your theme or create empathy for your client.

    d. Describing the facts accurately.

    e. Omitting factual arguments, references to the law, legal conclusions, and factual conclusions.

2. Includes the proper persuasive tone by:

   a. Emphasizing favorable facts;

   b. Strategically including unfavorable facts (the facts the opposing party likely will rely upon) by burying them within favorable facts;

   c. Having a parallel tone and theme with the Argument section; and

   d. Using an appropriate and persuasive organization.

3. Has strategically selected an organization to most persuasively tell the story: chronological, topical, or a combination of chronological and topical. The organization you select must be a strategic choice based on the best approach to persuasively tell the reader the story of your client's case.

4. Provides closure to the persuasive Statement of Facts by not ending abruptly; connect to the theme of the case and end with significant relevant facts as readers will best remember information they read last.

EXAMPLE PERSUASIVE STATEMENT OF FACTS:

Tasha V. Anchor is a local television reporter for KTV-LA. She has had a successful career as a reporter for the last ten years. During that time, she has won numerous awards, including an Emmy for her journalism, co-hosted national shows, interviewed A-list celebrities, high-ranking politicians, and well-known authors, and reported live from the Democratic Headquarters in Los Angeles as Barack Obama was elected President.

Ms. Anchor recently began a relationship with the Mayor of Los Angeles, who has been legally separated from his wife for two years. Ms. Anchor and the Mayor have been in a committed relationship for approximately six months. Currently, Ms. Anchor hosts the morning show for KTV-LA called, "Good Morning So. Cal." and the Mayor is running for re-election. While both are busy with their careers, they try to make as much time as possible to spend with each other.

In the summer, news of their relationship was made public, which was followed by a frenzy of media attention. Ms. Anchor could barely leave her home without being hounded by paparazzi. The Mayor had to add additional security just to be able to get to work each day. The media ran stories alleging everything from Ms. Anchor being the Mayor's second cousin to the Mayor influencing Ms. Anchor's reporting on his re-election campaign.

Ms. Anchor denies these recent allegations, as she is not the Mayor's second cousin and she never reported on the Mayor's re-election campaign or on any matters that directly or indirectly relate to his position as Mayor. However, Ms. Anchor did conduct two short of interviews with the Mayor last October and November, but these interviews were on topics unrelated to his re-election campaign and the general manager for KTV-LA said "There is no concern as to Ms. Anchor's ethics whatsoever."

Soon after the relationship was made public, Ms. Anchor came across a t-shirt for sale in a Beverly Hills boutique with her photograph on it. The t-shirt featured her photograph combined with a photograph of a miniaturized Mayor, wearing a suit and devil horns, sitting on her left shoulder. Ms. Anchor did not consent to the use of her photograph and its use on the t-shirt is offensive to Ms. Anchor because it inappropriately implies that she unethically reported on the Mayor's re-election campaign or that he somehow controlled her reporting. Ms. Anchor vehemently denies both allegations.

The t-shirt was created and sold by T–Shirts for Fun (TFF), a company that designs, produces, and distributes t-shirts, which are pri-

marily meant to be humorous and provide commentary on public events. Despite the $29.95 received for each t-shirt, with over 100 sales, TFF claims the t-shirt at issue was only intended to provide subtle commentary on the possible conflict of interest created by Ms. Anchor's relationship with the Mayor. However, according to information posted on TFF's web site, it admits that the t-shirt is its "best seller" and that its business objective is more about making money than providing social commentary.

Seeking to prevent further manufacture and distribution of the t-shirt and for damages against TFF, Ms. Anchor filed a Complaint alleging TFF violated her statutory right of publicity.

Case File Assignment:

Write a persuasive Statement of Facts for your client's case. To help you write a persuasive Statement of Facts, answer the following brainstorming questions:

1. What is the theme or the story of your case?

2. Identify the relevant facts:

   a. What are the legally significant facts? Read your Argument section and highlight all of the facts from your client's case that you used to support your arguments. These are the legally significant facts and they must be included in your persuasive Statement of Facts. If you have not yet written your Argument section, then determine the legally significant facts by asking yourself: what are the facts the court will consider in ruling on your client's case?

   b. What background facts are necessary to provide context for the legally significant facts identified in response to Question 2(a) above, to tell your client's story, and to establish the theme of your case?

c. What emotional facts are needed to establish your theme or create empathy for your client?

d. What are the unfavorable facts? What are the facts the opposing party likely will rely upon?

3. Looking at your answers to these brainstorming questions and using your understanding your client's case, identify the organization that will most persuasively tell your client's story: Chronological? Topical? Combination of chronological and topical? The organization you select must be a strategic choice based on the best approach to persuasively tell your client's story.

Using the answers to these brainstorming questions as your guide, write a persuasive Statement of Facts for your client's case. Start by cutting and pasting your answers into paragraph form and then mold them into readable paragraphs.

When writing your persuasive Statement of Facts, consider the following:

1. The first paragraph must tell a compelling story and establish the theme of the case.
2. The overall substance and tone must:
   - Strategically select the most persuasive organization (avoid stream of consciousness writing);
   - Represent the record accurately;
   - Describe the facts persuasively;
   - Have a parallel tone and theme with the Argument section;

- Emphasize favorable facts and bury unfavorable facts (but not omit them);
- Omit factual arguments, references to the law, legal conclusions, and factual conclusions; and
- Maintain a persuasive tone.

3. The last paragraph must:
   - Connect to the theme of the case;
   - Conclude with significant relevant facts—readers will best remember information they read last; and
   - Avoid ending abruptly: create a transition between the Statement of Fact and Argument sections.

WORKSHEET NO. 10: CONCLUSION

The Conclusion in persuasive writing is similar to a Conclusion in objective writing. Like an objective Conclusion, the persuasive Conclusion summarizes the individual conclusions that you reached in your Argument section and reminds the court of the relief requested.

A persuasive Conclusion is complete if it includes:

1. The ultimate relief sought by your brief (NOTE: This must be consistent with the information provided in your Introduction);
2. Each rule applied to your client's case (the R in each persuasive paradigm included in your brief).
3. The conclusion for each rule applied in your client's case (the C in each persuasive paradigm included in your brief).
4. A summary of the reasoning that supports those conclusions (summarize the A sections in each persuasive paradigm included in your brief); and
5. A restatement of the ultimate relief sought by your brief.

Throughout each of these components, use a persuasive tone and incorporate the theme of your client's case.

> EXAMPLE CONCLUSION:
>
> Ms. Anchor's Complaint states a valid statutory right of publicity claim against TFF and TFF's motion to dismiss should be denied. A motion to dismiss should only be granted in extraordinary cases where the plaintiff can prove no set of facts in support of her claim. Ms. Anchor has alleged more than sufficient facts to prove her claim. First, under California Civil Code § 3344(a), use of another's photograph is unlawful unless there is consent. Ms. Anchor's Complaint sufficiently alleges that TFF knowingly used her photograph without her consent in violation of § 3344(a). Second, the only exception to this statutory consent requirement is if the defendant can show that the use of a photograph was in connection with a matter in the public interest; but, if the unauthorized use of a photograph is for commercial purposes, consent is required. Ms. Anchor's Complaint sufficiently alleges that TFF used her photograph for commercial purposes, not to provide social commentary. Third, if the defendant uses a celebrity's photograph in a manner that disseminates false information, the defendant violates the celebrity's right of publicity and the use is unprotected. Ms. Anchor's Complaint sufficiently alleges that TFF's use of her photograph on the t-shirt falsely implied that Ms. Anchor unethically reported on the Mayor's re-election campaign and that this false implication is exactly what the statute is designed to protect against. For these reasons, Ms. Anchor's Complaint properly states a right of publicity cause of action and TFF's motion to dismiss should be denied.

Case File Assignment:

Write the Conclusion for your brief. To help you write the Conclusion, answer the following brainstorming questions:

1. What is the ultimate relief sought by your brief? (NOTE: This must be consistent with the information provided in your Introduction)

2. Identify each rule applied to your client's case (the R in each persuasive paradigm included in your brief).

3. Identify the conclusion for each rule applied in your client's case (the C in each persuasive paradigm included in your brief).

4. Summarize the reasoning that supports the conclusions on each rule (summarize the A sections in each persuasive paradigm included in your brief).

5. Restate the ultimate relief sought by your brief.

Using the answers to these brainstorming questions as your guide, write the Conclusion for your brief. Start by cutting and pasting your answers into paragraph form and then mold them into readable paragraphs. When writing the Conclusion, maintain a persuasive tone, incorporate the theme of your client's case, have the organization of the Conclusion parallel the organization of the Argument section, and avoid simply repeating the Introduction.

SAMPLE TRIAL BRIEF

MEMORANDUM OF POINTS & AUTHORITIES IN OPPOSITION TO DEFENDANT'S MOTION TO DISMISS

INTRODUCTION

Tasha V. Anchor, a well-known television reporter, has a valid right of publicity claim against T–Shirts For Fun (TFF) under the California statutory right of publicity. TFF knowingly used a photograph of Ms. Anchor on a t-shirt combined with a photograph of the Los Angeles Mayor as a miniature devil sitting on her shoulder. Ms. Anchor did not consent to this use of her photograph. Furthermore, TFF admits that it used the photograph primarily for commercial gain, not for social commentary, and admits that the image was designed to imply that Ms. Anchor was influenced by the Mayor to unethically report on his re-election campaign. Ms. Anchor denies this implication. Because TFF knowingly used Ms. Anchor's photograph on its t-shirt without her consent, did not connect the use of her photograph to a matter in the public interest, and provided false information about Ms. Anchor's reporting, TFF violated her right of publicity. Therefore, Ms. Anchor has stated a valid claim and TFF's motion to dismiss should be denied.

STATEMENT OF FACTS

Tasha V. Anchor is a local television reporter for KTV-LA. She has had a successful career as a reporter for the last ten years. During that time, she has won numerous awards, including an Emmy for her journalism, co-hosted national shows, interviewed A-list celebrities, high-ranking politicians, and well-known authors, and reported live from the Democratic Headquarters in Los Angeles as Barack Obama was elected President.

Ms. Anchor recently began a relationship with the Mayor of Los Angeles, who has been legally separated from his wife for two years. Ms. Anchor and the Mayor have been in a committed relationship for approximately six months. Currently, Ms. Anchor hosts the morning show for KTV-LA called, "Good Morning So. Cal." and the Mayor is running for re-election. While both are busy with their careers, they try to make as much time as possible to spend with each other.

In the summer, news of their relationship was made public, which was followed by a frenzy of media attention. Ms. Anchor could barely leave her home without being hounded by paparazzi. The Mayor had to add additional security just to be able to get to work each day. The media ran stories alleging everything from Ms. Anchor being the Mayor's second cousin to the Mayor influencing Ms. Anchor's reporting on his re-election campaign.

Ms. Anchor denies these recent allegations, as she is not the Mayor's second cousin and she never reported on the Mayor's re-election campaign or on any matters that directly or indirectly relate to his position as Mayor. However, Ms. Anchor did conduct two short of interviews with the Mayor last October and November, but these interviews were on topics unrelated to his re-election campaign and the general manager for KTV-LA said "There is no concern as to Ms. Anchor's ethics whatsoever."

Soon after the relationship was made public, Ms. Anchor came across a t-shirt for sale in a Beverly Hills boutique with her photograph on it. The t-shirt featured her photograph combined with a photograph of a miniaturized Mayor, wearing a suit and devil horns, sitting on her left shoulder. Ms. Anchor did not consent to the use of her photograph and its use on the t-shirt is offensive to Ms. Anchor because it inappropriately implies that she unethically reported on the Mayor's re-election campaign or that he somehow controlled her reporting. Ms. Anchor vehemently denies both allegations.

The t-shirt was created and sold by T–Shirts for Fun (TFF), a company that designs, produces, and distributes t-shirts, which are primarily meant to be humorous and provide commentary on public events. Despite the $29.95 received for each t-shirt, with over 100 sales, TFF claims the t-shirt at issue was only intended to provide subtle commentary on the possible conflict of interest created by Ms. Anchor's relationship with the Mayor. However, according to information posted on TFF's web site, it admits that the t-shirt is its "best seller" and that its business objective is more about making money than providing social commentary.

Seeking to prevent further manufacture and distribution of the t-shirt and for damages against TFF, Ms. Anchor filed a Complaint alleging TFF violated her statutory right of publicity.

ARGUMENT

Ms. Anchor has a valid statutory right of publicity claim against TFF and TFF's motion to dismiss should be denied. Generally, a motion to dismiss is disfavored and dismissal of a complaint is proper only in extraordinary cases. United States v. White, 893 F. Supp. 1423, 1428 (C.D. Cal. 1995). A complaint should not be dismissed for failure to state a claim unless it appears "beyond doubt that the plaintiff can prove no set of facts in support of his claim." Conley v. Gibson, 355 U.S. 41, 45–46 (1957). In evaluating the motion, the complaint is construed in the light most favorable to the plaintiff and the "court must accept as true all material allegations in the complaint, as well as reasonable inferences to be drawn from them." White, 893 F. Supp. at 1428.

Ms. Anchor has sufficiently alleged a right of publicity cause of action to survive a motion to dismiss. Specifically, Ms. Anchor properly alleges that (1) TFF's use of her photograph violates § 3344(a); (2) TFF's use of Ms. Anchor's photograph was not in connection with the public interest; and (3) TFF's use of Ms. Anchor's photograph was based on false information. For these reasons, Ms. Anchor's Complaint states a valid claim for which relief can be granted and TFF's motion to dismiss should be denied.

I. MS. ANCHOR HAS A VALID RIGHT OF PUBLICITY CLAIM AGAINST TFF BECAUSE IT KNOWINGLY USED HER PHOTOGRAPH FOR PROFIT WITHOUT HER CONSENT.

Ms. Anchor has a valid right of publicity claim against TFF under California Civil Code § 3344(a). The knowing use of another's photograph for commercial purposes without the person's consent directly violates California Civil Code Section 3344(a). See Downing v. Abercrombie & Fitch, 265 F.3d 994, 1002 (9th Cir. 2001) (right of publicity was violated when a clothing retailer's surf-themed catalog knowingly used a photograph of professional surfers in a surfing competition without their consent); Gionfriddo v. Major League Baseball, 94 Cal. App. 4th 400 (1st Dist. 2001) (right of publicity was violated when a web cast of baseball statistics knowingly used a photograph of a famous baseball player without consent). Because TFF knowingly used Ms. Anchor's photograph on t-shirts it produced and sold for profit without her consent, it violated Ms. Anchor's right of publicity under California Civil Code § 3344(a).

II. MS. ANCHOR HAS A VALID RIGHT OF PUBLICITY CLAIM AGAINST TFF BECAUSE TFF'S USE OF HER PHOTOGRAPH WAS NOT CONNECTED TO A MATTER IN THE PUBLIC INTEREST, BUT ONLY FOR COMMERCIAL GAIN.

TFF's use of Ms. Anchor's photograph was for commercial gain, not to provide commentary on a matter in the public interest. Under California Civil Code § 3344(a), use of another's photograph is unlawful unless there is consent. If there is not consent, then use of another's photograph violates the person's right of publicity. Id. The only exception to this statutory requirement is if the defendant can show that the use of a photograph was in connection with a matter in the public interest. Cal. Civ. Code § 3344(d). However, consent is still required if the unauthorized use of a photograph is for advertising purposes and is not directly connected to the public interest, even if the use relates to a matter in the public interest. Downing, 265 F.3d 994 (use of a surfer's photograph in clothing catalog, although on a topic in the public interest, not protected because the photograph was used as a "window dressing" to advance a surf-themed catalogue and promote sales).

TFF unlawfully used Ms. Anchor's photograph without her consent. TFF was required to obtain Ms. Anchor's consent to use her photograph because her photograph was used to further the company's commercial objectives, not to inform on a matter in the public interest. The use of Ms. Anchor's photograph is similar to the unauthorized use of a photograph in Downing and distinguishable from the authorized use of a photograph in Dora. In Downing, a clothing retailer used a famous surfer's photograph in its surf-themed clothing catalog. 265 F.3d 994. The court held that the photograph was only tenuously connected the public's interest in surfing because the retailer "did not explain that [the surfer] was a legend of the sport and incorrectly identifies where and when [the surfer's] photo was taken." Id. at 1003. Instead, the court held that the use of his photo only was used to sell clothing; therefore, its use required the surfer's consent. Id. Thus, where the use is commercial in nature, consent is required. Id.

Indeed, it is only if the connection between the use and the dissemination of information on matters in the public interest is clear that consent may be unnecessary. Dora v. Frontline Video, Inc., 15 Cal. App. 4th 536 (2nd Dist. 1993). For example, in Dora, consent to use a surfer's photograph in a surfing documentary was not required because the documentary was connected to the public's interest. Id. at 541. The court reasoned that because the "point of the program" was to inform the public about surfing and the people who impacted surf culture, the use of the surfer's photograph was connected to the public interest. 15 Cal. App. 4th at 543.

TFF's use of Ms. Anchor's photo was commercial in nature. Like in Downing, where the objective of the surf-themed catalog was to promote sales, TFF's primary business objective was to create and sell funny t-shirts for profit. The catalog used the surfer's photograph to capitalize on his fame and to "window-dress" the catalog, just like TFF used Ms. Anchor's photograph to capitalize on her highly publicized affair with the Mayor to sell t-shirts. Downing, 265 F.3d at 1003. Also, like the catalog's failure to properly identify the surfer and his relationship to the sport, TFF "did not explain" Ms. Anchor's situation with the Mayor and, therefore, did not connect the use of the photograph to the public interest. Id. Instead, TFF simply was trying to profit off of a highly publicized situation, like the catalog was trying to profit off the fame of the well-known surfer. Id. Furthermore, Ms. Anchor's is distinguishable from Dora because, in that case, the court reasoned that consent was unnecessary since the "point of the program" was to provide commentary on surfing. 15 Cal. App. 4th at 546. That reasoning does not apply here because the "point of the t-shirt" was to meet TFF's commercial objective of creating a humorous t-shirt for profit, not to inform the public or provide social commentary on that topic. Because TFF's use of Ms. Anchor's photograph on its t-shirt was not connected to the public's interest, but instead used to make a profit, TFF was required to obtain Ms. Anchor's consent.

III. MS. ANCHOR HAS A VALID RIGHT OF PUBLICITY CLAIM AGAINST TFF BECAUSE THE PHOTOGRAPHS ON THE T-SHIRT IMPLIED FALSE INFORMATION.

The implication that Ms. Anchor unethically reported on the Mayor's campaign is false and therefore unprotected. If the defendant uses a celebrity photograph in a manner that disseminates false information, the defendant violates the celebrity's right of publicity and the use is unprotected. Eastwood v. Super. Ct. of L.A. Co., 149 Cal. App. 3d 409 (2nd Dist. 1983). In Eastwood, for example, the court held Clint Eastwood's right of publicity was infringed when the National Enquirer published an article about Mr. Eastwood's alleged romantic involvement with two other celebrities; an article that was completely false. Id. at 414. Similarly, the implication that Ms. Anchor engaged in unethical reporting is also false. Ms. Anchor did not engage in any unethical reporting. Instead, and as alleged in her Complaint, Ms. Anchor never reported on the Mayor's re-election campaign and the general manager of her news station stated that "there are no concerns about Ms. Anchor's ethics whatsoever." The court in Eastwood reasoned that the veil of the public interest exception does not protect dissemination false information. Id. at 425. This reasoning applies to TFF's dissemination of false information regarding Ms. Anchor's reporting. Therefore, TFF's dissemination of false information is not protected.

Ms. Anchor's claim is further supported by the purpose underlying the statute. While § 3344(d) protects information that is directly related to matters in the public interest, the legislature did not intend to protect false information that is presented as news. Eastwood, 149 Cal. App. 3d at 425. The Legislature stated that the public interest exception cannot be exercised so as to abuse the rights of individuals. Id. This policy applies to Ms. Anchor's case. Ms. Anchor denies that she ever reported on the Mayor's campaign and the general manager of her news station stated that "there are no concerns about Ms. Anchor's ethics whatsoever." Yet, TFF created a t-shirt that directly challenged Ms. Anchor's ethics. It is exactly this type of dissemination of false information the Legislature did not intend the public interest exception to protect. Id. Therefore, Ms. Anchor's right of publicity supported by the policy behind the statute and TFF's unauthorized use of her photograph is not protected.

CONCLUSION

Ms. Anchor's Complaint states a valid statutory right of publicity claim against TFF and TFF's motion to dismiss should be denied. A motion to dismiss should only be granted in extraordinary cases where the plaintiff can prove no set of facts in support of her claim. Ms. Anchor has alleged more than sufficient facts to prove her claim. First, under California Civil Code § 3344(a), use of another's photograph is unlawful unless there is consent. Ms. Anchor's Complaint sufficiently alleges that TFF knowingly used her photograph without her consent in violation of § 3344(a). Second, the only exception to this statutory consent requirement is if the defendant can show that the use of a photograph was in connection with a matter in the public interest; but, if the unauthorized use of a photograph is for commercial purposes, consent is required. Ms. Anchor's Complaint sufficiently alleges that TFF used her photograph for commercial purposes, not to provide social commentary. Third, if the defendant uses a celebrity's photograph in a manner that disseminates false information, the defendant violates the celebrity's right of publicity and the use is unprotected. Ms. Anchor's Complaint sufficiently alleges that TFF's use of her photograph on the t-shirt falsely implied that Ms. Anchor unethically reported on the Mayor's re-election campaign and that this false implication is exactly what the statute is designed to protect against. For these reasons, Ms. Anchor's Complaint properly states a right of publicity cause of action and TFF's motion to dismiss should be denied.

†